DIVORCE IN WASHINGTON
A Humane Approach

Lowell K. Halverson
and
John W. Kydd

Eagle House Press
Mercer Island, Washington
(2d ed. 1990)

Portions of Chapter One, "The Psychological Divorce," were adapted from
REBUILDING: WHEN YOUR RELATIONSHIP ENDS, ©1981 by Bruce
Fisher. Reproduced by permission of Impact Publishers, Inc., P.O. Box
1094, San Luis Obispo, CA 93406. Further reproduction prohibited.

Eagle House Press
P.O. Box 1357
Mercer Island, Washington 98040

Printed in the United States of America

TABLE OF CONTENTS

CAVEAT (WARNING)

No book on family law can possibly substitute for the sound judgment and advice of a lawyer dealing with the particular facts of your case.

This book cannot give you legal advice. At best it can acquaint you with some of the factors lawyers, judges, and family counselors consider in resolving marital dissolution disputes.

The reader is urged to approach the complexities of family law described in this book with caution and then obtain the best legal advice and counsel you can to assure your optimum result.

PREFACE TO THE SECOND EDITION

We dedicate this book to our clients and their families.

A traditional step-by-step guide to a marital dissolution is like a step-by-step guide to surgery: regardless of how well it is written, the client cannot be spared the pain of the procedure. In a marital dissolution, this pain stems from the relational conflict and the legal procedure used to resolve it.

We have seen many costly court battles erupt solely from the parties' failure to understand their feelings of hurt, anger, or guilt. We have also seen many simple dissolutions degenerate into bitter feuds as the parties pass through a legal procedure.

Relationships are founded on feelings, not facts and finances. Ending a relationship demands considerable attention to the parties' feelings. The present marital dissolution procedure, however, is designed to deal with critical facts (*i.e.*, parenting, support, property division) and not the parties' feelings.

Since our first edition was published, Washington State has taken three major strides toward reforming divorce law in the area of determination and allocation of child support, protection of abused children or spouses, and, significantly, a complete revamping of the concept of custody and visitation with our new Parenting Act. Washington is in the vanguard of opportunity to set a new standard for humanity in our divorce laws, as we set a new standard for quality in our parenting law.

No one can predict how the courts will interpret our new laws. We have spoken with many judges and the authors of the new legislation, and have incorporated their insights into our book.

For the second edition we gratefully acknowledge the contributions of lawyers Steve Gaddis, Dan Radin, Marlin Applewick, Katie Moore, and Judge Joan DuBuque, and accountant Nadine Morgan.

Our thanks also go to attorney Joel G. Green for reading and editing the manuscript, for once again making consistently perceptive comments and suggestions, and for ensuring that the book was typeset and published in a highly readable fashion.

Lowell K. Halverson

John W. Kydd

INTRODUCTION

Mary Ellen sat across the desk from me, forcing a half smile. It was obvious that she felt uneasy visiting an attorney — not unlike many of the clients we have seen in our offices over the last sixteen years. When she arrived for our first meeting, experience told me to expect certain questions, concerns, and fears.

After sixteen years, her marriage was not what she and her husband wanted it to be; yet, she was not sure a marital dissolution was what she wanted either. I have to be candid with my clients: I am a lawyer, not a marriage counselor. I can advise prospective clients about the *legal* aspects of dissolution that they may encounter, but I cannot advise them whether or not they *should* dissolve their marriage. My colleague, John W. Kydd, is trained in both law and counseling and can give both legal and psychological advice. When clients are uncertain or fearful, clarification of the legal and psychological issues involved frequently can help them to make more informed decisions about marital dissolution.

That is why Mary Ellen found herself in my office: she needed to know about the emotional and legal process of a dissolution. She is not alone. Annually, there are over 1,300,000 marital dissolutions granted in the United States. Her story is not unusual, and because of that, she agreed to allow her own words to be used. Perhaps you, the reader, will hear your own concerns.

MARY ELLEN'S STORY

"I'm not here because of wife-beating or alcoholism. Basically, Jim and I just grew apart. Everyone thinks we're the all-American family. Justin is fourteen and Kristin's eleven. Jim and I are proud of our family.

"We're also proud of what we've achieved. I don't really know where to start. We've worked so hard and it just now appears to be paying off.

"I may as well start with Jim. He has really accomplished a lot, but I was alongside him every inch of the way. He has an M.B.A. I guess I feel it is my degree too, because I put him through school during the first years of our marriage. I taught high school English in California. We lived on my income. That made me feel very important because I knew I was really making a contribution.

"We came back to Washington fifteen years ago. Jim produced the MBA, and

I produced Justin. I haven't worked since then, at least not for pay. Oh, I've spent many, many hours working in the kids' schools and doing other volunteer work, but I haven't had a *real* job. I guess I believed my duty was to be a good wife and mother, so I never even updated my teaching credentials. The education field is so saturated, I probably couldn't get a job anyway.

"Anyhow, after we moved back home, Jim got a good job heading the marketing research department of a pharmaceutical firm. He stayed there for five years and then, nine years ago, he and two other fellows from the company started their own business. They formed a corporation that designs and produces medical supplies. Jim is responsible for the sales end of the operation. Now it is really starting to go, but I sure was frightened in the beginning. The loan we needed to start the business was overwhelming to me. For six months Jim did not draw a salary. We lived off our savings.

"It really didn't take long for the business to get off the ground. So six years ago we were able to buy our present home. Of course, we had the profit from the sale of our first home to help with the down payment, but it seemed like a huge financial commitment at the time.

"Over the years we grew into a comfortable lifestyle; but when you strip away all our material possessions, there isn't much left. Of course, we have the kids, and maybe that is enough to keep us together but aside from them, it gets awfully lonely in this marriage. Jim and I can barely agree on the time of day anymore. In fact, I'm just now recognizing all the subtle put-downs Jim has been handing me over these last years. Now I see how his put-downs have been eating away at my self-esteem, and the crazy part is that Jim still isn't even aware of what he has done. I guess I'm saying we might not be good for one another anymore.

"I don't know what is right for us, all of us, including the children. Kristin needs braces — you know what that costs — Justin was just accepted into a very expensive private school. I want the kids to have all the advantages we can give them. What would a divorce do to *their* future?"

Mary Ellen continued with some specific questions:

"The kids are used to our home. Do you think I could keep it? Even if I can keep it, how can I afford to live there, or anywhere else for that matter? I haven't worked for so long; I really don't know that I could get a job. Besides, women just don't seem to earn very much money.

"If we both want a divorce, does that mean that I am entitled to alimony? How about the kids? Who will pay for Kristin's braces and Justin's schooling, not to mention college, clothes, doctor bills, skiing, dance lessons, and soccer shoes? Wow, it's just so expensive to provide for children.

"If Jim moves out, what will I do for money? Or, what if he won't leave? Am I forced to move out? We're still friends; will we end up hating each other after a divorce? Does every divorce have to be ugly?

"What will happen to our kids? Our divorced friends' kids turn into monsters, especially when the parents bring home *their* new friends. I'm just assuming I would have custody of the children. Doesn't the mother always get custody?

"How do you start a divorce? Can Jim and I both use the same lawyer? How long does it take? It seems as though all our friends' divorces dragged on *forever*.

"I guess I'm just overwhelmed. Jim and I are unhappy in our marriage, but neither of us is sure that divorce wouldn't make a worse mess of our lives."

It is difficult to give "yes" and "no" answers to all of Mary Ellen's questions. Generally speaking, I could say, "Yes, you may get the house; yes, you probably will need to become employed; and don't worry, we'll make provisions for the children in the settlement agreement." But each dissolution is unique. The court considers many factors, including the age, income, and future earning capacity of the spouses, and every asset and liability of the marriage must be considered by the court before an informed judgment can be made. The court also considers the lifestyle to which they are accustomed. Few divorcing spouses will maintain their current standard of living.

In answer to the question about both spouses employing the same attorney, I answer with an emphatic, "No!" An attorney cannot ethically represent clients with conflicting or potentially conflicting interests, and every marital dissolution involves conflicting or potentially interests between husband and wife. A properly trained attorney, however, can act as a mediator for both parties, as you will see in the story of Jim and Betty in Chapter Three, which deals with divorce mediation.

What will Mary Ellen do for money if Jim moves out? The courts do provide for this. You will find an explanation of *temporary relief* in Chapter Six, entitled "Spousal Maintenance." In fact, as this book progresses, it is our intention to answer all of Mary Ellen's questions.

Although men and women face different factual problems, they often suffer from the same divorce-induced emotional problems. While my female clients fear that they will not be able to survive economically, my male clients often face the different and difficult fears of *losing* their house, *losing* contact with their children, and *losing* many of their assets in a court that seems biased towards women. Anger, guilt, hostility, anxiety, failure, rejection — these emotions don't favor men or women. Unwinding the legal relationship between spouses, although important, is usually only one act in a larger drama with many emotional scenes. Thus, we begin our book with "The Psychological Divorce," which summarizes specific stages of emotional recovery.

John Kydd and I co-teach a class entitled "Separation and Divorce" along with Mary Elliott, a psychologist. Much of the information in our book is in direct response to the concerns of our clients and students.

Clients often need both legal and psychological advice. I regularly recommend counseling to clients who might benefit. Because Mary Ellen and Jim were not convinced that a dissolution was the answer to their problems, that is what I did in her case. It is always wise to explore the alternatives before deciding upon dissolution.

Most non-violent couples should attend counseling sessions together because counseling involves three entities: the man, the woman, and the marriage. Patterns are evident when the couples go together that are absent when they go separately. Couples who are able to go to counseling together are more likely to remain together. Even if these couples do dissolve their marriage, they often have a much easier time of it because counseling teaches them to communicate better with one another. If they are communicating, they can cooperate.

After three months of counseling, Mary Ellen scheduled an appointment to start the marital dissolution process. She knew that she felt too much hurt and anger to stay in the marriage. The counseling had helped clarify their problems and now Mary Ellen was convinced of the need to end her marriage.

Making the divorce decision did not prevent Mary Ellen from having strong and sometimes frightening feelings about her dissolution. She said,

> "I feel guilty, and then I feel angry about the guilt, and angry at Jim because he never understood my needs. I know I wanted out, but still I feel a sense of failure. Why couldn't I make it work? I wonder if perhaps it was my fault.
>
> "I'm so tired. It's so hard to make a decision. I don't want to be responsible for making any decisions right now, but I guess I have no choice!
>
> "I had visions of the kids grouping together with me like little troopers, but they have really been difficult. Justin is surly; he seems angry at me. Kristin has become withdrawn and irresponsible."

Mary Ellen was clearly in the early stages of the psychological divorce process (*see* Chapter One). She was startled but a little relieved to hear she was fitting into a very normal pattern. I promised her that this would pass.

In spite of Mary Ellen's less than steady emotions, we had work to do. Prior to our meeting, I had sent Mary Ellen a large packet of preparatory materials, which she had completed and brought with her. Part of these materials are included in Chapter Four, "Preparing for Your Lawyer."

Mary Ellen had to gather specific information regarding all the tangible assets and liabilities of the marital community before I could prepare a Petition for Dissolution. I explained that the Petition starts the divorce process in the courts and includes provisions for parenting, visitation, support, and the division of property and debts. The chapters on "Property

Settlement," "Parenting Plans," "Child Support," and "Spousal Maintenance" address these issues in detail.

Chapter Two, "Choosing Your Lawyer," is meant to help you decide which lawyer out of thousands is the best one for you. The questionnaire at the end of the chapter could save you money. Whether you employ a lawyer or handle your own divorce, you may discover that being involved in preparing your case is an experience well worth the effort. Chapter Nine, "Self Help," explores these areas. Although I am an attorney, my own bias is that an attorney is well worth the investment, as will be demonstrated in later chapters.

Chapter Three, "Divorce Mediation: An Alternative," summarizes the process as well as the pros and cons of this exciting new area in the law. Mediation has great potential for those couples who are still able to communicate.

Chapter Ten, on "Cohabitation," is for those who choose not to (or cannot) be legally married. These family arrangements are increasingly common and explicitly supported in the courts. However, there are legal consequences that must be considered by those who choose this lifestyle.

Finally, no book on marital dissolutions would be complete if it did not provide resources for recovery and more constructive living. In the Appendices, you will find a representative sampling of services designed to help you through the rough spots. We have included hints to help with the healing process.

At the end of selected chapters, you will find a list of additional questions. Divorce issues are infinite in variety, so it is not practical to discuss every consideration at length. Study these lists; use them as guides. It is our hope that this book will help you define and effectively deal with the legal and psychological issues in your own marital dissolution and to enable you to use a humane approach to resolving your concerns and problems.

CHAPTER ONE

THE PSYCHOLOGICAL DIVORCE: PUTTING THE PIECES BACK TOGETHER

Divorce occurs in two places: in the court and in your heart. Those who fail to recognize this "divorce of the heart" often fail to learn from the mistakes of their first relationship and are likely to repeat these mistakes in later relationships. As we stated in the introduction, this book is about winning in both the court and in the heart. Too many people who win the court *battle* find that they have lost the *war* because their family is so shattered by the trial experience that neither parent can adequately function to meet their or their children's needs. The bottom line is: bitter divorce battles beget bitter post-divorce battles.

The purpose of this chapter is to help you to win that second divorce battle — the battle to become the best person or parent you can be in spite of the difficulties of your divorce. We believe that clients who learn the emotional and the legal processes of their divorce also learn how to have more satisfying personal and parental relationships in the future. Plainly, the psychological process of divorce is critical, and we need lawyers who are trained to deal with the divorce process as a whole, and not just its legal aspects in isolation. (Rainier Mediation in Seattle is one of many organizations nationally that is developing new approaches to divorce, which address both the psychological and the legal problems that men and women face.) The psychological divorce has stages just as the legal divorce does. Many of my clients find struggling with their feelings far more difficult than struggling with the legal process.

For example, late one afternoon a client, George, came by my office to see if we could *talk*. His face was drawn and I noticed that his cigarette trembled slightly between his fingers. He was usually confident and outspoken, with a *can do* attitude about life. Now his eyes seemed flat and tearful as he began to speak:

"You know, this may sound strange but I don't know where to start.... I'm usually so in control and on top of things but ... somehow..."

He looked out the window almost searching for words,

"Well today everything just collapsed. It felt like something in me shifted and my stable self just came down like a house of cards. I had to skip work. This is the first thing I've done today and it's 4:00 p.m.!

"I don't mind telling you this really scares me. For a moment there I thought, "So this is what it's like to have a breakdown.' I hope I'm not crazy, but you know that my chest actually hurts when I think about the divorce. I always thought that *heartache* was something in songs and romance novels, but this really hurts!

"Maybe you're not the right one to talk to about this, but I sure don't want to go to a counselor. All I want to know is how long will this last? I can't stay this empty very long or I'll be out of a job!"

George's feelings are not unique, and I find that many men struggle through them without talking about them. Thanks to a growing movement of support groups for men, the situation is improving. Still, I can't begin to count the number of men who haven't come in until after they gave up trying to drink, sweat, or work through their emotional problems themselves. The fact remains that men, like women, have feelings that need special attention and understanding during a divorce. We know that there are identifiable psychological steps or stages in a divorce. Every book on divorce has its own particular version of the stages of divorce. We have found Dr. Bruce Fisher's book, *Rebuilding: When Your Relationship Ends* (Impact Publishers, Inc. 1981), most useful in our practice, so we will use his work here. We have incorporated some of our concepts into his, so Dr. Fisher should not be blamed for any ambiguities or inconsistencies.

STAGES OF DIVORCE RECOVERY

We all know that divorce is a bitter experience that often engenders deep feelings of revenge, retaliation, despair, and disappointment. Many people going through divorce reconsider their basic values. Although many view divorce as a time of disability, self-doubt, and unresolvable fears, divorce is also an opportunity to answer serious questions about how to learn from the past, how to gain self-knowledge, and how to grow from the experience.

The process can be compared to a crab shedding its old shell to grow a new one. Just before breaking out of its old shell, the crab is very uncomfortable and almost unable to fend for itself because of the extreme pressures that have built up inside of its shell. When the crab finally breaks out of its old shell, it faces a dangerous world with very little protection. The crab's response is to bury itself deep into the sand for a few weeks until sufficient armor has built up to make it safe to journey into the outside world.

In human terms, the person initiating the divorce often spends a considerable amount of time being trapped and cramped inside of the old "shell" of the marriage. Spouses breaking out of their shells often find they are fearful about becoming single adults. Some will bury themselves with work or at home in order to gain time and sufficient self-confidence to reenter society.

One of the underlying themes is: *different people progress at different rates.* Normally, the psychological divorce takes at least one year. Some people begin their psychological divorce long before filing their legal divorce, while others do not begin it until long after their legal divorce is final. Also, there is significant evidence that men and women tend to react differently to the stresses created by divorce. Some men tend to act more upon the world as a means of coping, and they do so by working long hours, partying hard, *etc.* On the other hand, some women tend to act more upon themselves instead of the outside world, and seek counseling for an inner explanation of the failure of the marriage. Almost twice as many women as men seek help for personal, divorce-related problems. Some have suggested that this means that women are less able to handle their problems without help. Studies in emergency clinics indicate, however, that most men do not seek help until their problems have become acute and require extensive care. On the other hand, women tend to seek help earlier and more often, and usually require *less* care before they are fully recovered.

Lastly, remember that the children of divorce go through similar psychological stages of divorce recovery. Parents should be supportive but must also take care not to spend so much time helping the kids that they avoid dealing with their own problems. What follows is a summary of the stages of divorce recovery.

STAGE I. DENIAL: FACING UP TO IT

(1) THE INITIAL SHOCK

Each of us promises to be together until *death us do part,* and most of us believe that divorce is something that only happens to others. At this stage it is difficult to admit failure, partly because we fear rejection by our friends. In addition to the stigma of divorce, there is the fear that the fact of divorce means that we will never again have a satisfactory intimate relationship. Given these feelings, isn't it reasonable that many people prefer stunted, cramped relationships over the risks inherent in breaking out of a marital relationship?

Many people spend months trying to find precisely *what went wrong.* Sometimes it is easier to get clear answers by asking the question "Why were we married?" instead of "Why were we divorced?" People need to take some time for honest inquiry:

Were you and your partner friends?
Did you confide in one another?
Did you share friendships?
Did you go out together socially?
Did you make major decisions jointly?
Did you trust each other?
What interests did you share? Attitudes toward life? Politics? Religion?
   Children? Hobbies?
When you got angry with each other, did you deal with it directly, or hide
   it, or try to hurt each other?

Although these questions might be difficult to ask, the answers are often worth the effort. *Easy explanations of a divorce are usually incorrect.*

Many people spend weeks or months in this stage. The following checklist will help you to decide if you are ready to pass to the next stage:

1. I am able to accept that my relationship is ending.
2. I am comfortable telling my friends and relatives that my relationship is ending.
3. I have begun to understand some of the reasons why my relationship did not work out, and this has helped me overcome the feelings of denial.
4. I believe that even though divorce is painful it can be a positive and creative experience.
5. I am ready to invest emotionally in my own personal growth in order to become the person I would most like to be.
6. I want to learn to become fulfilled as a single person before committing myself to another relationship.
7. I will continue to invest in my own personal growth even if my former partner and I plan to get back together.

(2) FROM LONELINESS TO ALONENESS

It is natural to feel extreme loneliness when your relationship ends. Many people have great fear that this utter loneliness will *never end* and that they would *do anything* to get their partner to return. Even if the children are living with you and there are friends and relatives nearby, the loneliness is often greater than all of the warm feelings these loved ones have for you. Answers will emerge from your feelings.

This step is about learning how to grow *through* loneliness to the state of aloneness, where you are comfortable being by yourself. It begins with a *hiding in sand* period where many feel that they are safe only so long as they never venture out again.

Some dive into their apartments for weeks at a time while others dive into their work. Each is an equally effective avoidance mechanism that is healthy over a short term, but dangerous over a long term. A variation on this theme is diving into a *rebound relationship* where all the painful unanswered questions of the old relationship are avoided by devoting one's total energy to a new relationship. Such rebound relationships can be extremely exciting and dangerous, especially when relief is mistaken for love.

Getting to a point of "aloneness" involves being comfortable doing activities by yourself and for yourself. During the "loneliness" period, some say that food tastes flat, television is boring, and that it is impossible to read. There is a nagging feeling that you must do *something* but no clear idea as to what that "something" is. Eventually, the all-pervasive feelings of loneliness simply fade and cease to control your behavior. The need to hide in the sand, in your work, or in the arms of another falls away like an old and outworn shell.

(3) GUILT VERSUS REJECTION: DUMPERS AND DUMPEES

Dumpers are those who end the relationship while *dumpees* have it ended for them. The adjustment process differs since dumpers tend to feel more *guilt* while dumpees feel more *rejection*. Also, dumpers start their psychological adjustment while still in the relationship and dumpees often start adjusting later. Plainly, the adjustment process is easiest for couples who mutually decide to end their relationship.

The *fault* for a divorce is often placed upon whoever initiates it. Thus, both parties will often go to great lengths not to initiate the divorce. One party may terminate sexual relations, while the other may move out, yet neither is willing to take the first step to file for a divorce. For the dumpee, the divorce comes as a surprise and the dumpee feels totally unprepared to face the legal and emotional decisions that the dumper is *forcing* upon both of them. Frequently, the dumpee will plead for *more time* and may attempt last-minute changes or give up everything in hopes of buying a reconciliation. If this does not work, the dumpee is forced to acknowledge the reality of the divorce. The anger that often builds up along with this realization may create a revengeful cycle of retributive litigation, in an attempt to *get even*.

While dumpees strive to overcome feelings of rejection and anger, dumpers try to deal with the sense of guilt for terminating their relationship. Many punish themselves as a means of dealing with their guilt. Court settlements are often negotiated while dumpers feel so guilty they will give up everything and while dumpees will settle for anything in hopes of getting the dumper back. Some dumpers are willing to give up anything in order to *get out* and some dumpees are willing to ask for nothing in order to *get the spouse back*. In terms of individual consciousness, the dumpers often want to work on their relationship with themselves (*e.g.*, "I need to get out in order to straighten myself out"), while the dumpees want to work on their relationship with the dumper (*e.g.*, "I can't give up on it until I'm sure it's gone forever").

The dumper/dumpee concept helps explain why some children become very angry at the parent who decided to leave. These children often take out the fear, rejection, and frustration they feel on the parent most easily blamed. The children could be viewed as dumpees because they have very little to do with the divorce decision and often feel the same anger and frustration that dumpees do. In addition, they will often take responsibility for the entire breakup, feeling that if only they had behaved differently their parents would not be divorcing. Parents must do their best to maintain a quality relationship with the children during the entire separation and divorce process. Otherwise it is difficult for the children to realize that they are not guilty of causing their parents' divorce. Some children carry this stigma of responsibility for their parents' divorce into their own relationships as adults.

(4) GRIEF: BIG BOYS — AND GIRLS — DO CRY

Once you are past the cycle of guilt and rejection you are confronted with the painful reality of the death of your relationship.

According to Elizabeth Kubler-Ross, there are five basic stages (the grief cycle) in coping with a death:

1. *Denial*. There is a feeling of numbness, shock, and detachment from the world. Many report feeling and acting like robots.
2. *Anger*. The anger that has been turned inward to build depression now turns outward. Expressing this anger may create guilt that other persons (spouse and friends) will leave. The frustrations that have simmered for years in the relationship may suddenly boil over. Clients report that they try to convince anyone within earshot how absolutely horrible their ex-partner was. This is a stage of paradox: as long as the hatred continues it is difficult to answer why you chose to fall in love in the first place. On the other hand, if you choose to maintain that he/ she was a splendid person, then anger is difficult.

3. *Bargaining.* The bereaved feel that they would do anything to have the decedent return. This is a very difficult period when one partner is willing to do anything to keep the marriage going while the other often feels enormous guilt. Both try for another chance when the relationship is plainly dead. They come back together for the wrong reasons, such as deciding to have a child in order to save the marriage.
4. *Letting go.* This is a very depressing stage when the person finally comes to grips with the reality of facing life without the relationship. Thoughts of suicide are common at this point, but these same thoughts are a marvelous vehicle for asking deep questions about the purpose of one's life, for building a stronger identity, and for finding a deeper and more productive purpose in living.
5. *Acceptance.* Finally the day comes when the grief of the old relationship no longer needs to be carried from day to day. Once the loss is accepted, the burden falls away and there is no more need to invest in a relationship that is past.

Keeping in mind these stages, the sensitive parent will be aware that children go through similar stages. Everyone needs time to cry. Tears are a necessary part of leave-taking and mood changes may be rapid and surprising. Don't be shocked: you may be meeting new aspects of *yourself.* Go with the feelings and learn. The only sure way to be stuck in the grief cycle is to refuse to let yourself express the pain you feel. Divorce can be more traumatic than the death of a loved one.

Some who have worked through the grief cycle report that their constant depression has stopped, that they have recovered physical and emotional energy to work from morning to night, and that they have little trouble concentrating. In addition, they often report that they have stopped talking about their crisis, that they have no thoughts of attempting suicide, that their appetite is good, and that they no longer feel that they are operating as a robot from day to day.

Please bear in mind that grieving over one relationship also may trigger prior grief that has not been dealt with. For example, one man reported that he found himself dreaming about the death of his mother when he was a young boy. Such feelings and dreams are important because the more you deal with them, the better you will be able to pursue the rest of your life productively.

(5) ANGER: DAMN THE "*?!"

Once the depression cycle is broken, the pent-up anger often rushes out like water through a broken dam. Many people have difficulty letting their anger out, so they remain depressed while spending much of their energy containing *their angry water.* Basically there are three phases in dealing with anger: the first is to feel it, the second is to express it constructively, and the third is to forgive both yourself and your ex-partner.

Feeling anger can be difficult in a Christian culture because we have all been taught to *turn the other cheek*. The importance of feeling anger is that it creates *distance* from your ex-partner and allows you to function better on your own. Like grief, the anger may come from many sources and it can only be dealt with to the extent that it is honestly acknowledged.

The second phase is to express the anger constructively. Some spouses report having an active fantasy life where they dream of letting the air out of their spouse's tires, chopping down all the trees around the house, or covering the front walk with banana peels on a foggy morning. Others scream or cry out their anger, and some use the tremendous energy created by anger to their benefit by cleaning the house from top to bottom or doing a great deal of physical exercise. The key point in this phase is that unless you have had a structured experience in constructively expressing anger directly to your ex-spouse, it is best that you express your anger elsewhere. This is a dangerous period for those unable to acknowledge their feelings of anger, because repressed feelings can explode into domestic violence.

The last phase of anger is forgiveness of both oneself and of the other. Once the anger cycle has been fully experienced, it again becomes possible to communicate with your former partner in a calm and rational manner, and the need to *get even* and *blame* fades away under the force of forgiveness and the fact that you simply have better things to do with your life.

STAGE II. LETTING GO AND LEFTOVERS

(1) LETTING GO OF THE EMOTIONAL CORPSE

Normally, this is an easier phase for the *dumpers* who already have prepared for life beyond the relationship. It is difficult to let go of the past without some idea about where you wish to go in the future. The crab is reluctant to let go of its old shell until a new, inner shell has begun to grow.

Letting go involves redirecting one's emotional investments from maintaining the relationship to maintaining oneself. Those who insist on *staying good friends* throughout the breakup are often avoiding the reality that the relationship has died and needs to be buried. Burials can be ceremonial and some clients report scouring the entire house to purge it of anything that reminds them of their ex-partner. Others have simply rearranged their furniture.

If you find yourself stuck on the letting go stage, you might ask yourself what you are managing to avoid dealing with by not letting go. Parents who fail to let go often dwell either on all of the good things or the bad things about the other parent. The result is that the children will tend to get caught in either the positive or the negative dealings between the parents, and that will prolong their adjustment to the divorce. Plainly, letting go is a benefit to both parents and children.

Evidence that you are letting go can be found when you think of your love partner only occasionally, when you rarely fantasize about being with the partner again, when you stop trying to please the partner, when you accept that you will not get back together with the partner, when you rarely talk about the partner with friends, and when you stop generating excuses to talk with the partner.

(2) SELF CONCEPT: MAYBE I'M NOT SO WORTHLESS AFTER ALL

Many spouses define themselves by their marriage and thus are devastated by the prospect of divorce. If their marriage is a failure then so, too, are they. Rebuilding your self-concept is a difficult and time-consuming task, but it is well worth the effort. In terms of phases, it begins with the simple yet profound decision to change oneself and one's perceptions. This can occur simply by making a list of your good points as a human being. Many clients report having spent hours on such a list and coming up with only four or five points, while they are able to write pages on their faults. This reflects their self-esteem, and *the struggle to find positives is the first step to finding a new self-perception.*

Once positives are found and acknowledged, it is time to try to recognize some of the old patterns existing in the prior relationship and to make sure they do not continue. Many of these old patterns can be compared to negative tapes in which you mercilessly blame yourself for everything that goes wrong in the world while claiming it is a coincidence and refusing credit for everything you have done right. Once these blaming cycles are recognized, it is possible to look beyond them, to change behaviors, and to feel a growing confidence in your new self.

Once your new self begins to emerge, it needs to be fed by new friends, new experiences, and generally positive interactions. This is a great time to give and get hugs. Many find that working with a therapist at this point can be particularly beneficial.

Each child is also going through a self-concept cycle whereby the child redefines what parents and family mean. The struggle should be recognized and supported. This is a very exciting stage for most people when they finally come to the point where they can feel good about themselves, their bodies, and their capacities as creative and autonomous adults to deal with whatever life throws at them.

(3) FRIENDSHIPS: THE FAMILIAR AND THE NEW

One of the most painful aspects of divorce is the loss of old and cherished friends. Many women report being deeply hurt by the fact that they are no longer invited to parties with their married friends because some of the wives are suspicious of their single status. It is a sad fact that many friends cannot cope with the changes that occur in a person going through divorce. Although some friendships are lost, others are deepened, and there is great excitement in finding new friends who understand your emotional pain without rejecting you.

Getting to the point of establishing new friends, however, is not an easy task. Losing a number of your married friends can be a devastating blow to self-confidence, so many people find that their phones have begun to grow cobwebs before they are comfortable seeking out new friends. The first rule in seeking new friends is to seek *safe* friends. *It is too early to begin another intimate relationship.* Before you get together with someone, you need to get yourself together.

Interesting people can be met anywhere if you are interested in them. Clients report finding new friends in grocery stores, hardware stores, at church, in community groups, while bowling, while running around the park, and at lectures and concerts. The key at this stage is to find friends who are interested in you *as a friend* and *not* as a lover. Lovers will come and go and may take quite a bit of you with them. But, your new self deserves a better and more stable support system of friends who can be relied upon. Working through this stage, clients are surprised to find that people actually enjoy being with them and that they have deepened their relationships with some of their old friends. There is no greater security than having close friends who know and understand you and all of your faults, and still care deeply for you.

(4) LEFTOVERS: THEY'RE NOT ALL IN THE REFRIGERATOR!

Ending a relationship does not end the habits and problems that preceded it. Many people become married before they reach maturity. They simply move from obediently meeting their parents' expectations to obediently struggling to meet their spouse's expectations. Such people have never had or taken the opportunity to find out who they really are, and the fact of divorce forces them to confront leftover questions that should have been addressed years ago.

Leftovers have three phases: the shell phase, the rebel phase, and the love phase. The *shell phase* is completely *other-directed*. They live to please others as a means of avoiding the need to question themselves. Crises occur when the wishes of a spouse and those of the parents conflict, and it becomes impossible to avoid displeasing someone.

The *rebel phase* occurs most clearly in teenagers who attempt to define themselves in opposition to authority. Among divorced persons, this attitude is embodied in the recently divorced male who becomes a sudden playboy with his sports car, flashy clothes, self-centered behavior, and new-found attraction for significantly younger women. All of us *feel* like rebelling, and those who get through this phase the easiest are those who try to speak and feel their rebellion instead of acting it out. The first question is: who are you rebelling against? (Your spouse? Your parents? Your brothers and sisters? Society in general?) The next question is: what and whose expectations are you rebelling against?

The *love phase* begins once you are able to define your *self* in your own terms rather than according to the expectations of others. At this stage you are better able to risk and learn from your mistakes while responsibly interacting with others. Now your choices are made on the basis of facts instead of the need to meet others' expectations or to maintain a wall of defiance and denial.

In sum, this is an exciting period for both growth and prevention of a rebound relationship. Better relationships in the future demand that you confront your leftovers from past relationships. Clearly, this is a difficult task, but the effort is certainly worth it!

Leftovers also bother children because they have a limited number of behaviors with which to relate to adults. This is why many children relate to a step-parent in the same fashion that they related to the prior parent. The child may not change until old emotions are worked through and new ways of relating are learned.

(5) LOVE THY SELF AS THY NEIGHBOR

Some divorced people find it easy to love others and quite difficult to love themselves. They are basically *half-people* attempting to find wholeness through loving another. A love based on a fearful flight from emptiness and loneliness is unlikely to last. Realizing your self-love is basic to all productive, vital, and growing relationships. Self-love is accepting yourself for who you are. We must each be thankful for our strengths and equally thankful for our weaknesses.

Self-love does not mean that you love *only* yourself, but rather that your capacity to love and accept others is founded on your love and acceptance of yourself.

After a divorce, many people feel that they have no capacity to love either themselves or others. This is a self-esteem issue, and there are many exercises to improve the situation. For example, you could list five adjectives that describe yourself and then put a plus sign after each word that you think is positive and a minus sign after each negative adjective. After you have done this, look at the negative adjectives and see if you can find anything positive about that particular aspect of your personality. The more you work at this, the more likely you are to find positive things about yourself. Those who received little love as children often have a great deal of difficulty loving themselves as adults. Some turn to churches where they find, through God, the love they never felt from their parents. By accepting God, they develop the capacity to accept themselves and others. Many people, however, do quite well without the spiritual path. The choice of how to love yourself must be made by you alone.

Self-love is an important issue for children. Many children feel that they are unlovable because one of their parents has left the home. They fear that the remaining parent will leave as well. This is a critical time for parents to do their best to reassure their children that they are cared for and deeply loved. This is very difficult for parents, because children often are in need of the greatest love when their parents are least capable of providing it. Parents should make special efforts to explain to their children that even though they are having doubts about themselves and each other as parents, they have no doubts about the love they feel for their children.

Those who have passed through the self-love stage often report that they feel lovable, and that they are no longer afraid of being loved or of loving another.

Strangely, successful *reconciliations* can also occur once the old relationship is *let go*. If one spouse took on a lover to *escape* the marriage, then this is the point where she must choose between her husband or her lover, thus raising the possibility for reconciliation.

STAGE III. RENEWAL

(1) TRUST: FOUNDATION FOR HEALTHY RELATIONSHIPS

A frequent complaint of divorced persons is that persons of the opposite sex simply cannot be trusted or that *they are all turkeys*. Pointing out such things is like pointing to a mirror: the mistrust reflects more of you than it does of them.

Trusting the opposite sex again is a difficult task that must be accomplished cautiously. The key to this stage is to make friends, not lovers.

Many people plunge into a new romance before completing this stage, and the result is a relationship that is either dominating or desperate, and often smothering. We must learn to trust before we can safely love.

Our incapacity to trust is largely a function of the wounds created by our divorce. Some who have been deeply wounded find themselves either avoiding relationships or indulging in brief, exploitative relationships where the other party has little or no power. Others feel that they must make every relationship into a lifelong love relationship. Trying to *make* a lifelong relationship often does nothing more than prolong the adjustment process.

Trust is a two-way street: trusting yourself allows you to trust others. Trust demands openness and openness exposes you to the risk of disappointment or rejection. Start slowly and cautiously. Using caution, you can develop a healthier relationship style founded on your new sense of selfesteem. Clearly, the rewards are worth the risks.

Trust is an issue for the children of divorce. Children often will blame themselves for one parent's leaving, even if the reason for the departure is clearly explained to them. Children need to be protected from unhealthy parental conflict. They need to be certain that each parent will continue to love them, without either parent resorting to demeaning the other parent, in the children's presence. Children need to be able to trust that their parents will love *them* regardless of their parents' conflict. The more trust you place in your children now, the more trust they might place in you in the future.

(2) SEXUALITY: IT'S BEAUTIFUL!

Recently divorced people can be traumatized by the thought of dating. They feel they are old, unattractive, awkward, and that they no longer know the rules. To make it worse, they often have their parents' morality holding them back with the admonition to be *good*. Furthermore, their own teenagers may be dictating their dating behavior by less-than-subtle suggestions. No wonder dating is confusing and uncertain, and sexual hang-ups are so common.

Sexuality can be a major problem because it has been made such a big issue in this society. It is difficult to have a *normal* sexual relationship in a society where sex is used to sell everything from toothpaste to toenail clippers. There is considerable confusion as to the role each gender should play in the sexual revolution. Can a man still pay the check without making the woman feel dependent? Can a woman call up a man and ask him out without seeming forward? These and many other questions can make the resumption of sexual relationships frightening, but also fascinating.

During the early stages of divorce recovery, many divorced persons are totally disinterested in sex. This is often followed by a period of deep longing for sexual contact that many find very difficult to handle. Some cannot accept the idea of sex without marriage, while others are unable to accept their sexual feelings at all.

One way to deal with this problem is to recognize that our bodies need to be touched and held. A daily quota of hugs from friends can often be used as a substitute for fulfilling this sexual need. Regular exercise and massage from a licensed therapist can be helpful.

The key is to be both honest and cautious. Do not go beyond your comfort range, but do feel free to admit discomfort to your partner. The fact that there are no clear rules for courting today can be frustrating but it also provides you the opportunity to set your own rules and create the best possible intimate relationship.

The sexuality stage is important for children because they need adult role models of both sexes. Children are often confused, frustrated, or intimidated by their parents' involvement in another love relationship. Your attention and communication is critical at this point. You must make a clear, sincere effort to talk frankly about sex and relationships. Remember that your child's strong reaction may reflect less upon your new relationship than it does upon the fact that your child is just beginning to struggle with the whole notion of sexuality and independence.

Many people fail to progress beyond this stage, so it is very important to deal thoroughly with the issues raised here before proceeding to the next stage. Some indications of passing this stage are as follows: you are comfortable going out with potential love partners; you know and can explain your present moral attitudes and values; you feel capable of having a deep and meaningful sexual relationship; your sexual behaviors are consistent with your morality; and you are behaving morally, the way you would like your children to behave.

(3) RESPONSIBILITY: LET'S TREAT EACH OTHER AS ADULTS

This is a critical stage for learning from prior relationships in order to improve future relationships. Many marriages that end in divorce are relationships that lost the balance of responsibility. Where the responsibility for support, affection, and decisionmaking is not fully shared, the relationship is often not flexible enough to adjust to the stresses and changes in life. Accepting any rigidly defined role in your relationship can limit your capacity to grow within the relationship.

For example, some spouses fit the roles of *Prince* and *Princess*. The Prince/Princess relationship occurs where the Prince takes care of all of the Princess' needs, and lives only to defend and shelter her from a difficult world. The Princess responds by worshiping him and becoming increasingly *helpless* in order to create opportunities for him to rescue/help her. Unfortunately, people good at helping are often poor at being helped, so the Princess becomes increasingly frustrated at being unable to serve her Prince. She feels he only needs her when she is helpless and needs to be rescued. She is frustrated by her increasing dependence. The Prince is frustrated by her attempts at independence.

The Prince/Princess phenomenon is alive and well today. Many of us have friends who took in stray pets while they were children and seemed to continue the behavior as adults by taking a *stray person* in as their spouse. *These people feel they are not lovable unless they are helping someone.* By marrying such a needy person, the Prince is minimizing the possibility of risk and rejection that is inherent in an *equal and dynamic* relationship.

Givers and *Princes* need to practice *asking for help.* This is done first with friends and then can be extended to lovers. It is just as important for you to share the troubles of your day as it is for you to deal with the troubles of others. *Takers* and *Princesses* need to practice taking charge and helping.

Breaking out of these roles creates flexibility within yourself and your interaction with others. Relationships between parties are stronger when both are able to help and be helped.

Passing this stage involves being able to identify which of your behaviors are *over-responsible* and *under-responsible,* how they occurred in the past, and how they can be changed to create more flexible *adult* love relationships in the future.

(4) SINGLENESS: YOU MEAN IT'S OKAY?

Many people move directly from their home to the second home of college or trade school, and then into the third home of marriage, without a period of time where they are single and responsible for themselves. At this singleness stage, emphasis is on investment in your own personal growth rather than in other relationships. This period of singleness enables you to build confidence in yourself so that you can meet your needs and enjoy singleness as an acceptable alternative lifestyle instead of a state of utter loneliness.

Single parents often avoid new relationships by spending all their time at work or with the children and being *too busy* for dates.

The point of the singleness stage is simply to be comfortable with yourself, within yourself, and for yourself. The goal is to be free to choose whether to remain single or to remarry. Granted, there is still a considerable amount of discrimination against single adults, but the situation has improved greatly in the past ten years. Dealing with discrimination against singles can often make you even stronger inside. You may find yourself calmly and firmly educating others about the realities of singleness instead of walking away fuming mad from unkind but innocent remarks. This can be a peaceful and growing stage, as long as you do not use it to avoid all intimate relationships.

Lastly, singleness is important for children because they need to learn to be independent from their parents in order to succeed in their relationships. Children who are able to see and understand the importance of singleness are often better able to succeed in their future love relationships.

(5) FREEDOM

Freedom here is the freedom simply to be the person you were meant to be. This does not mean that your life will be blissful or that you will not run into any more *turkeys*. Instead, it means that you have freed yourself from the expectations that have controlled you. The greatest enemies of divorce recovery are not the other spouse or the legal process; rather, they are the enemies that we all carry within us. These are the enemies of guilt, selfdoubt, inadequacy, and fear of future relationships. At this stage, you no longer focus on the past and instead plan a future on your own terms and in your own direction where you can express feelings of anger, grief, loneliness, rejection, and guilt while actively pursuing a happy and self-fulfilling life.

SPECIAL CONCERNS

(1) ALCOHOL OR DRUG ABUSE

Alcohol or drug abuse shatters many families and complicates many divorces. If you suspect that this is a problem see a certified alcohol or drug counselor right away (Appendix L has a resource list.) Educate yourself about the problem and attempt to determine if and how you contributed to it.

It is surprising how many spouses act consciously or unconsciously in a manner that *enables* the abuser to continue. This is particularly true if one or more of your parents had alcohol or drug problems. There are many support groups for children of alcoholics. Even if you are a complete teetotaller, you could be a *co-alcoholic* or a *co-dependent*. Now is the time to break the cycle so it is not passed on to your children. If you suspect your spouse has a problem, please consider the following.

Most abusers deny their problem and seek to blame you and others for their behavior.

As one client, Ron, stated,

> My wife is a doctor and had me convinced that I was the problem, that I didn't help her enough or support her enough. When I found her misusing both alcohol and drugs, she claimed that I had "driven her to it."
>
> The scary thing is that she had me convinced that I was to blame and I'm no dummy.

Stopping the abuse doesn't mean you have stopped the addiction. Addiction is rarely broken without help. Many addicts can *stop* for months at a time to *prove you wrong*. If they stop cold they will often indulge in other addictive or compulsive behavior, *e.g.* food addiction (binge eating), excessive athletics, overwork, or infidelity.

Professional help is needed to get to the root of most addictions.

Don't settle for *quick fix* treatment programs. There are many program offers to cure the problem in just *ten* or *twenty* days at a hefty price, but long-term outpatient care is often needed.

While these programs can be helpful, they are never a substitute for you and the rest of the family getting a clear understanding of substance abuse and how each may enable it to occur in the family, so that the abuse can be stopped.

(2) DOMESTIC VIOLENCE

Family violence, whether physical or psychological, is a serious problem that has been long neglected. Like alcoholism and drug abuse, it is inter-generational. Children who witness abuse often enter into abusive relation-ships as adults. As with addiction, the abused party often enables the abuse to occur. Appendix L has a reading and resource list regarding abuse.

Abuse can be very subtle and very devastating. Abuse cuts across all classes, races, and cultures. In some upper-class families I have found victims of psychological abuse who have never been hit yet were pushed to the brink of suicide.

One *victim* went to a psychiatrist with severe depression and began an elaborate drug treatment program, which grew into an addiction. This woman was identified as the *problem* of the family. As her anxiety grew she couldn't sleep, she lost touch with reality, and was briefly institutionalized. After that, she moved into a battered women's shelter where she began to see that the problem was not *her* but her husband.

If you were abused as a child, the chances are high that you will pass this abuse on to your children, by abusing them yourself or by allowing your spouse to abuse them. With proper treatment, this intergenerational cycle of abuse can be broken.

(3) SEXUAL FAILURE — SEXUAL INFIDELITY?

For too long we have judged that a failure to perform sexually means that the love is gone from the relationship or that the one who fails is somehow defective. Recent research indicates that up to 40% of sexual failures are due to medication or other factors totally outside of the relationship. *Before you see a sex therapist, see your physician.*

Infidelity is also often misperceived. It can be more a cry for help than the end of a relationship. Recent research indicates that the majority of spouses, male and female, are unfaithful. I am not suggesting that infidelity be simply forgiven and swept under the rug. Rather, if it is honestly and deeply explored, it can lead to a deep renewal of commitment or to a clear decision to part, with each spouse having a better understanding of how to proceed in future relationships.

Life Cycle Crisis: Infidelity often occurs during a *midlife crisis.* Many adults have periods of disorientation and change every seven to ten years. These are periods where our basic purposes in life come into question and where everything that used to have meaning begins to lose meaning. Some have compared the experience to going through adolescence again.

These rites of passage are often hardest on those who endeavor to defer or control the crisis, and easiest for those who openly embrace the crisis as an exciting opportunity for personal growth and change.

(4) AIDS — FEARS AND FACTS

AIDS and other sexually transmitted diseases may prove to be a boon to monogamy. Accusations of AIDS are being used in custody battles and to limit visitation. A review of current research findings indicates the following:

AIDS is everyone's disease — no race, class, gender, age, or sexual preference is spared.

AIDS is *not* passed by normal parental contact such as touching, holding, sharing the same glass, or kissing.

Children are therefore generally *not at risk* living with an AIDS-exposed parent, although extreme caution must be taken when blood of the exposed parent is present. The question is the parent's fitness, not the exposure to AIDS.

Forced testing for AIDS is both unnecessary and dangerous. Forced test results used for court can often *leak* and be made public, causing loss of jobs, frustration of future employment, and loss of or inability to obtain medical coverage. If a party to a divorce has AIDS, steps should be taken to seal the court file so that all can be protected.

Appendix M contains a suggested policy regarding AIDS and parenting.

CONCLUDING REMARK

Many clients report that periodic review of this chapter is helpful in providing a better understanding of the stages of divorce and a clearer understanding of their progress. Before choosing your lawyer, it is important to know your emotional needs.

CHAPTER TWO
CHOOSING YOUR LAWYER

In all probability, your decision to divorce was painfully difficult. Now you are faced with another decision: how do you find a lawyer who is right for you?

A PERSONAL DECISION

With over 18,000 practicing lawyers in Washington and almost 1,000 more joining their ranks each year, you would think the task would be easy. It is not. Before you select a lawyer you must assess your own expectations of the attorney-client relationship. After all, you are buying into a highly personal, albeit temporary, partnership where mutual confidence is a key consideration. This relationship is highly individualized, so it is worth looking around before deciding upon the one attorney whom you trust above all others. Some lawyers can make a client feel instantly secure and comfortable. Others may not be as personable but they may be extremely imaginative in looking for solutions to your particular problems. You need to identify the qualities in a lawyer that are important to you.

It is advisable to do some serious soul-searching before you hire an attorney. Are you certain, for example, that it is a divorce you want? Do you expect the attorney to help you decide or to act as a marriage counselor? If so, you are making a mistake. Most lawyers are not qualified to aid you in this way unless they also are trained as marital therapists. Many will be concerned primarily with getting the legal process started, documenting your financial situation, readying forms for filing, and developing effective strategies. These are the tasks they have been trained to do. You may also wish to consider marital mediation, which is described in Chapter Three, "Divorce Mediation: An Alternative."

Look for a lawyer whose practice is principally involved with marital dissolution work. A lawyer's fine reputation in corporation law, for example, is largely irrelevant to your needs. Also make certain your divorce lawyer has experience with the courts and the legal community of your area.

19

REPUTATION AND RECOMMENDATIONS: KEY QUESTIONS

Most people choose lawyers through their reputations or by asking for recommendations from persons whose opinions they value. Divorced friends are a good source of information, particularly if their cases were satisfactorily resolved. Use caution, however. Do not assume that your friend's lavish praise (or angry denunciation, for that matter) should determine your final decision. Inquire closely about those qualities that your friend either admired or disliked in the attorney. You may want to ask some of the following questions:

1. Did the attorney's efforts interfere with or facilitate your friend's relationship with the former spouse?
2. Did your friend come away from the process feeling informed?
3. Did your friend feel that the attorney's fees were fair?
4. Did the attorney give an initial cost estimate before the proceedings commenced? (Remember, you have a right to ask for an estimate.)

If you follow this route, be sure you see the lawyer to whom you were referred, not his or her associate or partner. Remember that you may want to interview several lawyers until you find the one who suits you. This is your right. You are the employer, and in such a critical matter as divorce it is essential that you find an attorney with whom you can communicate and in whom you can place your trust.

For personal referrals you may also turn to various organizations, your employer, or your labor union. In King, Lewis, Pierce, and Spokane counties, the local county bar association will, through its Lawyer Referral Plan, refer inquiries to lawyers serving on a special panel. The Washington State Bar Association has a Lawyer Referral Service that may be reached through an in-state, toll-free number for Washington residents living outside of King, Lewis, Pierce, and Spokane counties. You can usually find a county Lawyer Referral Service ("LRS") or the Washington State Bar Association LRS in the Yellow Pages of your telephone directory under *Attorneys*. Under an LRS plan, a lawyer will consult with you for a half-hour without charge or for a prescribed low fee, usually $20 or $25; the Washington State Bar Association LRS fee is $15 for the first half-hour. The fee is usually paid directly to the referral service, not the lawyer. See Appendix G for phone numbers.

If your income is low, you may qualify for free legal services through a legal aid program. Look under *Legal Aid* or *Legal Services* in your phone directory.

If you are referred to a lawyer who is a stranger to you, you can sometimes get background information about the lawyer by consulting the *Martindale-Hubbell Law Directory* in the public library. This directory includes a roster of members of the bar in the United States, Canada, and some other foreign countries. Listings paid for by the lawyer or the lawyer's firm appear in the directory's biographical section and include the lawyer's biography and educational background. The biographical listing frequently includes those areas of practice that the lawyer or firm emphasizes. In some instances, ratings of legal ability may be found. Ethical standards, professional reliability and diligence, and other relevant qualifications may also be provided in the general recommendations rating. Those ratings are based upon the confidential recommendations of other lawyers and judges in the community who have been requested by the directory to rate that particular attorney. This directory should be used with caution, however, because not all lawyers choose to have their name listed in the free listings contained in the geographical bar roster and those lawyers who are listed in the directory's biographical section have paid a fee to be listed in that section.

LEGAL CLINICS: THE PROS AND THE CONS

An alternate method of employing a lawyer may be to take advantage of one of the *legal clinics* that have appeared recently around the country. These clinics often handle uncontested divorces at low rates. They are able to charge less because they work on a large volume basis and use simple, standardized forms, with extensive help from paralegal assistants. An uncontested divorce might cost anywhere from $150 to $500 not counting filing fees, depending upon where you live. Of course, the definition of *uncontested divorce* might vary from firm to firm and from state to state. Even in urban areas where costs are higher, legal clinic fees are still less than fees charged by traditional firms. Fees charged by legal clinics are usually set in advance and are based upon a published schedule.

The lower fee is not the only advantage legal clinics provide. Offices are typically located in places with plenty of free parking. Lawyers are available during the day, in the evening, and on Saturdays; also, credit cards are often accepted, and the initial consultation is often free.

There is no certain way to judge the quality of a clinic. One legal clinic proponent suggested,

> "First, you can call the local Bar Association to see whether there have been any disciplinary actions against the firm. Second, you can pay the small initial fee and talk to the clinic lawyers — see what the vibrations are, see what their set-up is, see what their office looks like. Then ask questions." (September 1979, *Consumer Reports*.)

The reader should remember that not all divorce cases lend themselves to the clinic approach. Standardized procedures will not work for complex cases. A law clinic is simply a high-volume, high-efficiency law firm. Since the cost per case is low, the firm can afford to set low fees. High volume, however, carries its own risks. There simply may not be the *horsepower* needed for complex and protracted cases. Clinics are most appropriate for cases that do not involve problems with property division or child custody.

Even if you do not choose to have a legal clinic represent you, you may find it advantageous to have a clinic check the quality of your own paperwork, if you are handling your own divorce. In the event you have concerns about your lawyer's work or if you are unsure whether you should sign an agreement, a visit to a legal clinic might allay your doubts. The consultation fee should be nominal.

THE INITIAL CONFERENCE: A CHECKLIST FOR EVALUATING YOUR LAWYER

Many of my clients confess that they were frightened by the prospect of our initial interview, but later discovered that their fear was unwarranted. I have found that the client's fear is often based on an assumption that he or she will be unable to deal with the lawyer. You can avoid this fear if you identify what you expect from your attorney.

During the initial conference there are some fundamental facts you should acquire. If you plan to see more than one lawyer, use an outline of the questions addressed below as a checklist for your later evaluation. With the answers to these questions, together with impressions gained from your interviews, you should succeed in choosing a suitable lawyer.

1. What are his or her credentials?
   a) Having attended the best law school in the state is no guarantee of outstanding ability, but it helps to know the lawyer's academic background.
   b) If the lawyer belongs to a city or county bar association, the lawyer's colleagues and peers who are also members of the local bar association might provide a ready source of information.
   c) You may check to see on which sections or committees of the state or local bar association the lawyer has served. If he or she has served on sections or committees related to family law, such as the family law section or the taxation section, or if the lawyer holds an office within the association, chances are you're dealing with one of the more committed lawyers in your area.

    d) Look around the office: you may see the degrees, diplomas, professional memberships, and honors the lawyer has attained. Perhaps you will not even need to ask about credentials.

2. What portion of the lawyer's time is spent in family law matters?

    a) Many lawyers in larger cities now deal almost exclusively in divorce cases.

    b) Try to gather information about the lawyer's recent contested divorce cases. Ask the lawyer how he or she felt about the outcome. You will get a good sense of the lawyer's interest in family law by discussing his or her past cases. If the lawyer's last trial was more than a year ago, however, use some caution. This could be a lawyer who will settle at any cost rather than face the rigors of trial. Few, if any, lawyers enjoy such an overwhelming courtroom reputation that no other lawyer in town will try cases against them. On the other hand, too many trials in the last year may indicate that this lawyer lacks the capacity to settle cases or the ability to compromise.

3. What is the lawyer's attitude toward arbitration and mediation?

    Many lawyers agree that the adversary process is inappropriate to divorce cases and are willing to explore alternative forums to resolve disputes between couples. If yours is a case that you feel can be resolved without a courtroom confrontation and this lawyer believes that *the truth* can only be found in the adversary process, then you had better look elsewhere.

4. Is the lawyer willing to discuss the attitudes of the local judges concerning issues relevant to your case?

    Some lawyers may be reluctant to discuss the actual personality of judges before they feel they can *confide* in you; nonetheless, encourage the lawyer to name some judges who have specific biases concerning child support and awarding the family residence, for example. Many lawyers are able to predict in 90% of the cases what the general outcome will be, based on the prevailing judicial attitudes. Getting the client to accept those predictions is often the hardest part of our job. This would be a good time to discuss specific strategies for your case.

5. What is the lawyer's attitude about shared parenting?

    In the recent past, most lawyers and judges discouraged even the thought of this kind of arrangement. Now that the Parenting Act requires joint decision making in many cases, more enlightened lawyers will consider a wider variety of residential parenting options

6. Does the lawyer recommend that only he or she represent both parties or that there is no need for another lawyer?

   If so, you should be advised that in the straight adversary process, lawyers are ethically compelled to represent only one party to the proceedings.

YOU ARE THE EMPLOYER: A CLIENT'S BILL OF RIGHTS

It is important to let your lawyer know exactly what quality and type of legal service you expect. According to some studies by J. Harris Morgan, there are "enormous differences between the client's view of what was wanted from legal services and the lawyer's view of what the client wanted." (Morgan, *Client and Public Relations, A Lawyer's Handbook,* Revised Edition [1975].)

Although lawyers assume that the result is the main criterion used by clients in evaluating their services, other less tangible factors are often more important to the client. One survey concluded that clients responded more favorably to friendliness, promptness, lack of condescension, and being kept informed by their lawyer.

You can control your own divorce proceedings by paying attention to what I call the "Client's Bill of Rights." Those rights are:

1. Insist on a written retainer agreement that explicitly sets out the lawyer's responsibilities.
2. Obtain a written estimate based on the lawyer's hourly rate, including an estimate of costs (such as filing fee, court reporters, and so on).
3. Stay informed about the progress of your case by requesting copies of all letters and documents prepared or received in the lawyer's office in your behalf.
4. Ask questions: communication is a two-way street.
5. Find out your lawyer's qualifications and experience in family law matters at the first consultation.
6. During the first consultation determine how the lawyer plans to represent you and what course of action is expected to be taken during the divorce process.
7. Be aware that you can always change lawyers even if you have signed an agreement. As long as you have paid, the lawyer cannot prevent you from taking your file with you should you decide to change lawyers.

Again, the relationship between client and lawyer is that of employer and employee. *You are the employer, and you have an absolute right to fire your employee at any time, even without cause.*

Conversely, there are a number of responsibilities you as a client must observe if the lawyer is to be an effective advocate on your behalf:

1. Use a checklist (like the one provided in the Chapter Four) when you first consult the lawyer so that a quick profile can be established regarding your case. Include with the checklist relevant documents such as title reports and car titles. This can save hours of work and can mean lower fees.

2. Do not expect your lawyer to guarantee results. Although the lawyer can, and probably will, make predictions about the outcome of your case, most legal problems cannot be predicted with 100% accuracy.

3. Always keep your lawyer informed on any new developments that might affect your case.

4. Take your lawyer's advice, or get another lawyer. You are wasting your money and the lawyer's time if you do not have confidence in the lawyer's special knowledge and skills.

5. Be utterly candid with your lawyer; tell the truth. Legal advice is worthless if it is based on faulty or partial information. Tell your lawyer every fact that is relevant to the situation, particularly facts that do not appear to be in your favor. Lawyers can plan effective strategies around adverse facts, but only if they are aware of them.

6. Avoid phoning your lawyer repeatedly about petty matters. If you write down your concerns in the form of a letter, you might be surprised to see how many of these matters are not consequential. You may decide not to mail the letter. Remember that the lawyer has other clients who require attention too. Indeed, if you involve your lawyer in irrelevant matters, attention will be diverted from the really important aspects of your case. Also, most attorneys charge clients for telephone consultations, so repeated phone calls may significantly increase your attorney's fees.

THE ATTORNEY'S ETHICS

You should expect and demand from your lawyer nothing short of the utmost zeal, confidence, and honesty. Once retained by you, the lawyer must, both by law and by the lawyer's own ethical code, be completely loyal to you. The lawyer should permit neither personal interests, interests of other clients, nor the wishes of third persons to diminish total commitment to you. This includes a commitment to accept employment only in matters in which the lawyer is competent. If the lawyer does not have the expertise to handle your particular divorce case, the lawyer is obliged to refer you to an attorney who does.

If you become dissatisfied with your lawyer and decide to use another lawyer, you should be aware that Washington permits the lawyer to assert a *lien* against whatever paperwork you have provided the lawyer in connection with your case. If the papers are originals that you need for your divorce or other matters, the lawyer has great leverage against you until you have paid the fee. Your new lawyer can help you negotiate this matter. *You can avoid this situation by giving your lawyer only copies of original documents.*

If you believe your lawyer overcharged you, acted unethically, or has failed to represent you fully, you should report this to the Washington State Bar Association. Our state has a mechanism for arbitrating fee disputes and for disciplining unethical lawyers. For more information on fee disputes or unethical lawyer conduct, write to the following address:

Washington State Bar Association
500 Westin Building
2001 Sixth Avenue
Seattle, WA 98121-2599
Telephone: (206) 448-0441

CHAPTER THREE
DIVORCE MEDIATION: AN ALTERNATIVE

Divorce mediation is a promising and increasingly popular method for settling marital conflicts out of court. The financial and emotional costs of a trial can be staggering and many couples are no longer willing to spend a sizable percentage of their earnings on retributive court battles. Instead, many couples now are resolving their divorces out of court with the help of trained divorce mediators and sympathetic lawyers. Divorce mediation is popular throughout California and is gaining acceptance in Washington.

Since our first edition, divorce mediation has begun to blossom:

1. Mediation or some other alternate method of dispute resolution is mandatory for all parenting disputes in King County.
2. Mediation or some other alternate method of dispute resolution is required in all parenting plans unless the parents are unfit.
3. Community dispute centers have been authorized by the legislature to provide *free* or *low-cost* mediation of all civil disputes. King, Snohomish and Spokane counties have dispute centers, which can be contacted through the local bar association.

Note: As of July 1, 1989, mediators must provide written records of the mediation and there is no confidentiality for post-divorce parenting conflicts. If you wish your mediation to be confidential you must make a written contract with the mediator and have all other parties do so.

Mediation means *to be in the middle* (from the Latin, *mediare*). Hence, mediators deal with both facts and feelings in teaching the parties new ways to negotiate in order to settle their disputes. Mediation is not for everyone. A careful reading of this chapter should help you decide if it is for you.

Since mediation pays more attention to the emotions than does litigation, this chapter begins with the story of Bob and Betty and their very personal decision.

For over six months Bob had been dreaming of being alone — away. He wanted a divorce.

But Bob remembered his friends Peter and Ann: they had just finished their divorce trial with experts and affidavits and *everything* — over $30,000 worth of everything. Ann *won* the parenting battle, but neither really liked the decision. The money they had put aside for the twins' college was spent on legal fees, but the real tragedy was seeing them break down under the pressures of court. Peter was sliding at work, hitting the bars late, and hustling — with a strange sort of blind fury — almost any woman he could find. He had liberal parenting rights, but he hadn't seen the kids since the trial, more than two months earlier. Ann seemed mechanical and inaccessible. It appeared that there was just no way for her to get through her bitterness.

What had happened to Peter's and Ann's twins was the worst part of it. Sherry and Sheila used to be near the top of their class, but now they were slipping in school and teachers reported they were *preoccupied, listless, apathetic,* and starting to hang out with the *wrong crowd.*

Bob felt there was no way he could put his family through that. Then he remembered Ben and Cindy.

Ben and his second wife, Cindy, recently divorced out of court, through family mediation. Bob remembered what Ben had told him:

> "The first time I went through divorce, you couldn't tell me *anything*. I had to find reasons and faults. Blame was the name of the game, and I really didn't care what it cost. I got the meanest lawyer I could find and told him to get that woman, but it didn't happen that way. It was all lawyers and experts fighting it out like prize fighters — more over their credentials than over the case.
>
> "That judge never got much of an idea of what our family was all about. My lawyer had me painted like the angel Gabriel and hers had me as Godzilla. Donna was really okay as a mother, but my lawyer got her on the stand and I've never seen *anyone* ripped apart like that. He really won it for me.
>
> "But now that I look at it, we all lost. Donna was really sick for a month after the trial and both the kids bounced in and out of therapy for years. It's been twelve years and we can barely *talk* to each other now. We really had to start from scratch.
>
> "I thought I was doing it for the kids, but it was for me and my pride.
>
> "This time I could see it coming. I didn't let my pride get in the way. After all, the kids didn't care who was right, they just didn't want to lose us.
>
> "So Cindy and I went to a mediator before we filed for divorce and it made a world of difference. He took the time to understand the family and he taught us how to fight fairly and pushed us to stick by our principles but drop the ultimatums. I know it doesn't work for everyone, but it certainly worked for us.
>
> "The kids see Cindy and me work out joint parenting every week and we're a united front. We're confident as parents and the kids seem happy."

Ben had compared the divorce process to dividing up the Thanksgiving turkey:

"In court the focus is on the bird, and the judge does the cutting with all these lawyers and experts arguing about who gets what piece and how much, and what the value of a wing or drumstick is. All you do is sit there and watch it happen until you're called on to say something. When you're done, you wonder whose bird it really is, because there isn't enough left for *anyone* to live on.

"But in mediation, it's the parents who do the cutting. The mediator suggests options and keeps you from getting too heated up. Whatever happens, it's your bird."

Ben and Cindy each had a separate lawyer check out the mediation settlement agreement and that was it — the rest they had done on their own.

Bob did some serious thinking in the next month and realized he had some difficult decisions to make. The problem was how to get a divorce without destroying his family.

TOWARDS A SOLUTION

Bob and Betty went to a trusted lawyer friend who advised them that they had too much property to handle a divorce on their own, and that she could not ethically represent both of them because they had conflicting interests. Court fights usually mean that one side *wins* the parenting-plan battle or a larger share of the property and the other *loses*. Neither Bob nor Betty could bear the thought of living without their children. As Betty said,

"In court I get a lawyer and Bob gets a lawyer and they argue for each of us as individuals. Who argues for our family? How do we save what we've earned for our children? Looks like we need a third lawyer, someone to come in the middle before we go at each other's throats."

When Betty called family court, she was told of the divorce mediation process in which she and Bob could hire a mediator to help settle their disputes. The mediator functions a little like a third lawyer, as the following sections will show.

MEDIATION — WHAT IS IT?

Mediation is often confused with conciliation and arbitration. There is considerable overlap in the techniques used for each process but, in general, proceeding from mediation to conciliation to arbitration involves giving an increasing amount of power to the neutral third party. Basic definitions are as follows:

Mediation: The process of bringing in a neutral third party to help two disputing parties come to a mutually agreeable settlement. The mediator does no counseling. The mediation role is limited to: (1) proposing basic ground rules for the parties' sessions to *keep them on task*; (2) helping the parties define or clarify the issues at hand; and (3) exploring alternative solutions so spouses can come up with a settlement best fitting their particular interests and circumstances.

Conciliation: The traditional distinction between conciliation and mediation is that the conciliator takes a more active role in resolving the conflict. That is, conciliators have a *therapeutic relationship* with the parties wherein they help each party with their negotiating skills and suggest their own solutions to the problems at hand. This traditional distinction is no longer accurate, however, because many divorce mediators use conciliation tactics as well. Therefore, anyone considering hiring a divorce mediator should ascertain whether the person does more than traditional mediation.

Arbitration: Again, a neutral third party is used here, but the arbitrator has the power to *decide the dispute,* as a private judge. In fact, many arbitrators are retired judges and both sides are often represented by lawyers. In *binding arbitration,* the parties agree beforehand to abide by the decision of the arbitrator, as if it were law.

Locally, some sources of arbitrators are the American Arbitration Association and the Washington Arbitration Service. A disadvantage of arbitration is that appeals from an arbitrator's decision are quite difficult to handle. Very few couples arbitrate their divorce. Most prefer mediation where the decisions are made by the parties and not the arbitrator.

Mediation is both a process and a product. As a process, it *forges a transition for the couple from a love/parenting relationship to a parenting relationship.* The product of mediation is more than a divorce: it is a mutually acceptable working agreement between parents who have an enhanced capacity to settle future disputes on their own.

Mediation keeps the power with the parents. It provides an opportunity to preserve the family on the participants' terms instead of the lawyers' and the court's terms. As Ben would say, "It's your bird, not theirs." The feelings and principles of the people involved will form the basis for any mediated settlement. According to O.J. Coogler, one of the founders of modern family mediation,

> "[T]he basic rule of structured mediation is that there should be no victims.... In court you don't know how it is going to come out. In most states, it depends on what judge you get that day, what mood he or she is in that day, and so on."

Coogler also believes that the participation and fairness of mediation prevents parties from being victimized. At a minimum, fairness means that family assets must be fairly distributed according to the needs of all and that children must have access to both parents.

Naturally each side's concept of fairness can change during mediation. According to John Haynes, a former partner of O.J. Coogler, "That's the magic of mediation." Mediation holds a mirror up to each party so that he or she can better see the impact of his or her demands and better understand the needs of the other.

Sometimes hard feelings between parties prevent the compromise necessary for negotiation. Mediation can provide a forum where these feelings are aired. Court rarely does so. Many people, like Ben and Donna, go to court to vent their anger or vindicate their position. When both sides present limited and unrealistic views of the family, the judge, despite his or her best efforts, can be forced into making a *limited* or *winner take all* decision. Courts must make their decisions on the evidence before them.

Mediators can help parties to deal with their anger, fear, and other feelings so that these do not block the progress of settlement. Mediation is not for everyone. It demands that spouses honestly communicate with one another in a structured setting where they are encouraged to clearly state their principles and positions and to negotiate in good faith. This can be difficult at first. Some spouses are simply unwilling to mediate or incapable of doing so. An exercise to determine your willingness and capacity to mediate is presented later in this chapter.

MEDIATION —HOW IS IT DONE?

The actual techniques of mediation differ with each practitioner and family. According to John Haynes,

> "[O]ne part of mediation is to lay out all the options. I look at every problem in divorce as a skein of wool that has to be carded. We have to look at each problem — children, finances, the family home — one by one. Then I will try to separate out each problem into component parts. Then I look at all the options I can think of and ask the parents to think of options of their own.... Perhaps it's the way we were educated, but most people come in with this idea that there is really just one way to do things; that there's just one way to think about dividing up the children's time, for instance, when there are perhaps five or six ways, or more, and we can begin to explore all the options before making any decisions."

With rare exceptions, mediation is future oriented. The past cannot be changed. The task is to determine how, starting right now, the parties can become cooperative, responsible, and separate parents.

MEDIATION — THE PROCESS

There are a number of mediation procedures. For illustrative purposes, O.J. Coogler's "Structured Family Mediation Method" will be summarized. Structured family mediation uses one mediator, who is not an attorney, and an advisory attorney is brought in later in the process to answer deferred legal questions and draft the Settlement Agreement. Mediation by two mediators (one a family attorney and the other a trained therapist) is becoming increasingly popular and has shown a greater effectiveness in dealing with difficult cases. In King County, this form of mediation (commonly called "co-mediation") is offered by Rainier Mediation and many other mediation services. The following schedule presumes a single, non-lawyer mediator.

Orientation Session

Here, the terms and conditions of mediation are explained and, if the parties wish to proceed, an agreement is signed and an advance deposit for ten hours of mediation is paid. Coogler has six basic rules for mediation, which are as follows:

1. The mediator cares about both parties and their children but will not represent any side.
2. Their participation in mediation is voluntary, but the mediator will not allow either side to coerce, abuse, or blame the other in an effort to force one spouse to agree to take any certain action.
3. Everything that occurs in mediation is confidential and should not be used in court if mediation does not succeed.
4. Any agreement the couple comes up with must be based upon adequate information, which means that both sides must agree to disclose fully what they know about family finances.
5. The mediator cannot require the mother and father to cooperate, but he or she can keep them from negotiating with one another in noncooperative ways. In other words, minimum civility is required during these sessions.
6. The mediator will not endorse any agreement regarding a parenting plan for children that does not provide for the children's contact with both parents.

Under Coogler's system, mediation sessions take place once per week and last two hours.

First Session

Hour 1

The first issue to be faced is the agenda — deciding the order in which issues will be considered. Parties are free to set any order they prefer. A common agenda is as follows:

1. Identification and division of marital property;
2. Spousal maintenance (if any);
3. Child support; and,
4. Parenting (child custody and visitation).

Next, parties will provide information on their finances and financial needs and the session will be concluded with a draft of a temporary Settlement Agreement. *The purpose of a temporary Settlement Agreement is to maintain the status quo during the mediation.* The agreement is in effect only during mediation and does not bind either party regarding the final decision.

Hour 2

If there is no custody controversy, the parties should agree on residency or visitation. The children can be present in this session but this often requires an extra session. After residency, marital property is considered. First, the property is fully disclosed, then valued, which may necessitate bringing in experts for property of a complex nature or uncertain value. Couples rarely bring full property information to the first session, so the final division is often deferred.

Once the combined budgets of the parties are provided, the mediator checks to see if they exceed the parties' combined incomes. If they do, then parties are directed to look separately for ways to reduce their budgets or increase their incomes.

Sessions II and III

Hours 3 to 6

Here parties work to flesh out the specifics of property division, support, and parenting. Parties needing more time can request it and pre-pay the fees to cover the anticipated costs. Extra time allows the mediator to suspend discussion on one issue (parenting, for example) on which the parties are deadlocked and return to it later after other issues have been resolved.

Session IV

Hour 7

If the parties are in agreement on all the basic issues, an advisory attorney is brought in to examine the settlement and to answer any deferred legal questions. Answers to legal questions often require further information from the parties, so more time may be scheduled here.

Hour 8

If the legal questions are fully answered during the prior hour, the advisory attorney will present the final Settlement Agreement to the parties for their examination and approval during this hour. Further time can be scheduled if substantial changes in the agreement are needed.

Session V

Hours 9 and 10

If parenting is still unresolved, then all financial issues should be resolved in a written agreement leaving custody and visitation for this last session. Prior to the session, agreement will be reached as to whether or not the children will participate in the session. The degree of participation by the children must be previously agreed upon and announced to the children during the session.

Parties with further difficulties are reminded that no parenting arrangements are permanent and that they might wish to opt for a temporary arrangement, after which time they can decide to:

a) Continue the arrangement;

b) Agree to change it; or

c) Agree to return to mediation if they don't agree on the changes necessary.

There are many other methods of mediation with different degrees of structure. All methods encourage the parties to proceed as they see fit.

Now that one method of mediation has been summarized, we shall consider its effectiveness.

MEDIATION — THE RESULTS

Mediation is booming. It has gained wide acceptance nationally and has been mandatory in California courts since early 1981. Mediation of visitation and custody issues has been mandatory in King County since August 1982, in an experimental program, and has been continued for all parenting disputes, although some other alternate method of dispute resolution may be used. Research has been done comparing mediation to litigation, but more time is needed to obtain definitive results. Two studies of mediation provide noteworthy results.

Fairfax County

This small study in Fairfax County, Virginia, involved couples who were asked to compare mediation to litigation regarding the relative costs, the fairness of the process, and their satisfaction with the results obtained. The cost of a mediated settlement was found to be approximately $550 less than the average cost of litigation. The *terms* of settlement were satisfactory to 100% of the mediated couples and approximately 50% of the litigating couples. Lastly, couples were asked to indicate their satisfaction with the whole divorce process. Fifty-three percent of the mediating couples were *very satisfied* compared to 15% of the litigating couples.

Denver Project

This extensive research study was undertaken by the Divorce Mediation Research Project in Denver, Colorado. In this study, couples contemplating divorce were randomly offered free mediation as an alternative to litigation. Initial results indicate that mediation does *not* consistently save money, but that there are other savings. Successful mediation results in less re-litigation of cases, generally saves time, and allows fewer misunderstandings between the parties and a greater satisfaction with the process.

To summarize the findings:

1. *Percentage of cases going to trial.* Eighty percent of those in mediation (including those failing mediation) settled before trial. Fifty percent of those in litigation settled before trial.

2. *Increased understanding and communication with spouse.* Approximately 50% of those mediating reported better understanding and communication with their spouses compared with approximately 10% of those in litigation.

3. *Increased visitation and joint custody.* Comparing the results of mediated and litigated settlements regarding *liberal visitation,* it was found that visitation occurred approximately 7.7 days per month for successfully mediated coupless and 4.9 days per month for litigated couples. Joint custody was agreed to by 69% of those successfully mediating and by 7% of those litigating.

4. *Re-litigation within 12 months.* Sixty-six percent of the successful mediating couples reported that the other spouse was in complete compliance. Thirty-four percent of the litigating couples reported their spouse in complete compliance.

5. *Savings in time and attorney fees.* Parties successful in mediation completed the entire divorce procedure in approximately 8.5 months. Those in litigation averaged 10.2 months. However, those failing mediation averaged 14.2 months. Mediation was less costly only for those who succeeded at mediation *and* who began mediation *before temporary court orders were entered.*

Again, the reader should be reminded that these results should only serve as guidelines in making a decision to mediate.

MEDIATION — ARE YOU READY?

Using the prior information, it may be profitable to make some decision about your readiness for mediation. Readiness depends first upon willingness and next upon capacity. Dr. Sheila Kessler, a prominent trainer of mediators, offers the following checklist to help determine if you are ready to mediate.

AM I WILLING TO MEDIATE

1. Is each issue (for example, custody of our children) negotiable? Yes No

2. Am I willing to make some compromises?   Yes ____   No ____

3. Do I trust my former spouse enough to think he or she will uphold a mutually satisfactory agreement regarding the children? (There is almost always some doubt.)   Yes ____   No ____

4. Am I willing to deal with my anger for a while so that I can confront the issues in a rational manner?   Yes ____   No ____

5. Can I truly live up to what I agree to (regarding the children)?   Yes ____   No ____

6. Am I capable of listening to the other person's side of the story?   Yes ____   No ____

7. Do I see this process in terms of compromise rather than winning or losing?   Yes ____   No ____

If your answers are mostly yes to these questions, you may be a good candidate for mediation. The next checklist will help you determine if you are ready. You should be able to answer most of the following questions. Do not be discouraged if you cannot provide detailed answers to the questions right now. Think of answering this checklist as an initial assignment.

AM I READY TO MEDIATE

1. Do I know what my current income is and what I can anticipate in the future?   Yes ____   No ____
2. Do I know what my former spouse's income is and what he or she can anticipate in the future?   Yes ____   No ____
3. Do I know what the household budget was before I separated?   Yes ____   No ____
4. Have I drawn up a reasonable budget for my household if a shared parenting plan is worked out?   Yes ____   No ____
5. Have I drawn up a reasonable budget for the parent with the *majority* of child-rearing responsibilities if a shared parenting plan is not worked out?   Yes ____   No ____
6. Have I drawn up a reasonable budget for the parent with the *minority* of child-rearing responsibilities if a shared parenting plan is not worked out?   Yes ____   No ____
7. Have I calculated the financial assets from the marriage (the value of the house, cars, investments, furniture, pension plans, *etc.*)?   Yes ____   No ____
8. Have I thought through how I would like the day-to-day parenting arrangements for my children to be set up for the next couple of months? For the next year or two? Until the children are of age?   Yes ____   No ____

MEDIATION — HOW TO FIND YOUR MEDIATOR

There are many mediators and many mediation groups in Washington State. Their experience, competence, and technique vary markedly, so there is probably one who will fit your needs. The Family Court of your county should have a list of mediators in your locality. If not, you may write to the Mediation Consortium of Washington State, an umbrella group of mediators in this state, and ask for a list of mediators for referral. The Consortium may be contacted by writing to P.O. Box 4323, Pioneer Station, Seattle, Washington 98104. You may also contact Rainier Mediation, 900 Fifth Avenue, Suite 1616, Seattle, Washington 98164.

Regardless of where you go to find a mediator, *do not choose one until you have interviewed a number of them.* Each person you interview will give you further insights into the nature of mediation, your expectations of mediation, and the results that professionals are willing to provide. The following interview lists are adapted from the work of Ciji Ware in her book *Sharing Parenthood after Divorce.*

Ask all the pertinent questions on the accompanying lists each time you talk with an attorney or a counselor. Each interview should allow you to further focus your questions. Attorneys and therapists not willing to answer your questions frankly should not be given further consideration.

ATTORNEY/MEDIATOR INTERVIEW

WITH: _____

NOTES:

1. What percentage of his/her work is in divorce and parenting matters?   _____

2. Where did he/she take legal/mediation training?   _____

3. How many years has he/she practiced family law?   _____

4. Is there a family law specialty or certification offered by the state bar association? (Washington has no such specialty.) Has this attorney been certified under such a program? For how long?   _____

5. Has he/she ever written any shared parenting agreements? How did they work out for the families?   _____

6. What does this attorney think about the concept of former spouses sharing parenting responsibilities?   _____

7. When does this attorney refer clients to mental health professionals?   _____

8. How often does this attorney find that clients need specialized help with the emotional aspects of divorce?   _____

9. Has this attorney ever served in a mediating capacity for spouses who think they might be able to negotiate a parenting and/or financial settlement? How often?   _____

10. If this attorney will mediate, will he/she agree *in writing* not to represent either side should the negotiations fail?   _____

11. What kind of formal training in mediation has this attorney taken?   _____

12. Does this attorney refer certain aspects of a divorce to tax specialists or other experts? Under what circumstances?   _____

13. What is the hourly fee charged by this attorney?   _____

14. What is his/her usual retainer?   _____

15. Is this attorney willing to submit to clients an itemized bill each month during the time he/she is employed by the client?   _____

16. Will this attorney be doing the legal work involved in this case, or will a junior partner or an associate have the major responsibility for this case?   _____

17. What is the approximate cost of divorces similar to yours, as you've briefly explained it.   _____

18. Will this attorney give you the names of one or two clients he/she has represented or mediated, after the clients have been contacted by the attorney and have given the attorney permission to release their names?   _____

19. Will this attorney agree to keep you apprised of all developments in your case and make no offers or agreements without first consulting you and securing your approval?   _____

20. How does this attorney deal with couples who have different bargaining powers? _____

COUNSELOR/MEDIATOR INTERVIEW

WITH:_____

NOTES:

1. What percentage of his/her work involves divorce counseling and mediation of parenting and financial settlement issues? _____

2. Where did the counselor/mediator take his/her training? _____

3. Has this person trained in *family systems* work? _____

4. How many years has this person worked in the divorce field? _____

5. What degree and/or licenses does this person hold? _____

6. Is this person affiliated with a clinic, community mental health association, family services group, or conciliation court in addition to, or exclusive of, a private practice? _____

7. What kind of specific training in divorce mediation has this person had? _____

8. How many divorces or parenting mediation cases does this person handle in a month? In a year? _____

9. What does this person think the *impact on the child* is when fathers share a significant portion of child-rearing responsibilities? _____

10. Is this person a member of the Mediation Consortium of Washington State, Family Mediation Association, the Association of Family Conciliation Courts, the Family Service Associations of America, the American Arbitration Association, or church-related professional counseling associations? _____

11. Is it this person's practice to see all members of the immediate family if possible or practical? _____

12. Does this person ever testify in court or through affidavit on behalf of *only one side* (mothers or fathers only) in parenting matters? _____

13. What does this counselor or mediator think of the concept of former spouses sharing parenting responsibilities equally? _____

14. Has this counselor been divorced? Does he/she have children? Does he/she have a working spouse? Has he/she remarried? Has he/she participated in the day-to-day care of his/her own children? _____

15. What is the hourly fee for this person's services? _____

16. Does this person call in or refer certain aspects of a case to a certified public accountant or other expert? Under what circumstances? _____

17. What is the anticipated number of sessions for the mediation process? At what total (estimated) cost? _____

MEDIATION — THE DANGERS

No balanced consideration of mediation can avoid addressing the known shortcomings of mediation, chief of which is the fact that the long-term effects of mediation are not yet known.

The relative newness of mediation is one problem because many persons flock to mediation with hopes unreasonably raised by numerous articles that provide a less-than-balanced appraisal of mediation. Others have jumped on the mediation bandwagon because it is new (and therefore better) or because mediation appears to be anti-lawyer and pro-consumer. None of these factors, however, has any bearing whatsoever on the mediator's capacity to resolve a family dispute.

The second major problem is that the informal, trusting atmosphere of mediation provides an opportunity for deception and bad faith. Parties may chose mediation to avoid responsibility for their actions. For example, choosing mediation to:

1. Convince your spouse that you are right;
2. Have the mediator tell you what to do;
3. Reconcile you with your spouse; and,
4. Delay the divorce.

A party may also use mediation in bad faith to:

1. Get shared parenting in order to have better leverage in later property bargaining;
2. Fool a spouse into accepting less than he or she would in court; and,
3. Avoid legal discovery in order to hide some of the party's assets and income.

The third major problem is intimidation between parties of unequal power. Where a spouse has been subject to emotional or physical abuse, the fear is likely to continue through the mediation sessions. The fear and intimidation could cause the spouse to settle for much less than is really needed. This is particularly dangerous where only one mediator is used because the single mediator cannot support one party without appearing to be partisan. With two mediators (co-mediation), much more support can be lent to the victimized spouse while still maintaining the objectivity of the mediation. However, the victimized spouse may, in many cases, need legal representation in order to gain equal power in the mediation.

Lastly, mediation creates many ethical problems for lawyers and laypersons. Some states have discouraged or disallowed attorneys from being mediators because they feel lawyers cannot ethically represent both sides of a conflict. Layperson mediation is also discouraged by some bar associations because they believe it constitutes an unauthorized practice of law. Comediation with an attorney and a mental health specialist gets around some of these problems but, in the end, each spouse should have the Settlement Agreement examined by a separate attorney prior to final approval.

One problem with this *unauthorized practice of law* criticism is that it assumes that all people can afford separate attorneys. If the choice is between having no attorney whatsoever or a mediator, the parties would likely be better off with the mediator, especially in light of the ethical problems involved where one lawyer agrees to represent both parties. These problems should be kept in mind and raised when interviewing potential mediators.

For the sake of contrast, a few problems of litigation are:

1. It can be exceedingly costly;
2. It can escalate conflict between parties and their children;

3. It can undermine the commitment and cooperation necessary for post-divorce parenting; and,

4. Orders of the court are often resisted or defied and securing compliance can cause further expense.

In conclusion, mediation has both significant promise and significant problems. If chosen after careful consideration, it can reduce the potential harm of litigation, increase the parties' communication skills, decrease the trauma to the children, and increase the value and strength of the family.

For Bob and Betty, the goal of family mediation is to humanize the divorce process. Their success will depend upon their initiative. There are no shortcuts in marriage, in raising a family, or in family mediation.

CHAPTER FOUR
PREPARING FOR YOUR LAWYER

Many people believe that the only person who will benefit from their divorce will be the lawyer!

Time is what a lawyer sells, so the more background work you do on your case, the less time you will need to buy from your lawyer. Unless your hourly rate is greater than the lawyer's, your efforts to prepare your own background and financial information are bound to save you money.

I have included Mary Ellen's fact sheet in this chapter. Use it as a guide. Most of my clients complete a similar questionnaire prior to our first conference.

TAKING CHARGE: REDUCING YOUR COSTS

In addition to saving attorney fees, the process of committing your assets and liabilities to paper is a learning experience. This exercise is consistent with my belief in fully involving the client in the divorce process. This is a particularly valuable experience for dependent spouses, who have less experience with the family finances. For the first time, they are required to account for the tangible assets and liabilities present in their marriage. This *mastery of the facts* provides these spouses some measure of control over what is happening to them. Although I recognize that many of my divorcing clients feel they cannot cope with the arduous task of filling out a family budget, it is well worth the effort. In fact, completing this difficult task as best you can is really an investment in the future because I have found that *those who take control at this point are better able to solve post-dissolution problems without the aid of a lawyer.*

THE BACKGROUND QUESTIONNAIRE

There is truth in the adage that *two can live cheaper than one*. The aftermath of a divorce includes the creation of two households where one previously existed. That means that the same family incomes and resources will now have to stretch to serve two homes. I will use the information below in order to assess the financial impact of the divorce on your future lifestyle.

Furnish this information for both spouses, not just yourself. Unlike a medical history, a legal history involves three parties: you, your spouse, and that entity that you are about to dissolve, the marriage. The lawyer needs to know details, sometimes even intimate and embarrassing details, about all three entities to do a good job.

What follows are the questionnaires Mary Ellen completed:

A. GENERAL BACKGROUND

		WIFE	HUSBAND
1.	Birthday	7/7/44	9/6/43
	a) Age now	45	46
	b) Age when married	22	23
2.	Date of marriage	8/20/74	8/20/74
	a) Place (city)	Seattle	Seattle
	b) County	King	King
	c) State	Washington	Washington
3.	Extent of education	4 yrs college	4 yrs college
	a) Other (list)		
	b) Other (list)		Grad. School
4.	Vocational skills	Education	M.B.A.
5.	List when used such skill		
	last	6/74	Currently
6.	Religion		
7.	State all health problems since marriage		
	a) List doctors currently seen		
	b) List medications currently taken		

B. EMPLOYMENT, EARNINGS

		WIFE	HUSBAND
1.	Employer		Med-Equip, Inc.
	a) Address		
	b) Telephone number		
	c) Job title		President
	d) Length of employment		9 years
	e) Work schedule		Flexible

2. Information Regarding Family Income from All Sources

	WIFE	HUSBAND

a) List gross income for past two years (attach copies of tax returns; if unavailable, copies of W2 Forms)

	WIFE	HUSBAND
(1989) $		$50,000
(1988) $		$48,000

b) **Present annual gross** wage or income; (attach pay stubs for last two pay months)

c) Other present and projected **annual** income, including commissions, bonuses, rentals, real estate contracts, pension, profit sharing, disability, unemployment or sick leave benefits, interest, public assistance, Social Security, dividends, child support.

		WIFE	HUSBAND
Identify source:	profit sharing	1) $	1) $ 5,940
Identify source:		2) $	2) $

d) Projected **annual gross** income (items 2(b) and 2(c))

	TOTAL GROSS:	TOTAL GROSS:
1983	$	$ 60,440
1984	$	$
1985	$	$

3. **Projected annual** reductions from gross income:

1) FICA SS	1) $ _____	1) $ 3,605
2) Income tax	2) $ _____	2) $ 6,142*
(# of dependents)		4
3) Union dues	3) $ _____	3) $ _____
4) Health, life insurance premiums	4) $ _____	4) $ _____
5) Pension contributions	5) $ _____	5) $ _____
6) Industrial insurance	6) $ _____	6) $ _____
7) Other compulsory deduction Identify:	7) $ _____	7) $ _____

4. **Total annual reductions** $ _____ $ 9,747

5. **Annual net income**
(line 3(d) less line 5) $ _____ $50,693

6. **Monthly net income**
(line 6 divided by 12) $ _____ $ 4,224

7. If any child of yours
works, either part- or
full-time, list child's
total net earnings
per month. $ _____ $ _____

*Assumes husband will claim interest deductions on house payments, *etc.*

Children of this Marriage

	Name	**Birthdate**	**Age**	**Custodian**
(1)	Justin	5-1-77	12	Mother
(2)	Kristin	12-2-80	9	Mother
(3)				
(4)				

Mother's Children

	Name	**Birthdate**	**Age**	**Present Custodian**
(1)				
(2)				
(3)				

Father's Children

	Name	Birthdate	Age	Present Custodian
(1)				
(2)				
(3)				

Are any children handicapped or disabled?	Yes	No
If yes, indicate which child and detail problem.		
Are any children adopted?	Yes	No
If yes, indicate if by step-parent or other.		

C. LIVING EXPENSES

Most of us have never made a budget, much less lived within one. However, spiraling inflation makes budget planning just good economic sense. The hard facts of a divorce demand that you start planning your future living expenses now. You may want to consult a financial planner.

To prepare a budget, start reviewing your check register or canceled checks. If you pay by cash or credit for most household expenses, start keeping receipts. Even if you pay by check you will be surprised at the number of items purchased with cash or credit, so do not forget to factor in these outlays too. The following sample budget, with Mary Ellen's household expenses, will help you prepare your budget.

In answering budgetary questions, calculate your expenses for the future, after separation. Take into account whether you or your spouse will have primary residency of the children. Calculate the children's expenses as if you are the one who will have primary residency. Many expenses, such as clothing and insurance, are not regular monthly expenses; the annual costs of such expenses must be amortized on a monthly basis and funds set aside each month in order to meet the expenses.

1. HOUSING:

Rent, mortgage, or contract payments	$	875.00
Installment payments for improvements	$	
Installment payments for furniture, appliances	$	
Taxes and insurance (if not in monthly payments)	$	125.00
Other:	$	
TOTAL HOUSING	$	1,000.00

2. UTILITIES:

Heat (gas and oil)	$	90.00
Electricity	$	50.00
Water, sewer, garbage	$	30.00
Telephone	$	18.00
Other:	$	
TOTAL UTILITIES	$	188.00

3. FOOD AND SUPPLIES:

For (3) people	$	500.00
Supplies (paper, tobacco, pets)	$	
Meals eaten out	$	50.00
TOTAL FOOD AND SUPPLIES	$	550.00

4. CHILDREN:

Babysitter	$	50.00
Clothing	$	80.00
Special health care or treatment not included in paragraph (6.) below	$	
Lessons, sports, clubs	$	50.00
School expenses (not tuition)	$	
Tuition (if any)	$	
Haircuts, personal expenses, allowances	$	40.00
TOTAL EXPENSES OF CHILDREN	$	220.00

5. TRANSPORTATION:

Vehicle payments or leases	$	208.00
Vehicle insurance and license	$	38.00
Vehicle gas, oil, ordinary maintenance	$	40.00
Vehicle repairs — identify	$	25.00
Parking, toll bridge	$	
Taxi or public transportation	$	
TOTAL TRANSPORTATION	$	311.00

6. HEALTH CARE (omit if fully covered):

Insurance, if **not** itemized in (4.) above	$	150.00
Uninsured dental expense	$	27.50
Uninsured medical expense	$	27.50
Uninsured eye-care expense	$	
Uninsured drugs, prosthetics, *etc.*	$	12.50
TOTAL HEALTH CARE	$	217.50

7. PERSONAL EXPENSES

Clothing (include credit card payments)	$	75.00
Cosmetics	$	20.00
Clubs and recreation	$	50.00
Education	$	100.00
Books, newspapers, magazines, photos	$	20.00
Gifts	$	50.00
Other:	$	
TOTAL PERSONAL	$	315.00

8.   MISCELLANEOUS:

Life insurance (if not deducted from income)	$	50.00
Court-ordered support or maintenance		
Identify beneficiary of such payment:_____	$	
Savings	$	100.00
TOTAL MISCELLANEOUS	$	150.00

9.   DEBTS (not included above):

Creditor	Amount	Monthly Payment
MasterCard	$1,200	$ 50
Visa	800	50
Nordstrom	650	50
Sears	300	40
TOTAL MONTHLY DEBT PAYMENTS	$	190.00

10.	TOTAL MONTHLY EXPENSES		
	(Total of lines 1 to 9)	$	3,141.50
11.	MONTHLY NET INCOME		
	(From item 6 under "wife's income")	$	—0—

PROPERTY: LISTING AND VALUING

The next major area to explore with your lawyer is property distribution (see Chapter Five, "Property Division"). To advise properly, the lawyer will need to be adequately informed about all your assets and liabilities. When listing and valuing your property, try to be as specific as possible. The hardest part of this will be placing a valuation on each item. I have included some methods to help you with this task. For example, to find the present market value of your home, enlist the aid of a realtor. He or she will be happy to evaluate your home in the hope of acquiring your listing if you choose to sell. A commonly used source for valuing vehicles is the N.A.D.A. Official Used Car Guide or blue book, which is published monthly and is available through most automobile dealerships and some public libraries. Insurance adjusters can give you a more accurate value of your car than a car dealership, as they use additional sources for valuing a car, such as the *gold book* and the *Cars of Particular Interest* (CPI) book. A few telephone calls should give you an idea of the current value of your vehicle, but a physical inspection is the only reliable method for determining your car's value. The same methods apply to boats and trailers. In some cases you may need to check with your banker or insurance agent.

Mary Ellen filled out the following questionnaire after a week of inquiry. As she gave it to me she said,

"I never thought I could get this done because I really had no idea where to begin. Once I found a good realtor, things became a lot easier because the realtor explained so much about property that I didn't know before and didn't charge me a cent! You know, I feel a lot better about the future now that I have an idea of what we own and what it's worth."

1. Family home
    a) Address _____

    City, state, ZIP _____
    b) Date of purchase   July 1981
    c) Purchase price $ 75,000
    d) Down payment $ 35,000
    e) Source of down payment   Sale of previous home
    f) Monthly payment $ 375
    g) Current mortgage balance $ 38,000
    h) Present market value $175,000
    i) Present annual taxes $ 1,100

2. Other: List details as above
    Vacation property _____

3. Investment Property
    a) Duplex: 110 Riverton Dr.
    b) Owned equally with   R.G. Walker
                              Mike Overton
    c) Date of purchase   September 1979
    d) Purchase price $125,000
    e) Down payment $ 12,500
    f) Monthly payments $ 250
    g) Taxes $ 666.66 each

    a) Condo: 1411 Mirror Lake
    b) Partners   As above
    c) Date of purchase   July 1980
    d) Purchase price $ 47,500
    e) Down payment $ 3,000 each
    f) Monthly payments $ 170 each
    g) Taxes $ 266.66 each

a) 12 acres undeveloped land
b) (See attached paper
  for boundaries)
c) Partners as above

d) Date of purchase	February 1981
e) Purchase price	$ 60,000
f) Down payment	$ 4,000
g) Monthly payments (paid directly from Med-Equip)	$ 600 each
h) Taxes	$ 173 each

4. Automobiles Owned by Community (including motorcycles and recreational vehicles):

Year	Make	Market Value	Amount Owed	To Whom	Who Uses Car
1987	Honda	$ 4,800	$1,200	Washington Mutual	Mary Ellen
1985	Jeep	$10,500	$ 0		Jim

5. Boats and Trailers:

Year	Make	Market Value	Amount Owed	To Whom	Who Uses
1973	Ranger Sailboat	$14,000	$2,000	Prudential Mutual	Jim

6. Furniture and Appliances*:

Room	Item	Balance Owing	Market Value
Living room	Brown wool sofa		$ 350
Living room	Brown wool sofa		$ 350
Living room	2 wing chairs		$ 200
Living room	Glass cocktail table		$ 300
Living room	Etagere		$ 250
Living room	2 end tables		$ 200
Dining room	Table & 6 chairs	$ 600	$ 800
Dining room	Buffet		$ 300
Laundry	Washer & dryer		$ 50

Room	Item	Balance Owing	Market Value
Laundry	Freezer		$ 150
Master bedroom	Dresser, 2 night stands, bed		$ 400
Kristin's room	Dresser		$ 100
Kristin's room	Desk		$ 75
Justin's room	Bunk bed/desk	$ 300	$ 300
Family room	Hide-a-bed		$ 250
Family room	T.V.		$ 200
Family room	Coffee table		$ 100
Entry hall	Antique rug	$ 600	$1,500
Kitchen	Oak table/4 chairs		$ 700
Rec room	Pool table		$ 100
Rec room	T.V.		$ 75

* Be sure you do not place too high a value on your home furnishings. A good measure of value is what you would probably get for it at a *cash only* garage sale and *not* the item's retail price or the replacement value.

7. Unusual Items (anitques, stamps, coins, sporting equipment, other):

Item	Date Acquired	Price at Acquisition	Current Market Value	Balance Owed and To Whom	Who Uses
Antique rug	May 1988	$1,500	$1,500	Pande Cameron	Both
Tent	June 1985	$ 259	$ 200		Jim
Club membership	June 1982	$2,500	$2,500		Both

8. Life Insurance:

Face Amount	Company	Type Policy Number	Person Insured	Benefits	Cash or Loan Value	Outstanding Loan
$ 50,000	Mutual of Wash-ington	Whole Life/ 7654012	Jim	$11,000		
$100,000	Mutual of Wash-ington	Term/ 6542301	Jim			

9. Bank Accounts:

Name of Bank	Branch	Type of Account	Current Balance	Who May Withdraw	Balance at Separa-tion	Name	Date Open
First In-terstate	Main	Pass-book	$6,500	Both	$7,300	Jim, Mary Ellen	7/10/76

10. Stocks, Bonds, Commodities, Margin Accounts (see Appendix):

Name	Number of Shares	Purchase Price Per	Current Price	Total Current Value	If Bond, List Current Value
Celanese	500	45-1/8	55-1/2	$27,750	

11. Certificates of Deposit:

	1.	2.	3.
Face amount	_____	_____	_____
Maturity date	_____	_____	_____
Where located	_____	_____	_____
Interest	_____	_____	_____

12 Loans and Other Debts:

	Security Deposits	Earnest Money	Loans	Promissory Notes	Mortgages and Contracts
Amount					
Owed by whom					
Due when					

13. Pension, Retirement, Profit Sharing:

	WIFE	HUSBAND
a) From whom	_____	Med-Equip, Inc.
b) Your contribution		
c) Company contribution	_____	$2,000 per year
d) State if vested or not	_____	Vested
e) If not vested, years to go before vested		
f) Lump sum entitled to now	_____	$20,000
g) Monthly amount entitled to now	_____	_____
h) Date and age when entitled		
i) Current age	_____	_____

BUSINESS VALUATION

A business may appear to be worth nothing because almost all profits are consumed by salaries. Salaries do, however, help determine the value of the business. In any event, you will probably need a Certified Public Accountant or an appraiser to find out exactly what the business is worth. The company's most recent financial statements would help this process along.

14. Does your spouse own or operate a business?   Yes__X__ No_____
    a) Name: Med-Equip, Inc._____ When started: __1980__
    b) Were you married then?   Yes__X__ No_____
    c) Is it incorporated?   Yes__X__ No_____
    d) If yes, total no. shares outstanding: __300___
    e) How many do you own?   __100___
    f) Does your spouse hold any shares?   Yes_____ No_____
    g) Are you or your spouse an officer?   Yes__X__ No_____
         If yes, indicate who and which office: Husband,_____President
    h) How many employees in business?   __25___
    i) Net worth (latest quarter or last year):   _____
    j) Profit or loss made last year:_____ Last quarter:_____
    k) Where are the books kept? _____

15. Did you provide your spouse with an education?   Yes__X__ No_____
    a) If yes, list when: _____Sept. 1974 - June 1976_____
    b) What education was received: ____M.B.A._____
    c) If you worked then, your monthly take-home pay: ____$475.00_____
    d) If your spouse worked, his or her monthly take-home pay: _____
    e) The source of each of your incomes: H _____
                                             W ___Teaching_____

16. Have you completed any financial statements
    or loan applications: Yes__X__ No_____
    Date made: 1-30-89_____
    For whom: First Interstate_____
    Present location: Main office_____

17. Have you ever signed an agreement that altered the
    ownership rights between you and your spouse
    (*e.g.* community or separate property agreement)?   Yes_____ No__X____
    Date: N/A____
    Where located:? _____
    Reason for agreement: _____

18. Have you ever signed a guarantee or indemnification
    agreement making you or your spouse liable in the
    event another breaches that agreement?   Yes_____ No___X___
    State when signed:___N/A_____
    For whom: _____
    If in default: _____
    Amount guaranteed: _____
    What security was given?_____
    State where agreement located: _____

19. When you married did you give up social security,
    alimony (maintenance), retirement?   Yes_____ No___X___
    a) If yes, list what you gave up: _____
    b) Monthly amount received: _____
    c) How long would you have received it?_____
    d) Can you get it back?_____

20. Separate property — any property that you or your spouse
    a) owned at the time you married: _____
    b) received through inheritance: _____
    c) received as a gift: ____ring_____
    d) acquired after a permanent separation: _____

21. If you own such property, list and describe it below:

List Property	Date Acquired	Balance Owed at Time of Marriage	In Whose Name Is Title Held	How Acquired
Diamond ring	At marriage	None	Jim	Inheritance

22. If you contributed separate property to the marriage, list what property that was,
    when you contributed it, what the value is, and why you contributed it to the
    marriage:

    _____

Be prepared to tell your lawyer whether you kept this property strictly in
your name or commingled it (mixed it into the common pot of assets) with
other marital assets. In Washington, a community property jurisdiction,
separate property can be converted into community property if steps are not
taken to preserve its separate character. Remember, if you and your spouse
can deal fairly and openly with each other, you can divide much of the
property yourselves without the help of lawyers. (For further information on
this topic, see Chapter Nine, "Self-Help.")

KEY DOCUMENTS: A CHECKLIST

You can shortcut some of the questions posed in this chapter by supplying your lawyer with photocopies of various documents. As a general rule, all documents that tend to establish ownership of assets, existence of debts, and current income should be assembled and made available.

To begin, you should gather the following documents:

1. Federal income tax returns for the last three years;
2. Last three pay stubs for both spouses that show deductions from gross pay;
3. Your current check register (which tends to establish your spending patterns);
4. The most recent annual statement of pension or retirement benefits furnished for each spouse;
5. Savings passbooks;
6. Certificates of deposit, Treasury bills, and the like;
7. Financial statements given to a banking institution in connection with a recent loan;
8. Monthly or quarterly bank statements for all checking and savings accounts;
9. Charge card (MasterCard, Visa, American Express, *etc.*) statements for the last few months;
10. Warranty deeds, contracts, title insurance and other documents establishing ownership to real estate such as your home;
11. Title certificates and registration statements for cars, trucks, recreational vehicles, boats, *etc.*;
12. If a business is owned, the most recent tax return, annual profit and loss statement, and most current monthly or quarterly profit and loss statement;
13. List of all current debts, monthly payments, and reasons for debts; and,
14. Each employer's annual statement describing medical/life insurance benefits and profit-sharing plans, *etc.*

The list could go on and on. Use your own common sense to assemble those documents that you feel would be pertinent during your first or second interview with the lawyer. Your lawyer will be able to guide you further as you proceed.

CHAPTER FIVE
PROPERTY DIVISION

Mary Ellen returned to my office shortly after Jim moved out. She brought the checklist discussed in the previous chapter to this meeting. The task of accounting for her monthly expenses was proving to be difficult. It was hard to focus on utility bills, insurance premiums, taxes, and the like. She wished she had been more familiar with those figures during her marriage. I had to assure her that, although this exercise was very trying, it was essential.

Mary Ellen commented,

> "Each time I sit down to *attack* those financial forms you gave me, my mind blurs. I just can't keep my thoughts straight. Then when I got to the questions about our insurance and Jim's pension plan, I knew I didn't have a clue! I felt so helpless. Jim and I plan to get together so he can help me list *our* assets.
>
> "It's so mechanical and stark putting dollar values on sixteen years together and dividing everything up. It's hard for me to do that when I'm still feeling so emotional."

I gave Mary Ellen information on the emotional stages of divorce (see Chapter One, "The Psychological Divorce") to show that her feelings were not unusual. I explained that our first priority was assessing the property to be divided. Until this was accomplished, we would be without a clear picture of her future resources. Washington is a community property state.

> "The fundamental premise of the community property system is that both spouses contribute to property acquisitions in a joint effort to promote the welfare of the relationship."

Therefore, all property acquired and wages earned during the marriage should be equitably divided upon dissolution. I assured her, however, that property division did not occur in a vacuum. Many factors are considered, including the future earning power of each spouse.

Mary Ellen was convinced she could never find a job that would pay enough to allow her to adequately support herself and two teenagers. She loved her suburban home and their newly acquired membership in a country club. Would this divorce cause her to lose her present lifestyle?

This is why, I answered, the division of property is one of the most critical aspects in the divorcing process. Two households are about to be created out of a single household, and in most families this demands changes in the living standards of both parents and their children. The goal of most courts will be to preserve the spouses' prior standard of living as reasonably as possible. The court will consider all the resources available when determining whether and how much support should be paid.

Except in cases involving marriages of short duration, no children, and limited marital property, the task of property division is not easy. The current Marriage Dissolution Act and the presence of tax problems require detailed accounting of the marital assets. The cold mathematical facts of property settlement do not abide well with the emotional aspects inherent in any dissolution. Divorces include feelings as well as facts. Unfortunately, property division demands that spouses detach themselves from some of their cherished objects. Today more lawyers are becoming aware of the fact that property division demands consideration of a client's emotional as well as financial needs.

Most courts will go through a four-step process to reach a full and fair division of the spouses' assets. By completing the questionnaire I had given Mary Ellen, she and Jim had already started the first steps in the process, which are:

1. Determine which property belongs to the marital community and which property belongs solely to one party thereby making it separate, or non-marital, property.

2. Value each significant item of property.

3. Consider how debts, attorney fees, and other *closing down* expenses should be provided from the economic resources at hand.

4. In light of all of the above, the court will decide how to divide the assets the most equitably. Sometimes an equitable result can be best achieved by providing for monthly or periodic payments from one spouse to the other, rather than dividing a chunk of property. Under Washington law, *equitable* does not mean equal; it means fair in view of all the circumstances.

CHARACTERIZING COMMUNITY AND SEPARATE PROPERTY

In Washington courts, marital (or community) property will be equitably divided between the spouses.

Washington courts view the marriage as a partnership, so that any accumulations during the marriage are presumed to be the result of joint efforts. Therefore, those accumulations should be shared equitably upon the conclusion of that relationship. Separate property will generally be awarded to the owner-spouse.

Generally speaking, *separate (or non-marital) property* consists of all property acquired before the marriage and all property acquired after marriage by gift or inheritance.

Community property generally consists of all non-separate property acquired during the marriage. This includes all purchases, wages, and the value of improvements to property from the labor of either spouse. A separate property can become community property if either spouse spends a significant amount of time or community funds on its improvement. This conversion process is called *commingling*.

Equitable distribution does not mean that all community property will be divided down the middle, nor can we conclude that each spouse will receive all of his or her separate property:

> "The court in a divorce action must have in mind the correct character and status of the property as community or separate before any division of property is considered.... *Characterization of the property, however, is not necessarily controlling;* the ultimate questions being whether the final division of the property is fair, just ,and equitable under all circumstances." (Emphasis added.)

Mary Ellen lowered her gaze to her hand. Upon one finger was a truly lovely diamond ring. The ring had been left to Jim upon his grandmother's death. Mary Ellen had enjoyed wearing it for the last ten years. Did this ring constitute Jim's separate property? Possibly, unless Jim had given it to her.

COMMINGLING: CONVERTING SEPARATE INTO COMMUNITY PROPERTY

Separate property can become community property in many ways. For example, the husband inherited a number of shares of stock; he later sold his inheritance in order to be able to purchase a home jointly with his wife. In this transaction the property became commingled, thereby losing its separate character. Assuming the husband was unable to trace or specifically identify his separate property through the transitions, the resulting home could well become community property.

When property is acquired during the marriage with partly marital and partly non-marital assets, the courts generally will apply the *source of funds* rule to reach a fair division. The proportionate value of the marital and nonmarital contribution *at the time of acquisition* will be applied to determine the marital community's present interest in the property.

Employing the source of funds rule, the court will attempt to credit both the owner-spouse — in this case the husband — and the marital community with a share of those assets that have become commingled. Thus, if one spouse purchases a house and takes out a mortgage before marriage but makes mortgage payments from marital funds, many courts will reimburse the marital community for the contributions. They will develop a formula that accounts for the marital contributions applied to the separate asset.

Property acquired after the parties separate, but before their marriage is dissolved, is generally viewed to be the separate property of the spouse who acquired it. The rationale is that the spouses are no longer working together in the interest of the marriage partnership. Because there is no hard and fast rule that determines when a marriage is in fact defunct (especially when there is still the possibility of a reconciliation), the date of separation does not necessarily determine whether the property is separate or community. Courts generally will honor the effective date set forth in a negotiated Separation Agreement.

If spouses are able to bargain in good faith, they are legally authorized to determine the character of their assets. That is to say, they may agree on what is community property and what is separate property. In fact, our state encourages such agreements by providing legislation directing the courts to honor them. To make these agreements enforceable, the spouses must clearly describe each asset and liability to be divided. It does not matter whether the agreement was entered into before or after the marriage, as long as it is comprehensive and fair.

IMPROVEMENTS OF SEPARATE PROPERTY

As a general rule, any income or increases in value attributable to separate property remains the separate property of the owner-spouse. Otherwise, the right to own separate property would be meaningless. However, income from that property may be considered in determining a *fair and equitable* division of all property. For instance, if the court realizes one spouse will be receiving monthly rent from an apartment complex, it may award the other spouse a greater portion of the community assets.

Improvements made with community funds or the personal efforts of either spouse are community property. Even this rule has its exceptions. The improvement or addition to separate property, even if made with marital resources or efforts, does not become marital property if the marital community is repaid for the value of the improvement or addition.

If the value of separate property has been enhanced by community efforts or community funds, the source of funds rule can be used to set a value on those enhancements. The value of the marital community's interest in the separate property is the ratio between: (1) the value added and (2) the value of the property immediately before the enhancement was made.

HAL'S CASE

Hal presented another graphic example of the use of the source of funds rule to determine the marital community's percentage of a separately owned business. Prior to his marriage, he bought a small dry cleaning shop. Although he did not draw a salary, he invested 50% of his workday managing the business. During the course of the marriage, Hal greatly increased the volume of business at the shop and doubled its value. This *enhancement* was due 75% to Hal's personal efforts and 25% to inflation. Hal got to keep the 25% due to inflation, but the balance of the enhancement was due to marital efforts and went into the community pot.

A 1982 case, *Marriage of Elam*, speaks to this point. The issue there was whether the marital community or Mrs. Elam was entitled to the increase in value of a home she purchased prior to marriage. Because community funds and labor were used to make improvements on her home, the community was entitled to share in a portion of the increase due to inflation.

The court presumes that all property acquired by either spouse during the marriage is community property. This is true regardless of whose name is on the title to the property. This presumption is not conclusive, however, if it can be proved that the property was acquired by gift or inheritance. The burden of proving the asset is separate falls on the spouse asserting its separate character

CHANGING THE CHARACTER OF YOUR PROPERTY

Spouses can agree in writing to change the status of their property at any time. For example, a husband may wish to make a gift of the family home to his wife. The courts will uphold the spouses' right to contract with or exchange gifts between one another. However, transactions of this nature demand a closer look when the spouses later obtain a divorce. The courts will look closely at the ostensible gift or sale to make sure that the community property is now truly separate. Usually, the burden of proof will be on the spouse who is presently displeased with the character of the property. An argument can be made that the transfer of property from one spouse to another was part of a larger estate plan, or even for protection against creditors.

If the spouses become embroiled in battle concerning characterization of property, the courts will decide the nature of the property. Because a *fair and equitable* division is the goal of the courts, judicial exceptions may take precedence over general rules. In Mary Ellen's case, an antique rug became one of those *exceptions*. Realizing the investment potential of Persian rugs, Mary Ellen and Jim purchased a magnificent rug at considerable cost nine months prior to their separation. They referred to it as Mary Ellen's birthday gift. If they were unable to agree upon the characterization as either community or Mary Ellen's separate property, then the court would consider the following:

1. The source of the funds used to acquire the property;
2. The underlying circumstances at the time of acquisition;
3. The dates of the marriage and its breakup relative to the acquisition and change in character of the property;
4. The reasons that commingling or transmutation occurred; and,
5. The value of the property and its significance to the parties.

Thus, it would be unfair to treat one spouse's substantial cash inheritance as community property merely because it was placed in a joint and survivorship account to avoid probate. It would also be unfair to uphold a gift between spouses if the marriage broke up shortly after the gift was made. *Even if the court cannot* set aside *the gift transaction, it still retains discretion to compensate the injured spouse by making an appropriate adjustment in the division of other property.*

VALUING YOUR PROPERTY

Every item of property has its value. Spousal agreement upon the value of property can be a difficult but not insurmountable task. Just as one person's junk is another's antique, some items of personal property have a very high value to one spouse.

On the birth of their first child, Jim gave Mary Ellen a solitaire diamond, which cost $3,000. Jim felt the diamond was probably worth at least $4,000 today and, for sentimental reasons, Mary Ellen believed it was beyond price. Imagine their surprise when the gemologist put its market value at $2,500. Mary Ellen felt the ring should not even be considered part of their property settlement — after all, it was a gift from Jim. Negotiations almost broke down when Jim insisted it be valued and put into the community pot.

Eventually Mary Ellen compromised. She *bought* the diamond from Jim by giving him an equal offset against other marital property.

Often, divorcing couples let sentiment cloud their judgment when valuing their assets. Each views their accumulations, whether a residence or a bird cage, as somehow intrinsically part of them and therefore not to be parted with, except at great price to the receiving spouse. I have seen carefully drafted, complex million-dollar settlements evaporate over the disputed value of a dining room table or a set of encyclopedias. To paraphrase the poet Robert Burns, would that we could see ourselves as others see us — when we wrangle over the bird cage.

MINIMIZING THE VALUATION DIFFICULTIES

To the extent that they can, spouses should each sit down and rationally set market values on all their personal property (furniture, appliances, jewelry, *etc.*). If they are unable to agree, each should set his or her value on the item. The high bidder can then take the item from the community pot at the high bid price, resulting in a credit to the other spouse at that value. (Imagine the husband's shocked expression when, after setting a $10,000 value on household furnishings actually worth $4,000, the wife declares, "All right, I'll take the cash, you keep the furniture.") It's surprising how close this bidding process comes to setting a true *market value* on these personal items.

Once sentiment is removed from the process of valuation, the spouses should be able to determine a reasonable value for most of their personal property. In valuing furniture and other household items, they should be guided not by what they paid for the item but by what it would sell for in the market place. (Some call this *garage sale* value, especially when dealing with used furniture.)

Market value is technically defined as the amount of money that a buyer (who is willing but not obligated to buy) would pay an owner (who is willing but not obligated to sell) for a particular piece of property. Market value is not the amount of money required to replace the item, nor is it what the item might bring at a distress or liquidation sale.

Expensive or rare items of property, like the residence, unimproved land, expensive jewelry, antiques, and paintings, will probably require the services of an appraiser for proper valuation. Even then, a mathematically precise valuation is impossible because appraisers (like lawyers and spouses) can honestly disagree. Nonetheless, the court will require present values based on the realities of the market place. The owner may give the court his or her opinion on an item's value, but the professional appraiser's opinion backed with facts, figures, and particularly information on recent sales of comparable properties, will probably carry more weight with the court.

SPECIAL CONSIDERATIONS AFFECTING VALUE:
TAXES AND SALES COSTS

For many items of property, particularly real estate, the cost of selling the property should be considered when fixing its net value. If the home is to be sold right away, the net equity on a residence will be reduced by the cost of selling it (*i.e.*, about 10% of the gross sales price). (See *Guidelines* in the Appendix.) However, a sale must be imminent for this deduction to be allowed.

The court may also consider reducing the market value of an item by the amount of taxes incurred upon a subsequent sale. An example would be two shares of Boeing stock, one purchased earlier in the marriage at a lower price, the other purchased later on in the marriage at a higher price. Depending upon the actual initial cost of the stock, if Mary Ellen took the earlier share purchased at a lower price and Jim sold the share costing substantially more, Mary Ellen would realize less from the sale of her share than Jim, even though they sold at the same market price. Although the sale of Mary Ellen's share might realize more dollars than Jim's sale, the tax on Mary Ellen's sale could be so much greater than the tax on Jim's sale that she would realize less income from the sale after taking into account the greater capital gains tax she would incur. This is because Mary Ellen's share would be subject to a greater capital gains tax than Jim's. *Taxes affect the sale of most items.* If the tax consequences are substantial enough, the court may be persuaded to consider them when setting a value on the item. A brief summary of pertinent sections of the 1984 Tax Reform Act is included in Appendix I. *See your tax attorney or accountant for specific information.*

DIVIDING COMMUNITY PROPERTY

If the spouses have some capacity to work together rationally, they should be able to divide their assets without court intervention. Obviously, where valuation of property or a business is involved, this may require the professional help of accountants and appraisers. In most instances, however, spouses will be equipped to handle the division. Who but the spouses themselves are more aware of the importance of the assets to each individual? By dividing the community property themselves or with the help of a mediator, the divorcing spouses can save attorney fees and perhaps reduce the cost of litigation.

IF YOU CAN'T AGREE, THE COURT WILL DECIDE

If the spouses disagree on the division of their marital assets, the courts will complete the task guided by the legal principles of equity and fairness. As noted earlier, this does not necessarily mean there will be an equal division of the assets. Equality is not always equity. For example, in the 1980 case *Marriage of Donovan,* 25 Wn. App. 691, 612 Wn.2d 387, the superior court awarded almost two-thirds of the assets to the wife. On appeal, the husband contended that this division was unfair. The court of appeals responded that

> "At first blush it may appear that the division is inequitable, the wife's award being valued at close to twice that of the husband's award. However, the scales of equity are balanced by the circumstances of the parties. This marriage lasted 14 years during which time three children were born. The husband is a commercial pilot and earns a substantial salary. His future, in this regard, is reasonably secure. The wife, on the other hand, is not prepared, without additional training, for entry into the labor market. Even as she trains for future employment, she will have to arrange for child care of her youngest child, who was two years at the time of trial. The two older children are young teenagers who require parental supervision, if not mother's care. Even after training, the salary potential will undoubtedly be less than a third of her husband's present salary.
>
> "Upon full review of the facts and circumstances, we find the property division to be just and equitable. We hold that the trial judge did not abuse his discretion in his division of separate and community property between the parties." (25 Wn. App. at pp. 697.)

It is perfectly normal to stack property on one side, and by stacking the property on one side either eliminate maintenance (alimony) completely or at least severely limit it.

In dividing marital property the court considers:

1. The nature and extent of the community property;
2. The nature and extent of separate property;
3. The duration of the marriage; and,
4. The economic circumstances of each spouse at the time of the division as well as *all other relevant factors.* (Relevant factors include age, health, education, employment history, the burden of custody, and future earning potential.)

The disparity in job skills and income potential between the husband and the wife in the *Donovan* case was readily apparent to the court. The short-term maintenance to the wife was balanced by an unequal award of property to her.

Each case that comes before the court is unique. The result must be tailored to the individual needs of the disputants. As one court put it,

"The key to an equitable distribution of property is not mathematical precise-ness, but fairness. This is attained by considering all of the circumstances of the marriage, past and present, with an eye to the future needs of the persons involved. Fairness is decided by the exercise of wise and sound discretion, not by set or inflexible rules."

GROUNDS FOR UNEQUAL PROPERTY DIVISION

The following factors may make a 50-50 split of the property less than equitable. It may be necessary to consult an attorney to see if these factors apply to your situation.

1. *Commingling of separate property.* Earlier in this chapter we dis-cussed the commingling of separate property, thereby changing it into community property. The reverse may also be true: marital property may be inrately deemed separate property. If an inequity has occurred, the court will make an adjustment.

2. *Squandering or wasting community property.* If one spouse unilater-ally sells, gives away, hides, or squanders community property, he or she may be charged for the loss.

3. *Willful abuse or harrassment.* The courts will also recognize the willful abuse or harassment of one spouse by the other. They note any spousal abuse that results in the other spouse becoming physically, mentally, or emotionally disabled to a degree that decreases his or her ability to be self-supporting. Similarly, if one spouse deliberately harasses the other so as to cause loss of employment, an adjustment may be made to compensate for the loss.

4. *Disability.* If a spouse has become disabled during the marriage, the courts may consider making an adjustment in the property division and/or periodic support to assist that party.

5. *Reimbursement or compensation for the support provided a spouse to obtain an education or degree.* In recent years, the courts have come to view intangible assets such as an education, the acquiring of a degree or a license, as property. Those assets may be considered to be marital property if they were obtained during the course of the marriage. In some instances, particularly those involving young couples, the col-lege education may be the only asset of any value in the marriage.

A PRACTICAL APPLICATION: JIM'S M.B.A.

After graduating from college with a degree in education and acquiring a brand-new marriage certificate, Mary Ellen moved with Jim to California where he earned a master's degree in business administration. The income from her teaching position fed, clothed, and housed the couple, and paid Jim's tuition through two years of graduate school. Of course, each case is judged independently. Nonetheless, many courts would provide Mary Ellen with compensation for her contribution to Jim's master's degree.

Whether the supporting spouse provided financial support or just plain *moral* support is not necessarily a determining factor. The existence of any support may be construed as an *investment* in the wage earner. Therefore, if one spouse helped put the other through school with the expectation that they would mutually share the economic benefits from the schooling, the spouse who made the contribution or sacrifice should be reimbursed. It is the effort and sacrifice that is being compensated, because the education or degree cannot be divided.

THE CASE OF MARILYN AND RICK: AN EXAMPLE OF REIMBURSEMENT

While Rick was in school pursuing a B.A. degree in parks and recreation, Marilyn contributed $7,000 in separate property to the community. Together they purchased a home, and Rick completed his studies. Equipped with his B.A., Rick found employment in his chosen field.

Rick and Marilyn separated after ten years of marriage. At their separation, Rick was earning $1,891 net per month. Without benefit of a college education and possessing only limited employment abilities, Marilyn worked as a waitress, earning $800 net per month. She was also receiving $400 per month child support for their two children. (Had the support been awarded after the effective date of the Child Support Schedule, Marilyn would have received $800 per month for child support.) Understandably, the $1,200 total income did not stretch far enough to cover all of the living expenses of three people, including daycare, food, and clothes.

Rick, it would appear, received a significant increase in earning capacity. The college degree, which increased his earning power, was gained through community efforts. Lacking the same benefits, Marilyn's economic future was truly shaky. Relying upon the concept of a college degree being marital property, Marilyn requested and received reimbursement for her *investment* in Rick's education.

A 1984 case, *Marriage of Washburn,* illustrates the point. Mr. Washburn acquired a veterinarian's degree and the Washburns separated within several years thereafter. Only modest assets were available for distribution. The Washington Supreme Court held that

"When a person supports a spouse through professional school in the mutual expectation of future financial benefit to the community, but the marriage ends before that benefit can be realized, that circumstance is a "relevant factor" which must be considered in making a fair and equitable division of property and liabilities pursuant to RCW 26.09.080, or a just award of maintenance pursuant to RCW 26.09.090. A professional degree confers high earning potential upon the holder. The student spouse should not walk away with this valuable advantage without compensating the person who helped him or her obtain it.

"We have said that the supporting spouse may be compensated through a division of property and liabilities. In many cases, however, the wealth of the marriage will have been spent toward the cost of the professional degree, leaving few or no assets to divide. Where the assets of the parties are insufficient to permit compensation to be effected entirely through property division, a supplemental award of maintenance is appropriate." (101 Wn.2d at 168.)

There is no precise formula prescribing the amount of property to be distributed or maintenance to be awarded to the supporting spouse. The following factors, however, will influence the court's decision:

1. Amount of community funds expended for direct educational costs (*e.g.,* tuition, fees, books, supplies);
2. The amount the community would have earned had the student spouse not been pursuing an education;
3. Educational or career opportunities the supporting spouse gave up to foster the educational attainments; and,
4. Future earning prospects of each spouse, including the earnings potential of the student spouse with the professional degree.

THE WINSOR REASONING: SHORT — PAST; LONG — FUTURE

A highly respected Court of Appeals judge, Robert Winsor, while serving in the King County Superior Court, published an article explaining the judicial reasoning he used to reach fair results in the distribution of marital property. I try to make sure every one of my clients takes that article home after the initial office interview. (Back copies of "Guidelines for the Exercise of Judicial Discretion in Marriage Dissolutions," 14 *Washington State Bar News* 114-19 (January 1982) by Judge Winsor can be ordered by calling the Washington State Bar Association at (206) 448-0441. There is a slight charge for a copy.)

Judge Winsor begins by stating something that cannot be overemphasized: the trial judge has broad discretion in awarding the property. This poses a dilemma to lawyers, because this discretion prevents us from predicting with acceptable racy the outcome for our individual clients. Predictability encourages settlements. Settlements save the client money and diminish the emotional confrontations that often plague the spouses' capacity to get over their divorce. Judge Winsor has shared some of the concepts of *fairness* he employed as a trial judge, thus giving lawyers an opportunity to help clients analyze their own situations as the court might see them.

Judge Winsor believes the length of the marriage is extremely important in determining how the property is divided and maintenance established. He believes, for example, that in *short* marriages (five years or less) different considerations should apply than in *long* marriages (twenty-five years or more). In short marriages, the judge looks to the past to restore the spouses to their respective pre-marriage economic positions. In long marriages, he looks to the future to put the spouses on an approximately equal economic footing for the rest of their lives. Judge Winsor stated that

> "In the case of a short marriage, the marriage has in fact not been the significant event that normally is presumed. Particularly, there has not been a long reliance on the marital partnership. Therefore, the emphasis should be to look backward to determine what the economic positions of the parties were at the inception of the marriage and then seek to place them back in that position, including provision for interest or inflation, if feasible. After doing that, if there are properties left over they presumably would be divided about equally. Presumably, in a short marriage, maintenance would not be paid, except in extraordinary circumstances or perhaps for a very brief adjustment where necessary, *e.g.*, if one of the parties gave up a job to relocate or otherwise accommodate to the marriage, that would be an extraordinary reason to either adjust the decision regarding property or allow brief maintenance during a relocation period."

In contrast, Judge Winsor's analysis of a long marriage is

> "In the case of a long marriage, the goal should be to look forward and seek to place the spouses in an economic position where, if they both work to the reasonable limits of their respective earning capacities, and manage the properties awarded to them reasonably, they can be expected to be in roughly equal financial positions for the rest of their lives. Long-term maintenance, sometimes permanent, is presumably likely to be used unless the properties accumulated are quite substantial, so that a lopsided award of property would permit a balancing of the positions without (much) maintenance. *In re Marriage of Rink,* 18 Wn. App. 549 (1977). (In a twenty-four-year marriage two-thirds of the property was awarded to the wife, along with maintenance for a brief time.)"

Judge Winsor explains the difference in treatment accorded long marriages and and short marriages

"In the traditional marriage relationship where one spouse devotes prime energies outside of the home earning money for the family and the other devotes prime energies raising children and maintaining a nurturing household, there is in a sense a contractual relationship entered into at the time of the marriage where the parties understand their respective primary obligations and undertake them willingly, understanding that they both expect that the marriage is a long-term (presumably lifetime) commitment and that each will be protected and provided for by the other. When a traditional long marriage fails, however, one of the spouses usually is stranded in a situation where she (sometimes he) is very much behind the other in earning capacity. The judge should redress the balance."

DIVIDING THE INDIVISIBLE: SPECIAL ASSETS

By their nature, some assets are not easily divisible. If the court must award a specific asset to one of the spouses, provisions are made to compensate the other. What cannot be divided can often be traded.

The family residence is usually an indivisible asset. Most courts will award the family home to the spouse having custody of the children. This is done partly in an attempt to minimize further disruptions to the children's lives. Therefore, if there is no additional property of equal value to award the non-custodial spouse, the custodial spouse may be left exclusive possession of the home for a number of years, provided that the residence then be sold and the proceeds of the sale be divided fairly between the spouses. In the meantime, the non-custodial spouse would be given a compensating lien against the residence. The dissolution decree often provides that the home will be sold should the custodial parent remarry, enter a cohabiting relationship, no longer use the home as his or her primary residence, or die, whichever occurs first.

Some courts will adjust maintenance or the division of sale proceeds to reflect the fact that the custodial parent has had the exclusive use and possession of the home. The custodial parent may be responsible for an interest-bearing note on the property with a balloon payment due when the home sells. Plainly, there is no end to the number of ways to deal with this major chunk of marital property.

The spouse out of possession could receive a share of the proceeds based upon the actual sale price rather than the residence's value at the time of trial. In determining the division of proceeds, consideration should also be given to the spouse responsible for house maintenance, major replacements, insurance, mortgage payments, and taxes.

Any such arrangement should involve a deed of trust in favor of the spouse who is not in possession that is recorded, along with some form of a promissory note.

PENSIONS: HIDDEN DANGERS FOR SOME

Pensions are often the largest assets in many marital communities. An actuary will often be necessary to determine the value of each specific plan. Pensions or other entitlements of employment will often be allocated to the employee spouse, while awarding other property to the non-employee spouse. If there is not enough property available, then distribution of the pension could be accomplished by two methods.

METHOD ONE: WAIT FOR FUTURE VALUE

A share is allocated to the non-employee spouse based upon the ratio between the number of years of the employed spouse worked during the marriage and the total number of years of employment. For example, assume Jim had worked four years prior to marriage and sixteen years during marriage before retiring at the point of divorce. Sixteen of the twenty years on pension occurred during marriage, in this case, so Mary Ellen would be entitled to a share of sixteen-twentieths or 80% of Jim's pension. Under this method, the non-employee spouse will not receive the benefits of the pension *until the employee spouse retires.* Under the terms of most pension agreements, an employee cannot withdraw his or her interest from the fund until retirement, so a court will not order an early withdrawal.

This method has its risks. If the employee spouse loses the job or dies, there may be no benefits left for the non-employee spouse. If the fund goes bankrupt, the non-employee spouse suffers, but then so does the employee spouse. Lastly, the ex-spouses' affairs are still entangled with one another, requiring the need for further cooperation, association, and communication. This may be neither desirable nor realistic. Two illustrative methods of dividing a pension have been provided in Appendix H.

METHOD TWO: DISCOUNT FOR PRESENT VALUE

The second method offsets or substitutes the present value of the non-employee spouse's share with other marital property and will require the employment of an actuary. Actuaries have training in methods to figure out how to *discount* a pension for various risks. The actuary will use charts and calculations to determine the *odds* for and against the employee's receiving the full benefits offered by the pension plan. Among the risks the actuary discounts is the likelihood of the employee spouse not surviving to enjoy his or her pension benefits at retirement. Employing the necessary calculations, the actuary will arrive at a lump sum equivalent to the value of the pension earned to date. The attractiveness of this method lies in its simplicity. A present value is placed upon the pension. The figure can then be used equitably and fairly when dividing the value of the pension between the spouses.

GOODWILL

Goodwill is defined as *property of an intangible nature*. This concept concerns mainly professional people. It is assumed, by virtue of the professional's training and skills, that he or she has established a reputation that promises a certain future economic expectancy. The non-professional spouse has been a *silent partner* in this enterprise and is now forced to withdraw from the partnership. Valuing *goodwill* invariably requires the services of an expert, usually an accountant or an economist. Assuming a value for that goodwill is established, the professional spouse must compensate the supporting spouse for the loss of future earning potential. Goodwill is a relatively new marital asset similar to the concept of an education or a degree being divisible property.

As an intangible but divisible asset, goodwill can be expected to increase the size of the property settlement for the spouse of a doctor, lawyer, accountant, or other professional than would be possible from a simple division of the tangible assets of the community. The spouse can also expect to receive an offsetting award in property or maintenance.

PERSONAL PROPERTY: YOUR WISHES

Specific items in the marital community have a great sentimental value to one spouse or the other. The court will attempt to award each party the items in which a spouse has a personal interest, such as sporting goods, tools, and special collections. The court will also try to allocate items that common sense dictates should be awarded to one party: a business traditionally operated by only one of the spouses or jewelry worn only by the one spouse. Lastly, the court will take into account the expressed wishes of each of the parties insofar as they do not conflict with an equitable distribution of all of the property.

ADJUSTMENTS: MAKING THE BALANCE

If the assets cannot be divided equitably, the court may use the mechanism of periodic payments to make up the difference. For example, if the asset to be distributed consists of shares in a family-owned corporation, the court will probably require payments over time rather than compel a forced sale of the corporation.

Whenever these types of payments are made, the court will ordinarily designate them as a division of property, not maintenance. Thus, the payments should not terminate upon death, remarriage, or other contingencies. Therefore, consideration should be given to secure these payments properly by using insurance, stock, or treasury notes, for example. In addition, the parties must decide whether interest is to be included in the payments. The effects of future inflation should be considered as well.

TAXES

See Appendix I for information on taxes.

GUILT AND THE UNEQUAL DIVISION

With so many options available in the courts to assist an equitable settlement, why, in retrospect, do some decrees appear unfair? What obstructs a fair division in those cases? Sometimes our greatest enemy is ourselves: our guilt! Guilt underlies many lopsided property divisions. It motivates some spouses to give up claims to assets they should rightfully share.

In Mary Ellen's case, experience told me to caution her. She was a prime candidate to fall prey to guilt. Her desire to be out of the marriage was similar to that of other people I have seen who relinquished far too much as a trade-off for their desire to get out of the marriage or as their way of punishing themselves for that desire. A lawyer is often powerless to prevent clients from punishing themselves in this way.

On the other end of the spectrum, some spouses allow themselves to be bullied. In the divorce, overpowering spouses continue to play the same destructive roles they played in their troubled marriage. Because *fault* as a legal reason for divorce has been denied to them as an offensive weapon, some spouses may resort to threats. For example, they may threaten a custody battle, a wasting of all assets, or to pay no support.

On occasion, I have had clients who insisted on being overly generous to their spouses purely out of hope. They have mistakenly believed that their spouses will come back to the marriage if they deal kindly with them. Giving up property that is rightfully yours will not heal a failed marriage.

Some of the following questions may be applicable to your own situation. Many of the issues are sophisticated and will, no doubt, require professional assistance to resolve.

CHECKLIST FOR PROPERTY DIVISION

1. If you own a home, who is named on the title? Are there any other parcels of real property? What is the title status? Are there any mortgages, liens, or encumbrances on the title? Who will assume which obligation?

2. Have the taxes been paid? What tax consequences will occur from any transfer of interest in real estate? If property other than real estate is to be sold, what are the tax consequences there? Will an appraiser be required to value the property? Who will pay for the cost of the appraisal?

3. If you are living in an apartment, is there a lease? In whose name is it leased? When does the lease expire? Who is to continue occupying the apartment? Who is to pay the rent? Is the lease assignable? Is it to be assigned? If there is a damage deposit, who is to receive that?

4. Is it necessary to dispose of a business? If so, should the value of the business be appraised? Is the business a partnership? Is the wife a partner? Is her interest to be purchased by the husband? Is the business incorporated? Is the wife an officer or director? Is she to resign? If she is a stockholder, what disposition is to be made of her holdings? If she is a creditor, what disposition is to be made of her claim? What tax consequences will result from any transfer of interest?

5. Does the business or profession have *goodwill* value? How should it be valued?

6. Is one spouse holding in his or her name any property belonging to the other spouse, or vice versa? Is so, is he or she to retain it?

7. Has the wife any real estate of her own? Is the husband to quit claim to her any interest he may have in it? What tax consequences will occur if he does?

8. Is there any insurance on personal items: jewelry, furs, cameras, *etc.*? Are any of the policies to be transferred?

9. Does either of the parties have an interest in any profit sharing plans, pension plans, or other retirement funds? Are they fully or partially vested? Will an actuary be required? What disposition is to be made of these interests? Why?

10. Does either spouse owe the other any money? Is there an outstanding note or other evidence of the debt? How is the indebtedness to be treated?

11. Are you and your spouse jointly liable on any obligation? If so, what disposition is to be made when the obligation matures? Is one spouse to assume the debt and indemnify the other?

12. Is there any litigation pending between you in addition to the marital dissolution litigation? Is there any pending litigation in which one or both of you are involved, either as co-plaintiffs or as codefendants?

13. Are there any outstanding bills or obligations that were incurred by one spouse, but for which the other is or may be liable? Who is to discharge that obligation? When is there to be indemnification?

14. When should credit cards and accounts be canceled and surrendered? Can each spouse's credit be preserved by opening new accounts?

15. Are schedules to be prepared, listing exact debts each spouse is to assume and pay?

16. Have the parties filed any joint income tax returns in the past? If there is a refund, who is to get it? If there is a deficiency assessment, who is to pay it? Is one spouse to indemnify the other as to any liability regarding prior income tax returns?

17. Who is responsible for other tax matters, such as estate taxes, and corporation and partnership returns?

18. Are authenticated copies of future tax returns to be exchanged?

19. Is each party to waive their rights in the estate of the other?

20. Has either party an existing will in which the other is named executor or executrix, devisee, or legatee? Should this be changed?

21. Should either spouse be required to leave the other or the children a specific sum or sums by will or is that spouse's estate to be charged for future support, medical obligations, *etc.*?

22. Are there revocable *living* trusts that should be changed because of the altered marital relationship?

23. Are the children beneficiaries under any existing *living* or testamentary trusts? Should they be? Which parent is to receive and control the income on the children's behalf?

24. Is the husband's obligation (assuming there are continuing payments) to survive his death and be binding upon his estate? If so, may the obligation be capitalized so that the estate may be promptly closed?

25. Is a spouse to furnish any security for the performance of his or her obligations under the agreement? If so, what form will the security take?

CHAPTER SIX
SPOUSAL MAINTENANCE

"Does alimony still exist?" Mary Ellen asked me. Over the years the term *alimony* developed a negative connotation. It has been replaced by a legal euphemism: *spousal maintenance*. Whatever it is called, it represents monetary support to the needy spouse. The concept of support that will last indefinitely, however, has fallen from favor.

Today, when over half of the women between the ages of eighteen and sixty-two are working outside the home, the trend is to give lower spousal maintenance over a shorter time.

> "It is not the purpose of the law to place a permanent responsibility upon a divorced spouse to support a former wife indefinitely. She is under an obligation to prepare herself so that she might become self-supporting." *Berg v. Berg,* 72 Wn.2d 532, 534, 434 P.2d 1 (1967).

Mary Ellen was correct when she assumed she would have to return to the job market, because today the purpose of spousal maintenance is generally considered to be rehabilitative in nature. Simply stated, that means support will be provided only so long as it is necessary to train the spouse for suitable employment. See Appendix I for a summary of the new tax law, which significantly affects maintenance payments.

TEMPORARY SUPPORT AND MAINTENANCE

Mary Ellen was understandably frightened when Jim reluctantly packed his bags and left. They had not yet made provisions for her financial support. She realized this oversight was caused by the unusual circumstances of Jim's departure, but she feared being left without money for the duration of the dissolution proceedings. She honestly had no idea how she would maintain the house and feed the two children and herself without Jim's paycheck safely deposited in their checking account.

Fortunately, the courts can intervene if one spouse (often the wife) is left with insufficient funds during the dissolution proceedings. *Temporary* support is designed to maintain the status quo as nearly as possible while the divorce is pending. Your lawyer can obtain an Order to Show Cause and a subsequent Temporary Order, which will provide temporary payments until the final decree. In theory, temporary support (or relief) maintains the current standard of living. However, this is rarely possible in reality. Mary Ellen did not require an accountant's expertise to realize that Jim's income must now provide for two homes, their respective living expenses, and two lawyers. It was unlikely that she would receive the amount for household expenses she had been receiving prior to the separation. Courts will not impoverish the supporting spouse. They must leave both spouses with sufficient resources to cover their own individual and necessary living expenses or the employed spouse may stop working. Based upon Jim's current take-home pay, Mary Ellen and I agreed that $3,000 per month to support both herself and the children would be a fair temporary award.

PERMANENT MAINTENANCE: A VANISHING SPECIES

The word *permanent* is misleading. As I explained to Mary Ellen, permanent support rarely occurs today. In most instances, spousal support is short-lived. Furthermore, because alimony is *not* a matter of right, wives are not automatically awarded support. It is awarded according to the need of one spouse (most likely the wife) and the financial ability of the supporting spouse (usually the husband) to pay. When the wife has the ability to earn a living, courts rarely give a perpetual lien on her former spouse's income. The courts also put considerable emphasis on the wife's desire or lack of desire to work.

All courts generally consider similar factors when deciding the need, the amount, and the duration of spousal maintenance. The following are necessarily considered by the court in making a determination:

1. Earning capacity;
2. Ability to pay (a wife may need an accountant to detail her husband's ability to pay);
3. Duration of marriage;
4. Work experience;
5. Educational level;
6. Age;
7. Number and ages of children;
8. Health; and,
9. Nature of separate estates.

COMPARABLE WORTH

Earning capacity and need tend to be a function of many factors. A study by the National Organization of Women found that women earn 59.6 cents for every dollar a man earns while doing comparable work. Furthermore, women with college degrees generally earn less than men with no more than an eighth-grade education. Mary Ellen had a college degree, but her work experience was limited. In the past, women with teaching or secretarial skills were assured of employment. That is not true today, particularly in Mary Ellen's field of teaching. Although educational level and work experience contribute to earning capacity, the courts will use discretion before assuming employability. A degree in history or a job as a clerk/typist fourteen years ago does not place one in high demand in today's job market. An award of spousal maintenance may be designed specifically to train the supported spouse for better employment through a return to college or a trade school.

Ability of the husband to pay necessarily limits the amount of support and even the possibility of providing support. To determine Jim's *ability to pay,* Mary Ellen and I looked at their tax returns for the last two years. Next we studied her accounts of their living expenses prior to separation. This helped establish the *needs* of both parties. Only after deducting Jim's fixed expenses —rent, food, car, and medical— could we get an idea of what we might ask for support for Mary Ellen and the children.

It might be necessary to hire an accountant if the husband's income is tied up in his privately owned business. Perhaps many private expenses are incurred by the business for tax purposes rather than being distributed as personal income. Of course, it is to the husband's advantage to show a limited income. Obviously, the less income he produces, the less money is available for spousal maintenance!

The courts will ensure the husband has sufficient funds to cover necessary expenses. In one case, Frank earned $1,800 a month. Although Judy was awarded primary residential care of their three-year-old daughter, she did not seek spousal maintenance. Frank's limited income certainly could not have supported two homes. Judy voluntarily sought employment and made daycare arrangements for their daughter.

Longer marriages yield greater possibilities for spousal maintenance. Besides having invested a number of years in her husband, the wife will be older and will likely have less current work experience. These last two factors limit her capacity to be self-supporting. A woman under forty is much more likely to find employment than a woman over fifty. Whereas the younger woman may be awarded support and maintenance on a declining scale for a fixed period of time until she is employed and self-supporting, the older woman has a higher likelihood of being granted support until she remarries or receives Social Security.

The courts often consider the number and ages of the children involved. Perhaps it will be decided that it serves the best interests of the children for the mother to remain home rather than work. This often occurs when the wife has custody of pre-school-aged children. Those same little children tend to have a negative effect on their mother's chances for remarriage.

If health is a primary issue in seeking spousal maintenance, be prepared to substantiate the claim. It may be necessary to support the spouse's health problems with expert medical testimony. This, of course, would apply to either spouse: a wife who seeks support or a husband who claims that his ill health will reduce his future earning capacity.

Maintenance awards are not made without knowledge of the property division. The courts consider the obligations and assets of both parties, including their separate property and the extent of marital property awarded to each spouse.

Mary Ellen reviewed the list of deciding factors. Earning capacity: who knows? She knew she required more schooling. Her sixteen-year marriage was considered of *moderate* duration. That left the maintenance issues to the discretion of the court. At age forty-five she was still employable, and her children were fairly independent. Jim's ability to pay was certainly not endless. What did all of this mean in terms of a dollar amount? To give her a clue we reviewed some dissolution decrees in my files and the County Clerk's office.

SPOUSAL MAINTENANCE ARRANGEMENTS: SOME EXAMPLES

1. *Monica and Alan* present the classic case of the unemployed wife with a limited employment history. Alan's income was approximately $70,000 per year. They were accustomed to a very comfortable lifestyle, which afforded many luxuries. The couple had been married twelve years and Monica had not worked out of the home for the last ten years. She had fulfilled the traditional role of full-time wife and mother of two children. Although she was a college graduate, her degree in the social sciences did not prepare her for employment. In the settlement agreement, Monica was awarded $800 per month maintenance for two years, thereafter reduced to $300 monthly for three years. These sums were in addition to $600 a month child support for each of the two children. The agreement left little to chance. It stipulated that Monica's employment was not grounds for termination of support. It further ensured Monica's continued support in the event of Alan's death. (Unless otherwise agreed, spousal maintenance terminates upon the supporting spouse's death.) This particular agreement applied to Alan's estate, if he did not survive.

In this type of a case, I urge the provider to maintain an insurance policy with the recipient as beneficiary to cover the obligation in the event of the provider's death. There are many creative ways to guard against early termination of support. However, unless they are included in the decree, they will be of no help.

2. In the *Donovan* case, the trial court awarded the wife maintenance of $350 per month for the first 12 months and $250 per month for the next 12 months. This was in addition to awarding her almost two-thirds of the marital assets. The husband was an airline pilot who earned a substantial salary. By contrast, the wife was not prepared for entry into the labor market without additional training. The trial court estimated that even after training, her salary potential would be less than a third of her husband's salary. In setting the alimony, the court considered both spouses' financial condition, job preparedness, age, the duration of the marriage, and their current lifestyle.

It sometimes appears difficult to note the difference between spousal maintenance and property division. Maintenance may be allotted in periodic payments or in a lump sum. Similar means may be employed to disburse property awards. Although a $450 spousal maintenance payment is tax deductible to the provider and must be claimed as income by the recipient, a $450 monthly property payment is not income or taxable. It is to the advantage of the providing spouse to be making spousal maintenance payments rather than balancing a difference in property division. The Internal Revenue Service has, however, taxed an unequal property division. The Internal Revenue Service has issued complicated rules on deductibility of maintenance payments. A tax lawyer or tax accountant can provide further information.

3. The *Baker* case included alimony and property settlement payments. This decision involved a marriage of twenty-one years. The couple had a daughter in her early teens. The wife was awarded custody (now called primary residential care) of the child. Since their daughter's birth, Mrs. Baker had not been employed. During their married life, the husband had received a B.A. and an M.B.A. He supported the family by managing properties he inherited from his mother's estate. When the couple sought a divorce so that the husband could marry another woman, the trial court awarded the lion's share of property to him. It was, after all, his separate property by the nature of its acquisition. As a result, he received property valued at $105,000 and his wife's award was valued at $10,000. However, the court sought equity for the wife and awarded a judgment against the husband in the amount of $50,000 including interest. Rather than a lump sum, this award was payable at a rate of $450 a month. By virtue of its being

a property award rather than maintenance, this monthly payment was not a deductible expense by the husband.

Taking a further look at the wife's circumstances, the court recognized that her future was financially bleak. She had few job skills and had not completed her college education. She considered herself only capable of performing housework, and the court agreed. The court found that she was in a position of need and ordered alimony in the amount of $200 per month for one year to permit her to train for employment as a nurse.

4. Some circumstances do not warrant spousal maintenance and the case of *Laura and Robert* illustrates this point. When they divorced, Laura was awarded $20,000 in cash. Both parties agreed that it was in the best interest of their minor child to remain with Robert. Robert's income was limited, and although Laura had no current income, she was training for employment. In this case, no support payments were awarded.

5. In the Midwest, there was a spectacular case in which no spousal maintenance was awarded. A wealthy executive and his wife were divorcing after six years of marriage. She had lived a life of luxury and ease during the six-year marriage. Alas, the court concluded that she was not entitled to spousal maintenance because her *spousal services* were limited during their marriage. It seems she had a full staff of servants at her disposal. Thus, the court did not find her deserving of continued support!

There are no formulas to specify spousal maintenance. There is, however, room for creativity. Perhaps a maintenance award will take the form of a college education, particularly if the supporting spouse completed all education at the expense of the marital partnership.

A young woman I recently represented requested spousal maintenance to allow her to complete her education. My client suspended her education to support her husband while he obtained his education. Upon completion of his degree, her husband had significantly enhanced his earning power. Without her degree, my young client was likely to remain in the same lowpaying, dead-end position she currently held. We petitioned the court, maintaining that a *just and equitable result* may be obtained only by awarding spousal maintenance in the amount necessary for her to complete her education. The court agreed and fixed a monthly amount the husband was to pay her until her degree was obtained. Washington courts have the discretion to use spousal maintenance as a means to compensate the supporting spouse for her contribution to the husband's education.

My files contain many types of maintenance awards. The bottom line, of course, is individual circumstances. Wealthier clients may obtain up to $3,000 a month or more; other clients accept awards of $300 or less. Often maintenance payments decline in specified annual amounts on the theory that the wife should start becoming financially independent.

Spousal maintenance does not survive the death of the provider unless it is specifically stipulated in the settlement agreement.

Optimally, a settlement agreement is tailor-made for each family. The parties should not simply adopt maintenance guidelines from previous dissolution files. A review of some maintenance awards already on file in the County Clerk's office, however, will give you a better idea of what is considered reasonable. It is helpful to note that an award of child support is usually present as well. Both sums must be recognized when considering the total amount available for living expenses.

AVOIDING SPOUSAL MAINTENANCE

It follows that the spouse wishing to avoid paying spousal maintenance (often the husband) will employ the same factors, but to his or her own advantage. For example, the husband may try to disprove need by establishing that his spouse has sufficient funds available to support herself. Perhaps he will attempt to prove she is presently employable or will argue that she could liquidate her half of the community's assets and live off interest payments. If immediate employment is not possible, he may maintain that suitable training can be obtained in less time than she claims is required. In this case, he may need to employ expert testimony to corroborate his claim. An expert in employment counseling could provide this service. Witnesses could testify to the availability of suitable employment or to the ability of his spouse to complete her training on a quicker time schedule.

If the husband cannot prove his wife is without need, he may attempt to prove that he cannot pay. He may assert *living expenses,* which deny or limit the funds available for support. He may even try to reduce his future earning ability. Obviously, the wife's need and the husband's ability to pay is a two-way street.

The tax consequences of spousal maintenance are discussed in Appendix I.

ATTORNEY FEES

There may be a question of responsibility for attorney fees. The law does not entitle either spouse to free litigation. A genuine need must exist before the law will require one spouse to pay the other's attorney fees. A disparity in income is not reason enough for the husband to accept the responsibility.

The award of attorney fees must be based on the honest financial need of one party and the ability of the other party to pay.

SPOUSAL MAINTENANCE CHECKLIST

A well-drafted agreement guards against future problems and should help to eliminate the need for later modification. Therefore, it would be wise to have answers for the following questions before drafting your settlement agreement:

1. Is there to be a lump sum settlement or periodic payments?
2. If there are periodic payments, are they fixed in amount or subject to fluctuation? How much do they decline in value? What factors cause fluctuation?
3. When are the support payments to be made? On what dates?
4. To whom are the support payments to be made? What are the penalties if they are late?
5. Can the wife obtain income from employment or some other source without affecting the amount of her support allowance? If so, is there to be any limitation on the amount she can earn?
6. When does the allowance to the wife end?
7. How are the wife's Social Security rights to be handled? What benefits does she get?
8. What are the tax consequences of the payments?
9. Are there to be security provisions to ensure the payments?
10. Who is to pay the parties' respective attorney's fees and costs of suit? How much? When?
11. Can the tax laws be properly applied to make attorney's fees legally deductible? Can the form of billing assist in a tax savings?
12. Who pays for audits, costs of transferring real estate, and other expenses incident to the dissolution of the marriage?
13. Is one party to pay the other party's attorney's fees and costs arising out of any post-judgment litigation? Under what terms and conditions is the party responsible?
14. Is cohabitation a reason for termination of maintenance?
15. Is remarriage a reason for termination of maintenance?

These are just a few of the questions that must be answered to ensure that a spousal maintenance agreement meets the present and future needs of the spouse who is to receive financial support after the divorce.

CHAPTER SEVEN
PARENTING PLANS

As of January 1, 1988, the state of Washington stepped into the forefront of innovation with its new Parenting Act. Every innovation has its price, so the citizens of Washington will now address difficulties that have not been faced elsewhere. Our Parenting Act focuses on determining which parental functions and parental responsibilities best meet children's needs. The concepts of *custody* and *visitation* are no longer viable. The Act supports parents who are responsible and reliable, and limits parents who are inadequate.

INTERPRETING THE PARENTING ACT

Normally, statutory law is interpreted by case law. Case law interpreting the Parenting Act will take many years to develop. For now we can only look to the assumptions and comments of the drafters and early users of the Act. The law was designed to correct the following problems, inequities, and dilemmas in our divorce process:

1. *The win-lose court process.* By using words such as *custody* and *visitation*, our old law fostered an expensive competition where children were viewed as a prize to be won by only one parent, with the other frequently left only with an opportunity to pay support and not parent.

2. *Only the marriage is ending, not the parenting relationship.* In a divorce, only the spousal relationship ends. However, traditional divorce often does great damage to the parent-child relationship. Ambiguous decrees with few standards or guidelines for parenting after the divorce have led to inadequate parenting and many returns to court. The new law demands a clear explanation of how parenting relationships are to be continued.

3. *The crap-shoot custody battle.* Anyone reading court custody decisions may perceive the lack of clear guidelines or criteria for determining child custody. Too many cases went to trial over custody. Our prior law failed to recognize the harm done to the parenting relationship by the trial procedure.

The Parenting Act gives weight to demonstrated patterns of parental care and plans for continuity of care.

4. *Joint custody rarely is.* Joint custody does not cure the problem of the non-custodial parent feeling left out of child-rearing decisions. Nor does it prevent the unfairness of those who demand joint custody in order to reduce child support or make a less than equitable property division. Imposing joint custody on an unwilling party can harm the children. With the exception of physical abuse and neglect, parental conflict is the greatest source of psychological harm to children. *Parental conflict continued because of* joint custody *can harm children more than sole custody or the total absence of one parent.* However, in the few cases where there is a deeply shared parenting commitment, joint custody does work.

5. *Joint custody can be inefficient.* Children under joint custody arrangements may be passed back and forth on a time schedule with each parent performing the entire constellation of parenting functions. But, each parent taking on responsibilities to which he or she is most disposed or simply best at doing would appear to be a sounder approach. Division of time with the children in a viable family is divided according to parenting function, not time. This should continue after a divorce.

6. *Neither child support nor child time should be withheld.* As of 1988, $4.3 *billion* of child support remains unpaid in this nation and what support is awarded is often inadequate. In fact, it is estimated that single parents nationwide were awarded $19 *billion* less in support than they needed and deserved. Primary parents were further exploited by the support-paying parent through the reductions and set-offs that the support-paying parent demanded for each day the child spent with him or her. This is far from fair if the custodial parent's costs were not significantly reduced by having the child spend time with the other parent. Generally, our new Child Support Schedule significantly increases both the fairness of determining support and the adequacy of the amount paid. In some cases, our Schedule does not work well. Now that support payments better reflect need, we should also address the serious problem of withholding access to the children. Children need both parents. Spouses who were rarely involved during marriage often make quite a turnaround upon divorce.

7. *Lack of protection from abusive or over-reaching spouses.* The system protects spouses who are battered but not parents who are intimidated physically, emotionally, or economically into agreeing to custodial relationships that are simply unworkable. The Act limits an unfit parent's participation in future parenting and in mediation. Further, the new law specifies a procedure for changes in parenting functions and responsibilities.

8. *People change, children change, why shouldn't our divorce decree?* Under prior law, the divorce decree remained set in concrete unless a significant change in circumstance occurred. Under our Parenting Act, it is

presumed that the needs of the children will change over time and that a parenting plan format can more flexibly address these changes.

9. *Parenting itself is changing.* Mothers and fathers are redefining their roles in parenting. While our prior law appeared to set the standard that the wage earner would have only limited parenting desires and responsibilities, the new law provides opportunities for equitable parenting by each. Equitable parenting is rarely equal. Children's needs change. At one time one child may need more mother time and another more father time. Some of the most difficult parenting concerns letting go in favor of the other parent. Good parenting demands more than 50% commitment but not necessarily more than 50% time.

10. *Cheap shots vs. mediation.* Our court system prevented neither retaliatory withholding of child support or visitation nor the *race to the courthouse* where the first to file with the biggest fabrications often won. These costly *affidavit wars* created more heat than light and more bitterness than resolution. Temporary parenting plans demand more responsible information and tolerate less blame and rancor.

11. *Justice delayed is justice denied.* In King County, it took years to get to a trial. The wait alone created an intolerable degree of scarring. A child waiting the many months for a trial often experienced this time as living in a war zone between bitter parents. The Act requires clear plans for the child's care at the *outset* of the divorce process. The hope is that the child will be protected and provided with greater stability during the initial stages of the divorce.

12. *Returns to court.* The Act specifies procedures for discussion and the use of mediation before parties seek relief through the court system.

THE PARENTING FUNCTIONS AND THE NEW
BEST INTERESTS OF THE CHILD

There are six parenting functions recognized by our Parenting Act. They are based on an expanded definition of the best interests of the child, which is the standard used by the court to allocate parental responsibilities. Our new law provides:

> "The State recognizes the fundamental importance of the parent-child relationship to the welfare of the child, and that the relationship between the child and each parent should be fostered unless inconsistent with the child's best interest. *The best interests of the child* are served by a parenting arrangement that best maintains the child's emotional growth, health, stability, and physical care. Further, *the best interests of the child* are ordinarily served when the existing pattern of interaction between the parent and the child is altered only to the extent

necessitated by the changed relationship of the parents or as required to protect the child from physical, mental, or emotional harm." (Emphasis added.)

This expanded definition gives more guidance to parents about what factors the court will consider. It does not mean that the court will attempt to preserve the division of responsibility that existed while the two parents lived together. The court clearly recognizes that separation and divorce demand a new consideration of parental responsibility. This new consideration will be based on consideration of the past performance of each parent of the following six parenting functions:

1. Maintaining a loving, stable, consistent, and nurturing relationship with the child;

2. Attending to the daily needs of the child such as feeding, clothing, physical care and grooming, supervision, health care and day care, and engaging in other activities that are appropriate to the developmental level of the child and that are within the social and economic circumstances of the particular family;

3. Attending to adequate education for the child, including remedial or other education essential to the best interests of the child;

4. Assisting the child in developing and maintaining appropriate inter- personal relationships;

5. Exercising appropriate judgment regarding the child's welfare, con- sistent with the child's emotional level and the family's social and economic circumstances; and

6. Providing for the financial support of the child.

These parenting functions declare a strong preference towards the maxi- mum involvement of both parties in the act of parenting their children. But, the statute places more emphasis on the *quality* than the *quantity* of interaction. Active parenting is only encouraged where the parent is fit and not using his or her participation to harass the other or reduce the support obligation. The Parenting Act has no sympathy for manipulative behavior.

INADEQUATE PARENTING — SECTION 191

Our Parenting Act highlights two groups of inadequate parenting behaviors. *If these behaviors are found, traditional limited custody provisions are available.* There are two levels of inadequate parenting. The more serious shall be labeled *Inadequate I* and the less serious *Inadequate II*.

Inadequate I

Any analysis of your role as a parent must begin with whether you or your spouse have committed any of the following behaviors:

1. A willful abandonment of children or family that continues for an extended period of time or a substantial refusal to perform parenting functions;
2. Physical, sexual, or emotional abuse of a child; or
3. An assault or sexual assault, which causes grievous bodily harm or fear of such harm.

If a parent is found to have engaged in any of the above behaviors, the following sanctions *will* occur:

1. That parent *shall* be denied the opportunity to participate in mutual decisionmaking regarding child's future.
2. That parent *shall* be denied the opportunity to participate in mediation or any other method of dispute settlement outside of the formal court process.
3. That parent's residential time with the child *shall* be limited.

Inadequate I is the most severe level. These sanctions will be in effect both in a temporary and a permanent parenting plan. However, the Parenting Act does not condemn the *parent* if these acts occur, only that *parent's behaviors*. If a parent stops the inadequate behavior and tries to repair the injury of the past, the court *may* be lenient.

Inadequate I: Defining the Terms

Willful abandonment or *substantial refusal to perform parenting functions* have no definition in our case law. Under other statutes, the term *willful abandonment* is defined as "a settled intent to forgo, for an extended period, all parental responsibility despite an ability to do so." This rather narrow definition suggests that if there is contact between the parent and the child, even if it is not particularly supportive, there has not been a willful abandonment.

Under the Parenting Act, the definition seems more expansive. Abandonment seems to include the failure of a parent to perform parenting functions which they are capable of performing and the refusal need not be complete, but only *substantial. Substantial refusal to perform parenting functions* refers to the parent who largely refuses to help the children meet their emotional, social, psychological, and educational needs. One key to these criteria is that the parent's behavior is voluntary. Parents with a recognized disability limiting their earning or parenting capacity will not be found inadequate under this criteria if they do their best to parent well.

Physical or sexual abuse is already well defined by our statutes and agencies. Washington State's Child Protective Service is available to help with the determination. *Emotional abuse* can be broadly defined. It could cover unreasonably exposing the child to parental fights, unreasonably soliciting the child to take sides in a dissolution, or limiting a child's access to the other parent without a clear threat of harm to the child.

For example, Susan *might* be found to have emotionally abused her twelve-year-old daughter if she told her the following:

> "I'm sorry, Hillary, but your father just isn't paying enough money to us so you can't go to camp this year. Also, you're going to have to drop out of the private school that you've been attending for the past six years. The new support schedule just doesn't give me enough money and I've asked for more from your father but we both know that he's spending all of his extra money on that new girlfriend and we're not likely ever to get what we need."

One isolated incident may not rise to the level of abuse contemplated by the Act. If comments like Susan's are part of an ongoing pattern the court would consider them emotional abuse. No one knows how the courts will define *emotional abuse* of a child. For now, we should rely on common sense and a good-faith effort to avoid any act that could alienate the child's affections from the other parent, as well as acts that are intended to hurt the feelings of the child, cause needless shame, insult, or tend to damage the mental well-being of the child.

In basic terms, the Parenting Act recognizes that any *physical or sexual assault* of one spouse or the *serious threat* of physical or sexual assault is not appropriate behavior, unless it is used strictly to defend oneself against a physical attack. Strong disagreements and shouting matches are a recognized fact of relationships. Assault is not.

This sends the clear message that domestic violence is strongly discouraged. The court recognizes that many divorces have a few incidents of throwing plates, screaming and shouting, and non-injury physical contact, which do not constitute domestic violence. The court also recognizes that repeated acts of domestic violence create a *cycle of violence* that is passed on to the children. The cycle must be broken.

Please note, *an assault conviction is not required.* The abuse needs only to fit the description of a felony crime. If you have committed an assault and your spouse has not, your time with your children will be limited unless you can clearly demonstrate to the court that:

1. It was a one-time incident; and the chance of it happening again is so slim that the harm to the child of not seeing you is greater than the risk of recurrence; or

2. The incident did not have an impact on the child.

If both parents are involved in domestic violence, then there is some possibility that the children may be raised primarily by grandparents, relatives, or foster parents. The message of our court: domestic violence is intolerable. Provocation is no excuse, and if you must hurt something, break something replaceable or take it out on the woodpile.

If you have a problem with violent anger, you should seriously consider calling your local family court or the Harborview Memorial Hospital Anger Management Center in Seattle for a referral to an anger management group in your locality. Similarly, if you have a history of being victimized, you should consult Appendix K for information about how to break out of the cycle of being an abused spouse. If you act now, you may learn enough to stop the cycle of violence with you and not let it pass on to your children.

Inadequate II — Discretionary Limits to Parenting

The second, less serious, level of inadequate parenting includes seven behaviors, any one of which *allows* the court to omit or limit any aspect of parenting. Inadequate I *requires* limits; Inadequate II *allows* limits. These seven factors focus upon neglect, impairment, absence, abuse, and withholding access. They are as follows:

1. *Neglect or substantial non-performance of parenting functions.* This is lesser than Level I above where the standard was willful *abandonment* or *substantial refusal.* Rather, the focus will be on the parents' *conscious and continued failure* to parent as they are capable.

2. *Long-term emotional or physical impairment, which interferes with the performance of parenting functions.* This standard does not discriminate against parents with a history of mental illness or physical impairment unless their impairment limits their capacity to perform specific parenting functions. Parents who can show that their impairment is temporary and does not adversely affect their parenting should not be prevented from being active parents under this section. *Long-term impairment* may be construed to mean that it has lasted or will continue to last for at least one year.

3. *Long-term impairment resulting from drug, alcohol, and other substance abuse that interferes with the performance of parenting functions.* Any parent with a serious drug or alcohol problem must deal with his or her problem if he or she wishes to continue parenting. If you have a drug or alcohol problem, and your spouse files for divorce, hope is not lost if you act quickly to assess the problem and begin a rigorous recovery program. The court is likely to look kindly upon those who show initiative and act on their problems and unkindly upon those who deny them. Appendix L contains a listing of numerous

agencies that can help in dealing with drug and alcohol dependencies. A chemical dependency can be a very difficult habit to break and most of the experts in the field say that it is rarely done alone.

4. *The absence or substantial impairment of emotional ties between parent and child.* This section targets the parent who simply has not developed a warm parental relationship with the child or perhaps the parent who needlessly attacks the child such that the relationship is, at best, limited. All too often, children are the first victims of the divorce process. The upset parent, frustrated by the other spouse, may often lash out at the child instead. This section is not meant to penalize one or two outbursts unless they are quite severe. The focus is on the longer history and the purpose is to protect the children.

5. *Abusive use of conflict, which creates a danger of serious damage to the child's psychological development.* This is an expansion of Level I's *physical, psychological, or emotional abuse.* Abusive conflict involving the child is to be avoided. The abusive use of conflict can impair parenting capacity and thereby harm the child's development.

   Serious conflicts between parents should be dealt with by parents alone. In other words, serious disagreements should be resolved out of the presence of the children. Children often feel they are responsible for conflict between their parents and that causes them to internalize a great amount of guilt while attempting to bring their parents *back together.* They often assume that they are a part of the reason their parents are fighting. The Parenting Act clearly aims to relieve children of this anxiety.

6. *Withholding the child from the other parent for a protracted period without good cause.* Game playing with visitation will be penalized. Game playing on support payments will be penalized. So long as the other parent is adequate, there should be no reason for limiting the other parent's time with the child. Periods of a child's sickness or injury should be shared just like periods of health. Any failure to parent adequately should be brought up clearly and diplomatically — a letter may be best. Give the other parent clear opportunities to change before you consider limiting his or her time. *Do not limit time without a court order.* Conflict between parents should be resolved in a manner that does not involve the children.

   Note: If you are found in contempt of court for denying residency time, the denied time will be made up. If you are found in contempt for a second time within three years, your ex-spouse will be granted twice the denied time. You may also be charged with and convicted of custodial interference. That would constitute a significant change of circumstances sufficient for modifying your parenting plan.

7. *Such other factors or conduct as the court expressly finds in the best interests of the child.* This catch-all section allows the court to leave the door open for other behavior that it finds to be detrimental to the child. As of July 1, 1989, the parents' work schedule is a new factor under this category.

King County courts now provide drug evaluation where the court feels it necessary. If either parent has a problem with drugs or alcohol, the parenting plan should push that parent to seek help. If that parent refuses to seek help, then the residency time of the parent may be conditioned upon no consumption of drugs or alcohol.

Parents must be careful not to construe Factor 7 too broadly. A parent's religion or sexual preference is not, in and of itself, sufficient grounds for limiting parenting. Similarly, a parent's exposure to AIDS should not, alone, result in a limitation of residency time. The key concern here is whether the parent is capable of meeting the children's day-to-day needs. For example, there are many capable parents with AIDS and there is no record of AIDS being transmitted from parent to child from normal household contact.

Neither parent knows all the child's needs. Fathers meet certain needs that mothers don't and vice versa. Good parents learn to tolerate, then understand, the different parenting style of their spouse. If the children are misbehaving, look to your own parenting before blaming your spouse.

INADEQUATE PARENTING: WHAT IF I DON'T REPORT IT?

You are at risk if you do not report your spouse's misbehavior. For example, it is a well-documented fact that alcohol dependency and drug dependency are subtly enabled by the non-addicted spouse's failure to confront the dependent spouse. Likewise there are many incidents of abuse or neglect of a child that continue because the other spouse failed to report it to the proper authorities or to confront the spouse.

Just as we must say NO to drugs, the responsible parent must say NO to abuse, neglect, and inadequate parenting. Many of our clients ask if the Act should be interpreted to mean that they should immediately report an exspouse to Child Protective Services for abuse or neglect and to the spouse's employer or some other public agency for drug or alcohol abuse. We suggest that a qualified counselor should be consulted first in the event of possible child abuse and a qualified drug or alcohol counselor should be consulted first regarding drug or alcohol abuse. The reason for this is that your spouse's capacity to admit and modify these behaviors may be increased if the issue is aired first in private counseling rather than in open court.

PARENTAL RESIDENCY — THE NEW VISITATION

Thankfully, our new Parenting Act resolved many of the common visitation problems addressed in the first edition of this book. Under our new law, parental *visitation* no longer exists unless the other parent is found to be inadequate. It is replaced, in part, by the more neutral concept of residency time. Under our prior law (and most law nationally), custody fights were a *winner-take-all* affair. To the victor went the *award* of custody and to the vanquished went the *right of visitation.*

For parents considering a divorce or wishing to change their visitation arrangement, a parenting plan is necessary. A parenting plan must be filed within 180 days of filing the petition or within thirty (30) days of filing a notice of readiness for trial.

After reviewing the statutory requirements for residency schedule, Mary Ellen exclaimed:

> "Do I really *have* to be that specific? I have to write something that details where each child resided and when for the past year and then what each of us parents did for them. Then I have to summarize my work and child-care schedule for the past year. Then I have to state any parenting problems I'm concerned about regarding Jim. Once that's done, I also have to do a parenting plan, which requires a detailed daily schedule for the next twelve months!"

Three months after filing her parenting plan, Mary Ellen said:

> "I can see that I was really angry to have to answer all of those specific questions. They required so much work and so much *risk.* I mean, putting out a schedule for the next year with all the specifics makes the judge's job easier, but how do I give this to Jim without seeming like I'm a dictator? Thank God I could talk with Jim beforehand. I fear for those women who can't. A detailed parenting plan could upset them even more than they already are.
>
> "Now that I look back on the parenting plan, I feel really good about it. I realize that I didn't want to answer all of those questions because partly I wanted someone else to do my divorce for me. I wanted to avoid painful questions just like I wanted to avoid the pain of divorce. Now, I'm really glad I faced up to it — those specifics forced Jim and me to examine a lot of our unstated expectations.
>
> "With this parenting plan business, you've got to lay it all out on the table. As near as I can tell, the main reason people go back to court after divorce is not what your divorce decree says, but what it doesn't say."

Mary Ellen is partially correct. Parenting plans sometimes create more problems during the first stages of divorce than the prior divorce petition. Often, there is less hostility from the other parent if the requests are not as specific. However, many parents take advantage of the parenting plan as an opportunity to begin mediation and a constructive discussion of the children's needs. Paradoxically, the need to do a detailed parenting plan can create an opportunity for greater involvement by the less active parent. The more this parent is involved, the less intimidated or angry he or she is likely to feel.

It is our experience that most post-divorce conflict results from issues that could have been addressed in the dissolution decree. Little items, such as when the children are to be picked up or who does the transportation, can, over time, become major aggravations. Thankfully, our new law forces parents to spell out many of these issues, and to spell out how their decisions will be altered over time as the children's needs change. The bottom line is clear: the more specific the dissolution decree, the less there is to fight about, and the more specific the method of dispute resolution, the less there is to go to court about. IF YOU CANNOT WORK OUT ALL OF THE SPECIFICS OF RESIDENCE TIME WITH YOUR SPOUSE, THEN SPELL IT OUT IN YOUR PARENTING PLAN.

DRAFTING A RESIDENCY SCHEDULE

The following is designed to help you understand how to put together a residency schedule. Sample provisions are included for your use. *You must, however, use your own judgment in determining the provisions you would like to have in your temporary and permanent parenting plan.* Between some parents, there is a need to account for every possible contingency. For others, it is only necessary to have a detailed backup schedule in the event of disagreement. Common sense tells us that putting it all down on paper will provide a clear opportunity to deal with parental expectations and needs up front and reduce the risk of future misunderstanding.

With the help of their mediator, Mary Ellen and Jim developed their own temporary parenting plan. Mediation is encouraged under our new law. They identified their own needs and the needs of their children, and also reviewed their own particular parenting skills and the flexibility available in their work schedules.

For example, they agreed that Jim woul dparticipate as a coach for Justin's basketball team and assist on Kirsten's soccer team. They also chose to alternate Sunday ski trips during the winter months. Both parents decided to participate together in school conferences.

Although your attorney may have a more detailed procedure, doing a basic residency plan is a three-step process:

Step 1. Twelve Months of Family Background

In your initial declaration to the court, you must, for the past year, indicate: (a) where the children have resided during the past year, including the name and address, names of those residing with them, and time at each address; (b) what parenting functions were performed by each parent and when; (c) each parent's work and the child-care schedules up to the present time; and (d) whether there are any inadequate parenting behaviors.

Dissolution is difficult for children and the courts require this data, in part, to ensure that the parenting arrangements provide the least disruption to the child's prior routines.

For our purposes, there are three basic types of parenting:

A. *Inadequate parenting I and II.* These parents will likely have their time with the children reduced, if not eliminated, unless they address and change their harmful behaviors.

B. *Single primary parenting.* This is the typical family envisioned by the legislature where the husband or the wife assumes primary responsibility for the child and the other spouse assumes the job of primary wage earner.

C. *Dual primary parenting.* This is a less typical couple, where both have nearly equal parenting responsibilities. Special care must be taken to ensure that these arrangements are feasible, voluntary, and in the best interests of the children.

Step 2. Assessment of Children's Needs and Parents' Capacities

Both temporary and permanent residency schedules require a statement describing any inadequate parenting as described earlier.

Although the court considers the parental inadequacy factors in both temporary and permanent parenting plans, the key to temporary parenting plans is that the focus is *temporary*. The court's focus is directed by two factors:

> 1. Which parent has taken greater responsibility during the last twelve months for performing parenting functions related to the daily needs of the child.

This refers to the performance of the parenting functions (for example, feeding, clothing, providing for health care, supervision, and education). The nod is often given to whichever parent has been the primary care giver for the children unless, of course, both parents have shared that role. The courts recognize that divorce demands a change in parenting roles and responsibilities. While allowing this change, the court seeks, under the above factor, to maintain as much continuity of care and love for the children as possible. Here the law discriminates in favor of the active, involved parent. It is no longer wise to be just a wage earner — you must also meet the needs of your child in your marriage if you expect to be active in your child's life upon divorce. For temporary parenting plans, your future depends largely upon your past. For permanent parenting plans, more weight is given to the future and the potential that you have demonstrated under the temporary parenting plan. The second factor is as follows:

2. Which parenting arrangements will cause the least disruption to the child's emotional stability while the dissolution action is pending.

This factor demands that you address and determine the sources of your child's emotional stability. This is not a question that need be answered by a psychologist. There is no statutory definition of emotional stability, but the definition would certainly vary as each child's needs vary. It could involve how you can assure that your children continue to feel a sense of (a) *safety* — that they will be protected and provided for; (b) *love* — that they are unique, important, and not to blame for their parents' problems; and (c) *relationship stability* — that they will not lose touch with friends, family, and their academic and social activities.

During mediation of their temporary parenting plan, Jim stated:

> "I am really lucky that I have been a pretty active dad with the kids. If I had done the traditional long-hours-away-from-home breadwinner act, I wouldn't have had a *chance* to be an active parent under this new law."

While Jim may perhaps be correct for the purposes of a temporary parenting plan, he is not correct for the permanent parenting plan. If you are not satisfied with the temporary parenting plan, there is great hope, as our courts expressly discourage judges from using the temporary parenting plan to frame the permanent parenting plan. A parent's full-time work should not limit his or her residency time. Work *schedules,* not work itself, are important for residency time.

Step 3. Schedules and Conflict Resolution

One clear purpose of our new law is to help fit parents settle their cases now or to change their plan in the future without court intervention. Thus, once the residency schedule is agreed upon, there must be arrangements for how to change it. Some process, prior to court, must first be used. Dispute processes may include the following:

1. Counseling
2. Mediation (by an individual, agency or court personnel)
3. Arbitration (by an individual or agency)

Please see Chapter 3 for more information on mediation and dispute resolution.

Only court action is allowed if either parent falls under Inadequate Parenting I.

In deciding which method of dispute resolution to use, the parents must ask if it is affordable and must take care not to abuse it. Attorney's fees and costs will be awarded to a parent if the other parent abuses or frustrates the dispute resolution process.

Once conflict resolution is determined, it is time to address the residential schedule of the children.

Residential schedules must cover every day of the year. Do not settle for general ambiguous language because the courts now have a duty to review each permanent and temporary parenting plan. Parents with incomplete plans will not be granted divorces.

Residency schedules usually have two levels: the standard days and the exceptional days.

Standard Residency Schedule

When will the children reside with each parent (a) during the school year, and (b) during the summer?

Exceptional Residency Schedule

This concerns holidays and other exceptional days that supersede the standard schedule. This schedule can be determined by answering the following questions.

1. When will the children reside with which parent during the following:
   a. Winter vacation
   b. Spring vacation
   c. Thanksgiving
   d. Three-day holidays (Martin Luther King's Birthday, Presidents Day, Memorial Day, Labor Day and Veterans Day)
   e. One-day holidays (Fourth of July)
   f. Each child's birthday
   g. Each parent's birthday
   h. Mother's Day and Father's Day
   i. Observed religious holidays such as Christmas Day, Christmas Eve, Passover, Yom Kippur, Hanukkah, Chinese New Year, *etc.*
2. During each parent's annual vacation (a) how long may the children be with them, (b) during what months of the year, and (c) how much notice must be provided to the other parent and the children?

COMMON RESIDENCY PROVISIONS

The following language is typically found in parenting plans.

Weekends

Father shall have residency time with the children every other weekend from Friday at 6:00 p.m. through Sunday at 6:00 p.m. and every Wednesday overnight, commencing Friday, January _____, 19__.

Time and dates should be varied to fit the needs of the children and the parents. An alternative provision might provide:

> Father shall have residency time with the children on the first, third and, if applicable, the fifth weekend of each month from 9:00 a.m. Saturday through 4:00 p.m. Sunday, and Wednesday and Thursday overnights, commencing Saturday, January _____, 19__.

Holidays

Parents should carefully consider how holidays are to be divided. Keep in mind the child's changing needs as well as your own. After all, how many turkey dinners can a child eat on Thanksgiving?

After listing the national, local, religious, and school holidays, they should be divided in some reasonable manner, with consideration to each parent's special attachment to particular holidays. For example, Mary Ellen's family had a history of get-togethers on the Fourth of July and Jim's family had a history of get-togethers on Labor Day weekend. Since the children plainly benefitted from seeing their extended families, Mary Ellen and Jim decided that she would always have Fourth of July and he would always have Labor Day weekend. Holiday language could read as follows:

> During even-numbered years, the children shall reside with the father on Martin Luther King's Birthday, Memorial Day, Fourth of July, and Thanksgiving, and with the mother on Washington's Birthday, Labor Day, and Veterans Day. During odd-numbered years the children shall reside with the mother on Martin Luther King's Birthday, Memorial Day, Fourth of July, and Thanksgiving, and with the father on Washington's Birthday, Labor Day, and Veterans Day. Holiday visitation will begin at ___ p.m. on the first day of the holiday and end at ___ p.m. on the last day.

Vacations

Winter, spring, and summer vacations deserve careful planning. The non-primary parent has a benefit of longer residency with the children and the other parent has a break from the responsibilities of caring for them. The non-primary parent will be confronted with the day-to-day tasks assumed normally by the primary parent. These responsibilities might include car-pooling, day-care arrangements, medical appointments, illness, enrichment activities, and an increased food budget. Just as it is healthy for the primary parent to have a break, it is healthy for the non-primary parent to have an opportunity to shoulder the full parental responsibility and to reap the benefits. These longer periods of parenting require forethought and planning if the experience is to be successful.

A broad provision for spring vacation might read as follows:

> The father shall have visitation for a period of one week during the child's spring vacation. This week shall begin at ___ o'clock on the first day school recesses and end at ___ o'clock seven days later.

If the parents wish to alternate spring vacation, the same language can be used with the following additional language:

> Father's residence time shall occur only in odd-numbered years, and in even-numbered years, the same residency time shall be granted to the mother.

Christmas or winter vacation poses many problems for parents. A parent who celebrates Christmas wants to share the *package-opening* experience with the children. This special event could be divided on the basis of Christmas Eve and Christmas Day as follows:

> The father shall pick up the child at 9:00 a.m. on the 24th day of December each year and return the child by 9:00 a.m. on the 25th day of December.

The days could be switched, if desired, by adding the odd-numbered/even-numbered years language. In the alternative, the parents might desire to use Christmas Eve and Christmas Day as a dividing point for the entire vacation. In that case, the language for winter vacation might read as follows:

> The father shall have residency time during winter school vacation commencing at ___ o'clock on the first day that school recesses and ending at 9:00 p.m. on the 24th day of December each year. The mother shall have the children in residence from the 24th day of December for a period of time equal to half of the winter vacation, whereupon the children will reside with the father from that date until 5:00 p.m. the day before the children's school resumes.

Again, *odd-numbered/even-numbered years* language could be added to alternate days.

Summer Vacation

The summer vacation residency time with the other parent usually lasts from two to eight weeks, depending upon the age of the children, the distance between parents' residences and the employment requirements of each parent. To permit both sides to plan their own summer schedules, a notice provision should be included. Typical language could provide:

> Each parent shall have the children for a period of _____ consecutive, uninterrupted days during the children's summer vacation. Each parent promises to provide the other with notice of the time they would like to have the children on or before April 15th of each year and the parents pledge to resolve their vacation schedules on or before May 1st of each year. Parents further agree that, so long as their child is under ten years of age, neither will spend more than fourteen consecutive days with them. Once their child passes the age of ten, either parent may spend up to twenty-one consecutive days with them and this may be extended to thirty consecutive days when the child attains an age of fourteen years.

MAKING YOUR RESIDENCY PLAN WORK

Once you have drafted a residency agreement, you have to make it work. Changing from a full-time live-in parent to a part-time live-in parent creates a new and very vulnerable relationship. If the child and the non-residential parent have always shared a close bond, there will be additional pain beyond the emotional strains already created by the divorce.

With planning, there are ways to reduce the difficulty of building a new relationship with your children. Changes should be agreed between parents beforehand and implemented carefully. A *go-slow* pattern is crucial to the adjustment of very young children.

Each parent has the benefit of knowing far into the future when and where they will be seeing their child. The very young child has a different sense of time, and may perceive an absence of a few days as abandonment. That child needs special attention during the transition to the new custody arrangement. If, for example, one parent is to have residence time only on weekends, it will be better for the parent to visit every evening for a while, and gradually taper off to the weekend provision. Similarly, if your agreement allows you to take the child overnight, it may be advisable to begin with short, frequent visits to your new home. A very young child may be unnecessarily upset by being forced to spend the weekend in totally strange surroundings. Eventually, the young child will be confident enough for regular extended visits there. But don't rush it.

It will help if your children have a place of their own at your new residence — somewhere for their own bed and belongings. This will reassure them that they have a permanent place in your new life.

If your children are older, you may wonder what to do on your first few visits. These may be awkward times for you, especially if you are not already close to your children. Some parents make the mistake of perceiving the visit as an occasion for mandatory entertainment. They expect, subconsciously or otherwise, that excursions to the zoo or sporting events help to compensate the child for what he or she has suffered during the divorce. This concept, frequently called *Disneyland Daddy,* may lead the child to have an artificial view of that parent's place in his or her life, and undermine the establishment of a strong relationship between parent and child.

Children need fun time and work time with each of their parents. Avoid planning your visits only around fun time. After all, you will have to talk with them sometime. Both of you need time free from distractions to examine your feelings about the divorce and get to know each other in a new way. I have repeatedly witnessed the great satisfaction that blossoms between the non-primary parent (predominantly the father) and his child when the *entertaining* stops and they discover a far stronger relationship. The relationship simply flourished once they stayed home, talked, and worked together.

The presence of more than one child complicates conversation. If you have two children, you and your ex-spouse must consider whether your visit will include both children or alternate with each child visiting separately. This requires careful thought from both parents. You will need to consider the needs of the children and their relationship to you and to one another.

Whether you have one or several children, you should recognize that once your times are established, it may be good for your child to invite a friend along occasionally. This will vary your experience together. Your child's friends should get to know you. In so doing, you will both share more fully in each other's lives.

After settling into your residency routine, you may find that weekly or even less frequent visits are unsatisfactory to both you and your children. This is particularly true if you have a close, happy relationship. This may be a lonesome time for all of you. You miss the children and they miss you. You will all benefit if you maintain contact in additional ways. Daily phone calls may be one answer. You may also want to write notes to the children and encourage them to write to you. Additional means of communication may go a long way toward easing the pain of separation. A book entitled *Ways to be a Long Distance Super-Dad* by George Newman is full of good communication ideas.

To help you and your spouse minimize difficulties in living with a residency schedule, the following guidelines should be heeded.

RESIDENCY SCHEDULES: RULES FOR PLAYING FAIR

1. Do not be late; stick to the agreed-upon hours.
2. Do not make an appointment to see your child if you do not plan to keep it. Your child needs to be able to rely on you.
3. If you must cancel a day with the children, give at least forty-eight hours' notice, and at least a week's notice for missing a weekend or more.
4. Do not use your child to spy on or carry messages to your ex-spouse; do not question the child about the other parent's activities.
5. Do not belittle your ex-spouse to the child.
6. Be willing to compromise on residency time, especially as your child grows up. Your children have a right to a life and interests of their own.
7. Do not threaten to stop residence if child support checks do not arrive. The court cannot impose this sanction, and your interference with the residency schedule could affect your parenting status.

8. Do not make excuses to block visits. Your child has a right to see the other parent and needs both of you. Encourage your child to go, even if he/she is reluctant. Children often express reluctance to please you. If you are concerned, ask them for specifics. Discuss their concerns tactfully with your ex-spouse.

Remember, residency is a dual right. It involves the parents' right to share in the life of the child and the child's right to know both parents and to enjoy their companionship. If you and your spouse remember your child's interests, visits will be happier and more beneficial for all.

DUAL PRIMARY PARENTS — A RESIDENCY FORMULA

Dual primary parents are each recognized as capable of providing for all the parenting needs of the child and are able to parent in a cooperative fashion with the other parent. Under our prior law, these individuals commonly agreed to shared parenting. Under our new law, the court requires additional findings for parents whose children switch from house to house frequently and spend approximately equal time with each parent. This part of the law has been referred to as the *ping-pong provision*. The courts clearly fear that frequent residency changes will harm the children, their education, and their peer friendships. The criteria are:

1. Neither parent falls within Inadequate I or II.
2. The parents have agreed to the proposal and the agreement was knowingly and voluntarily entered into. (This factor is aimed at parents who, in the past, have often been coerced by the parent making more money to agree to a shared custody arrangement when, in fact, the parents did not get along well enough to agree to this. Under our new support schedule, there is a clear incentive for the primary wage earner to push for shared residency time in order to reduce his or her support payment. Don't be pressured into fifty-fifty residency and don't resist working on communication problems. Always leave the door open for more *child time* if differences can be worked out.)
3. The parties have a satisfactory history of cooperation and shared parenting in the past, they are available to each other, live near each other, and are clearly able to share parenting in the future.

The court does not have to find the third factor if there is clear evidence of the second factor. Either the second or third factor is sufficient for the court to grant such shared parenting, but both are preferable.

Part of the reason for this ping-pong provision is the clear recognition in the psychological literature that parental conflict can be quite harmful to children. Shared parenting demands frequent and continuing interaction between parents and, thus, a great opportunity for friction and conflict. If you are not comfortable with your spouse's demands for such shared parenting, clearly express this to your attorney and consider hiring a child psychologist or utilizing court personnel to determine if such an arrangement is, in fact, in the best interests of the children.

It is our experience that a mathematically equal division of time (50% with each parent) is rarely in the best interests of the children. The needs of the parents and the needs of the children shift over time such that in one year it may be in the best interests of the children to spend slightly more time with the mother and another year slightly more time with the father. Thus, you should consider replacing a demand of *equal* time with a standard of *maximum quality* time for each parent.

The following is a sample residency formula for successful shared parenting.

1. *School year schedule.* The children shall reside with the father from Monday after school through Friday morning when the children go to school and they shall reside with the mother from when they leave school Friday through Monday morning when they are taken to school. The mother shall be responsible for ensuring that the children are picked up and dropped off at school each Friday and Monday and the father shall be responsible for ensuring that the children are picked up from school each Monday through Thursday.

2. *Summer residency time.* The school year residency time shall continue through summer except that each parent shall be provided up to three weeks of uninterrupted vacation time with the children. Parents shall, on or before April 1st of each year, provide each other with the times that they request for summer vacation. On or before April 30th of each year, the parents shall agree to when each will take summer vacation. The non-residential parent shall, during these vacations, have an opportunity to talk with the children on the telephone at least once a day if they so desire. Parents pledge to consider the children's wishes for summer activities prior to agreeing upon their scheduled vacation time. Further, the parents may divide their uninterrupted residency into two periods of time if their schedules conflict. Normal school year residency shall be suspended during vacation times.

3. *Holidays.* The children's holiday time shall be allocated as follows:

    1. For 1990 and each even-numbered year thereafter the children shall reside with the father on Memorial Day, Labor Day, Veterans Day, and Easter and with the mother on Presidents Day, Fourth of July, and Thanksgiving.

2. For 1991 and each odd-numbered year thereafter the children shall reside with the father on Presidents Day, Fourth of July, and Thanksgiving and with the mother on Memorial Day, Labor Day, Veterans Day, and Easter.

3. The parent having the children for the weekend immediately before or after a national holiday shall have the weekend time expanded to include such holiday.

4. Thanksgiving shall be defined as beginning at 5:00 p.m. Wednesday preceding Thanksgiving until 7:00 p.m. Sunday following Thanksgiving.

4. *Birthdays and special holidays.*

1. The children shall celebrate their birthdays with their mother in even-numbered years, and with their father in odd-numbered years.

2. The non-residential parent shall be allowed to spend some time with the child to celebrate the child's birthday, within a week of that birthday.

3. The mother shall have the children every year for Mother's Day and the father shall have the children every year for Father's Day from 9:00 a.m. to 6:00 p.m.?

5. *Vacations, winter and spring break.*

1. The children shall spend a portion of the winter school holiday from the first day of school vacation until 10 a.m. Christmas Day with the father in evennnumbered years, and with the mother in odd-numbered years.

2. The children shall spend every other spring vacation as defined by the school schedule with the father.

No residency plan will succeed forever. Parents need change and the children's needs change over time. Residency decisions that are initially made by parents will often be largely made by children once they become teenagers. Children's needs rarely coincide with their parents' needs, particularly when they are young. Infants and toddlers are not always capable of the shared residency time that their parents seek. Many parents plan a mandatory annual review of their residency plan to adjust to the children's changing needs. A clause like the following in the parenting plan is helpful to reduce the need to litigate in order to effect a minor change in the residency plan. *Do not use this clause unless you and your spouse get along well.*

The parents herein recognize that the children's residency needs will change over time and that such change, if voluntary and reasonable, is in the best interest of the children. Therefore, parents agree that a change of up to 20% in either parent's residency schedule shall not require a petition to modify the parenting plan. Rather, it shall be considered a clarification.

To reasonably set the standard for appropriate residency time, we must consider the developmental needs of the children.

DEVELOPMENTAL STAGES OF CHILDHOOD

Children's parenting needs and residency needs change and grow as they mature through the different stages of childhood. Parents should continue to adapt the parenting plan to suit the various stages of the children. If a divorced family is flexible, it can accommodate these changes on its own or with the help of a mediator. Development does not stop with the end of childhood. There are many who argue that developmental stages continue throughout life and are behind such common phenomena as *mid-life crisis*. There is no agreement as to the precise number of stages that children pass through or the precise content of those stages. There is agreement that each child's rate of development is unique. Some progress more rapidly through the initial stages and more slowly through the latter whereas *late bloomers* do just the opposite. The development schedule in Appendix D is proposed by the King County Family Court Services for descriptive purposes. It should not be considered a binding model, but rather a series of signposts that could be useful in considering the needs of particular children. Stages may be identified as the infant, toddler, preschooler, early elementary age, later elementary age, and adolescence. Understanding the needs of each developmental stage will help you design your own residency plan. *See* Appendix D, *King County Family Court Services Access Guidelines*.

SPECIAL PARENTING PROBLEMS

The Reluctant Parent

There is, within that large population of *lazy, unreliable*, or *Disneyland* parents a group of *reluctant parents*. They were usually the primary wage earners during the marriage and had scant experience at parenting. They often assume that it was their primary responsibility to *work hard* to meet the economic needs of the family and that their spouse was primarily responsible for meeting the emotional needs of the children. Reluctant parents are distinguished from other parents by the fact that they do make their support payments on time. They do not regularly exercise residency time and their time usually consists of going to activities that do not require significant interaction between the parents and the children. The children often speak of having difficulty understanding what this parent wants. Strangely, the spouses of reluctant parents often engage in behaviors that subtly continue to discourage closeness between the reluctant parent and the children while com-plaining.

As one divorced wife explained:

> "Fred and I were together for almost twenty years and he was never what you could call the feeling type. He did well at work at his CPA firm and always kept a good roof over our heads. Fred has always been a shy sort of guy and that is what initially attracted me to him. I naturally thought I could *warm him up* and his self-doubt made me feel like I was really needed.

> "As our marriage progressed, the job of meeting the children's emotional needs became mostly mine. Fred was always there to help if need be, but his tasks usually focused on keeping the house and cars in good repair, maintaining the children's bikes and other equipment, and sometimes helping them with their lessons.

> "As our marriage turned sour, I now see that I looked more and more to the children for emotional support and Fred could never come close to matching the emotional intensity that I had with them. Thus, the children are much more comfortable with me than with Fred.

> "After our divorce, Fred visited the children rarely and constantly came up with excuses not to see them. At first I was really angry, thinking that he had another relationship or was somehow trying to get even with me. I *assumed* that Fred's absence was malicious. My anger boiled over on a number of occasions. This caused Fred to be even more distant. I started calling him a *dropout daddy,* but he would just take the insult like a slap and then walk away.

> "Finally, after one particularly vicious outburst by me about his failure to parent, Fred just stood there for a moment trembling and I saw tears that he was trying to blink back and it finally dawned on me that he was *afraid* of something. After talking with my friends, I went to see a therapist who helped me put two and two together to see that I had been driving Fred away from the children by continuing to point out his shortcomings. I began to see that Fred was so fearful of my disapproval of his parenting that he felt safer not parenting at all than risking failure in my eyes. I had to face the fact that I had made a series of serious mistakes by attempting to impose my standards of parenting and warmth on both Fred and our children.

> "I couldn't really explain all of this to Fred, so I sat down with a trusted mutual friend and tried to explain it. This friend met with Fred on a couple of occasions over dinners and came back with the fact that Fred did feel like he was an inadequate parent around me. He felt that since he wasn't the *warm and exciting* person that I was that the kids were better off being parented mainly by me. Fred's parents were apparently quite reserved and distant and he felt that he could do no better than they.

"Fortunately, this ended well. With the help of our mutual friend, Fred began to see a psychologist who helped him feel safer expressing his feelings. After about six sessions with the psychologist, the children were invited to meet with Fred and they gradually began to open the door. It has been about two years since our divorce and the situation between our kids and Fred has really improved and I think the children have benefitted."

Regrettably, Fred is not the normal reluctant parent. Most reluctant parents simply build a life for themselves away from the family that does not include parenting. The children grow increasingly more distant from that parent and seek substitute father or mother figures to compensate for the loss. Step-parents are rarely a good substitute for actual parents.

Recently, I spoke with one boy, John, whose father faded into the woodwork after the divorce:

"You know, when they got divorced I was only five and I didn't know what was going on. Now I'm twelve, and Mom treats me like I'm the man of the house or something. I don't know, but it is really sort of lonely just living with girls, you know.

"All the guys at school go out and do sports with their dads and fix cars and stuff, but Mom doesn't do that. You know, sometimes I get real mad that I don't have a dad. I get sad, too, because maybe it is something I did that keeps him away. It just sort of eats you up, you know.

Reluctance by one parent often reflects dominance by another, whether that dominance is passive or aggressive. Strangely, dominant homemakers are often reluctant wage earners, just as dominant wage earners are sometimes reluctant parents. Divorce demands that both parents perform both functions. In dealing with a reluctant parent, you may find success if you stress your parental shortcomings and seek advice or counseling while strongly praising any efforts at parenting by the reluctant parent.

Long-distance Parenting

Distance need not diminish love. With parental cooperation, proper planning, and extra money for transportation, a warm parent/child relationship can continue. It is not enough to provide large chunks of vacation time to the long-distance parent. The children need frequent contact and continuing reminders of this parent's support of the children from the residential parent.

For example, Jan and Dean have two children who are six and eight years old. Dean is the primary residential parent and Jan was transferred to New York shortly after the divorce. Since the children were well established in the neighborhood with relatives nearby, they remained with Dean, who was a capable and conscientious father.

As Dean described:

"Jan put her career on the shelf for eight years to focus on the kids. It was a tough decision that maybe contributed toward our divorce.

"Nine months ago, this incredible job offer in New York came through for Jan and she just *had* to take it. The kids were six and eight and wanted to stay here with friends.

"Suddenly I went from being a proud, *active* father to a fretful single parent. I never realized how much Jan was to the kids until she'd left.

"Things just started falling apart at the seams with the kids. They were cranky, upset, sick, depressed, and suddenly *good ol' dad* wasn't so good anymore.

For a few weeks I busted my rear end to do everything right for the kids. If it didn't work, then I felt that I was the problem and maybe I just couldn't give the kids what they needed.

Finally, I figured out that part of the problem came from the kids missing their *mom*. But they were also trying not to say anything about it. Fortunately, Jan was missing them as well, so Jan and I decided to do everything we could to make Jan a daily presence in the kids' lives. Here are some of the things we did:

1. We bought used fax machines for both homes. Everyday, there were new messages, pictures, jokes, and other fun things coming to the kids. The kids would fax their schoolwork and drawings and anything else they wanted to talk about directly to their mother. I learned the hard way that crayon drawings and fingerpaintings don't fax very well.

2. We linked up our home computers so the kids could play their favorite computer video games with their mom. It was great to watch them typing these messages back and forth about which moves to make next. It was almost like she was in the room with them.

3. We scheduled the children's TV time with Jan so they could watch the same shows *together* even though they were on different coasts. After the shows, Jan phones them and they talk about the show. Jan also sent videotapes of great shows from New York that we don't get here for the children to watch and then discuss. Sometimes they use these videos for school reports as well.

4. Jan is a great dramatic reader, so three or four times a week she reads a good-night story for one-half hour to the kids over the speaker phone in their bedroom. Then we *both* tuck them in at night.

5. The kids write three letters a week to their mom. They have special paper, bright envelopes, and all sorts of pre-gummed decorations such as stars and hearts to put on their letters. They mail out report cards and copies of their schoolwork. I think this has really increased their skills at writing.

6. The kids and Jan decided learning Spanish would be fun. They share tapes and practice Spanish conversation. Jan plans to take them to Mexico City as part of one of her extended business trips. The kids have a goal to practice for and they have made friends with a number of Spanish-speaking kids at their school.

"Frankly, I still resent Jan leaving our marriage and I initially resented all the attention she was getting from the kids. However, I noticed the kids felt my resentment and held back with their mom. It hurt them. I had to confront my jealousy and anger and let it go — for the kids' sake. Now my *single* parenting is much easier."

Jan and Dean's creative approach to long-distance parenting is no longer rare. More and more parents are seeing the benefit of long-distance parenting, both for themselves and for their children.

The All Thumbs Parent

The *all thumbs parent* is typically — but not always — the provider male who, prior to divorce, couldn't cook, clean, or minister to the children, not to mention interpret their emotional needs. Such parents strike fear into the hearts of their divorcing spouses, who often try to limit the children's time with them in order to *protect* the children. The *all thumbs parent* typically responds angrily that the kids are being *taken away* for no good reason and the stage is set for an expensive and unnecessary court battle.

To break this deadlock, one key fact must be realized: ALL THUMBS PARENTS ARE USUALLY INEXPERIENCED AND RARELY INCOMPETENT.

A recent study compared the parenting skills of single parent mothers and single parent fathers when interacting with their infant children. At the outset, most of the fathers were truly lacking in parenting skills. After nine months, the parents were retested and the researchers found that the fathers had equalled or exceeded the mothers in their parenting capacity.

Two of my mediation clients, Fred and Sally, struggled very successfully with this problem. As Sally commented:

"Fred was a good provider but a total loss in the kitchen. He came closer than anyone I know to burning water. With clothes washing he had this incredible knack for always tossing in at least one item of the wrong color so we perpetually ended up with light green underwear or pink T-shirts. There's no doubt that he cared for the kids but he tended to show it through listening, hard work, and buying them the things that we all needed.

"I was scared to death the kids would be neglected while they were with him. Fortunately, we worked out a *plan* for Fred's *inexperience* at parenting and for *my* fear. Fred took a cooking class and a parenting class offered by the local community college. I got some counseling and slowly came to realize that I was part of the problem. I had judged that Fred couldn't discern the needs of the kids or the household but the truth was that I had usually figured out the needs of the kids *faster* than Fred. I assumed that Fred didn't *know* their needs. He knew, but he just didn't catch on as quickly as I did."

As Fred commented:

> "On the homefront I majored in lawn mowers, tax preparation, and house repair. Sally was lightyears better than me at cooking, cleaning, and figuring out the needs of the kids. Over the years I figured I didn't have what it took in that area so I deferred to Sally all the time. I know now that Sally felt I had abandoned her to be the primary parent.
>
> "Now that we're divorced, I've gone back to school to be a parent. It was horrible — or I guess embarrassing — at first. But it is slowly becoming more natural. I'm not as quick as Sally to figure out the kids' needs but I think I can at least cover all the bases with the kids in the house now.
>
> "Besides, the kids really seem to like it so long as I don't take my mistakes too seriously. For example, I really messed up a clam chowder last month. And the kids are still ribbing me about it. My experiments, and particularly my failures at cooking, seem to give them more incentive to experiment themselves. They see their dad taking chances, blowing it, and going on and this seems to make them less fearful of taking chances and learning themselves. In the end analysis, we know we'll still love each other even if we blow it once in a while."

Fred and Sally have both come to realize that, for children, it is more important that their parents be present than perfect, and that parental conflict often creates more harm than divorce.

THE DANGEROUS OR IMPAIRED PARENT — FACTS ABOUT FAMILY VIOLENCE

Many American women and children find no refuge in their own homes. Figures suggest some form of violence is going on across the street or even next door.

1. At least 1.8 million women and children are battered every year.
2. Some form of violence occurs in 25% of all marriages.
3. 20% of women seeking emergency surgical procedures are victims of domestic violence.
4. More than 2,000,000 cases of child abuse were reported in 1986 compared with 669,000 in 1976.
5. More than 1,200 children die annually due to child abuse and neglect.
6. Parents who were abused as children are six times more likely to abuse their own children.
7. At least 40% of all abuse cases involve alcohol or drugs (*Newsweek*, 12/12/88, p. 59).

Sadly, an increasing number of parents are harming and neglecting their children. Drug addiction, poverty, and teen pregnancy take a mighty toll.

The single greatest source of dangerous or impaired parents are violent or dysfunctional families. Violence and self-victimization are *learned* from one's parents. Similarly, alcohol and drug addiction are often passed from parent to child. Add to this the increasing impoverishment of American families, and the already difficult matter of recovery becomes almost impossible. Because of cuts in federal budgets and the skyrocketing costs, quality medical, alcohol, and drug treatment programs are out of reach to all except those on welfare and those that are reasonably well-to-do. Similar problems are faced by those in abusive relationships despite the fact that the YWCA and many other groups make heroic efforts to counsel battered and battering spouses.

Dealing with a violent parent demands a focus on both the past (to root out the intergenerational history of domestic violence) and the present (to develop clear and demonstrable skills in anger management and prevention of self-victimization). Few succeed in stopping violence without extensive treatment.

Treatment should extend to both the batterers and the battered, for each often contributes to the continuance of the problem. Although physical violence is intolerable, rarely is the batterer solely to blame. Battered spouses must wrestle with how they may enable or provoke the battery just as the assaultive spouse, must deal with how they fail to control their temper. One of the best centers in Washington for treating and diagnosing domestic violence problems is located at Harborview Hospital in Seattle. Their treatment programs and groups deserve study and emulation statewide.

Battering parents are inadequate parents under the new law (RCW 26.09.191). *Both* parents usually need special help. Batterers need to manage their anger and the battered need to stop allowing themselves to be victimized. Simply leaving a violent relationship will *not* prevent more violence in your next relationship.

CHAPTER EIGHT
CHILD SUPPORT

After some genuine soul-searching, Mary Ellen and Jim agreed to a final parenting plan. Now we were faced with drafting a child support agreement that would fit the two families and their altered economic status. Neither Mary Ellen nor Jim wanted to see a change in the children's lifestyle if it could be avoided. Nonetheless, certain comforts were bound to be lost in the process of maintaining two homes rather than one.

A recent survey found that 20% of all children are living in single-parent families. This sizable number of single-parent homes points to the magnitude of the child support issue.

Today the courts are recognizing the obligation of both parents to provide for the support of the children. Support is becoming an equal responsibility of both parents. Each will be required to discharge the obligation in accordance with his or her capacity and ability. Thus, when the support order is considered, the court will determine what, if any, contribution each spouse should provide.

In Washington, this philosophy is born out by a statute, RCW 26.09.100 (RCW refers to a statute [law] adopted by the state legislature, and is short for *Revised Code of Washington*):

> "In a proceeding for dissolution of marriage, legal separation, declaration of invalidity, maintenance, or child support, after considering all relevant factors but without regard to marital misconduct, the court may order either or both parents owing a duty of support to any child of the marriage dependent upon either or both spouses to pay an amount reasonable or necessary for his support."

Right now Mary Ellen could not provide any support beyond the limits of her property settlement. Of course, we hoped to avoid selling this remaining property. Although it was difficult to convince Mary Ellen of this, she must eventually be earning an income on her own. The Dissolution Decree would have to declare what effect, if any, Mary Ellen's employment would have on Jim's support obligation. Child support is subject to modification at any time and the burden of proof necessarily rests with the parent seeking the change.

The courts will consider the income available to both parents. Of course, Jim's income would be a limiting factor. The most recent tax return showed a gross income of $60,000, so I assumed that his disposable income included some room for flexibility. Since Mary Ellen was not currently employed, we were able to deviate from the mandatory support schedule transferring some of Jim's income to Mary Ellen in the form of spousal maintenance. The net effect was to pass on the tax savings for the benefit of the children.

The Washington State Child Support Schedule became mandatory for all divorces after July 1, 1988. Its purpose is to apportion more equitably the expenses of child rearing between the parents. King County Superior Court Commissioner Steve Gaddis, chairman of the state panel that drew up the schedules, states:

> "Children will be the major beneficiaries. We've seen some remarkable statistics about the health of children and the level of poverty. We are attempting to provide the care that will improve child health and will improve their ability to take care of themselves later in life... the new Schedule makes everyone's life easier... the real issue is setting fair standards that are objective and are based on the actual costs of raising children."

The Washington State Child Support Schedule sets forth sixteen standards, which must be observed by parents who are preparing their own schedules. These include definitions of income, rules on how to handle health insurance payments and child care expenses, *etc.* An accompanying table shows how income is to be apportioned between the parents based upon the number and ages of the children.

Although the courts still have broad discretion, any support orders that vary from the calculations laid out in the Schedule must be accompanied by a written reason for the deviation. Thus, if one or both of the parents have significant wealth, there are disabled children, tax planning produces a better outcome, *etc.,* there can be deviations. Otherwise the schedule is mandatory. Agreement between the parents is no longer a valid reason for deviating from the schedule.

The law also requires that these worksheets be filed as part of the supporting record and that they be signed.

Mary Ellen and Jim worked on the Child Support Schedule together. Jim supplied his most recent earnings information from his job. Mary Ellen pulled together the day-care receipts from Better Homes Daycare, where the children had spent some time after school while she attended a displaced-homemakers program. They agreed that this day-care expense was appropriately considered in the Child Support Schedule because it was incurred in furtherance of Mary Ellen's search for employment. They then looked at their calendars to confirm that the children had not spent more than 25% of the nights (ninety-one nights per year) with Jim. Therefore, no residential adjustment was required. They spent several hours reviewing the standards to determine whether there was anything unusual in their assets that would merit deviation from the schedule. Finding none, it was agreed that a Child Support Schedule would be filed with the decree of dissolution, indicating that Jim was to pay $1,475 per month to Mary Ellen for the support of the children as well as 100% of the actual day-care expense while she sought employment. Later, when her job situation had stabilized and Mary Ellen was able to contribute more toward the children's support, they planned to modify the schedule to reflect both this new capacity and the enhanced living standard generated from her income contributions.

Because Mary Ellen was not employed, she and Jim could have negotiated a slightly different outcome whereby the amount Jim paid to Mary Ellen was increased but called *undifferentiated family support* rather than support. This outcome would have resulted in a transfer payment that was taxable to Mary Ellen and excludable from the income of Jim. Since her tax bracket was much lower the tax savings could have been passed on to the children in the form of increased cash flow. This approach would have been approved by the judge under Standard 12 (Tax Planning), which provides: "The transfer payment amount may deviate if tax planning results in greater benefit to the child." Mary Ellen chose not to agree to a deviation from the support schedule because she knew that she would be going to work within a year or less and she wanted both the certainty and the uniformity of a direct child support payment.

Mary Ellen and Jim's Child Support Worksheets are found in Appendix E attached to their Findings of Fact and Conclusions of Law. Two other illustrations (the "Weavers" and the "Hendersons") are kindly provided in Appendix J by Dan Radin, an Assistant Attorney General, who also served on the Washington State Child Support Commission.

DURATION OF SUPPORT

Beyond the dollar amount of support and the inclusion of escalation clauses, consideration must be given to the duration of support. Mary Ellen and Jim both agreed that the children should attend college. They were prepared to provide for graduate school if it was warranted. Jim had always hoped that Justin would become a doctor. He assured both me and his own attorney that he had every intention of providing a college education for his children. This is not always the case. Some parents share the costs of college equally; others share ratably in accordance with their respective ability to contribute. Perhaps the children may be expected to contribute as well. In other instances the court may order the father to pay for college expenses.

A recent precedent setting case in Washington required the father, a medical doctor, to provide a college education for each of three sons. The father argued that the children were adults at age eighteen and no further support was due from him. The court reasoned that emancipation from dependency does not always occur at age eighteen. Trial courts reserve discretion to determine dependency. In this case, dependency was determined from relevant factors:

> "age, needs, prospects, desires, aptitudes, abilities, and disabilities, and the parents' level of education, standard of living, and current and future resources."

The court ruled that the children of this medical doctor were entitled to a college education. The father had benefited from years of higher education, which afforded him a high income. Furthermore, the court maintained that *the children should not be denied an education that they would have otherwise been permitted if their parents had remained married.*

With escalating college expenses, many families are finding it necessary to plan ahead. One court ordered the husband to create a trust fund to be used for the purpose of funding a college education. The father was a salesman with an average annual income of $60,000. The decree required the father to pay child support in the amount of $475 per month for each of two children. In addition, the father was directed to pay into a trust the sum of $125 per month for his daughter and $85 per month for his younger son. The discrepancy in the amounts was adjusted because of their age differences, so that each would have the same amount in the trust at age eighteen. Payments into the trust were to continue until each child reached the age of eighteen, whereupon it would be made available to the children for educational purposes. The court ruled that because the trust provided for college, further support payments during college would be discontinued.

Like spousal maintenance, child support amounts vary with the circumstances of each family. For example:

1. Mike and Sue

Mike's monthly earnings totaled $800. He paid $75 child support and no spousal maintenance.

2. Robert and Vivian

Robert's most recent tax return showed a gross annual income of $109,000. Vivian earned $1,800 per month as an administrator. Vivian was awarded primary residential care of the couple's young daughter. She received $650 a month for her support. The figure of $650 was to be increased by 5% annually under their original dissolution decree. The couple shared joint custody of their son. No award of support was made for him. Robert agreed to provide medical insurance for the children. Vivian provided dental insurance. In the event of uninsured medical expenses, Robert would be responsible for 70% and Vivian 30%. Both parents agreed to contribute equally to college educations. With passage of the Child Support Schedule, Vivian became a prime candidate for a support modification action.

3. Paul and Denise

Dual primary parenting of their teenage daughter did not exclude child support for Paul and Denise. Paul paid child support and maintenance in one undifferentiated payment: $1,000 per month for one year, $800 per month for the succeeding year, and $650 per month for the remaining two years. Paul and Denise agreed to pay for college education in accordance with their circumstances at the time. Paul continued to insure his daughter under his health care policy. Denise agreed to pay the normal coverage of health care costs.

4. Frank and Gina

The following is an open-ended example of flexible child support in a highincome family. Frank paid Gina $1,800 monthly maintenance for eight years. However, his child support payments totaled only $100 per month for each of two children. The real measure of support was realized when Frank fulfilled his obligation to provide all reasonable clothing, medical, dental, orthodontia, and eye care expenses. In addition, he was responsible for all preschool tuition. It didn't take long to modify the decree. Gina's support was reduced to $1,200 a month, but each child's support was raised to $500 a month. In addition, Frank continued to provide medical, dental, orthodontia, and eye care expenses.

5. Monica and Alan

Monica and Alan's background was previously described in the "Spousal Maintenance" chapter. To ensure continued payment of support, Alan was required to maintain a life insurance policy to cover his obligation. Their dissolution decree contained the following provision:

> "*Life Insurance Trust:* Husband shall maintain sufficient life insurance for the benefit of his children to actuarily fund, in the event of the husband's death, the maintenance and support obligation herein together with the husband's medical obligation as defined in the Decree. In the event there is insufficient life insurance, less social security benefits payable for the children on account of the husband's death to fund the foregoing, the wife shall have a continuing lien against the husband's estate, which shall survive his death for the purpose of continuing the above payments."

In the event the non-custodial parent fails to honor his or her support obligation, the custodial parent does have some recourse. For a small fee, the

Washington State Department of Social and Health Services (DSHS) will help the parent collect child support if he or she is encountering difficulty. In addition, the federal government will withhold tax refunds if the parent is behind in support obligations.

New Washington legislation grants mandatory wage assignments against a non-custodial parent who is fifteen days past due on a month or more of support payments. The assignment cannot exceed 50% of the non-custodial parent's disposable earnings and employer is entitled to a small processing fee. Support orders should include language explaining the terms of the wage assignment.

A SUPPORT CHECKLIST

The following questions should help when considering support provisions:

1. How often and on what dates are the support payments to be made?

2. Are the payments made to the primary parent directly or through the Support Registry?

3. Are support payments reduced or waived in part when the children are visiting with the non-primary parent, when living away at school, or at summer camp, or when the non-primary parent contributes to day-care expenses? If so, by how much?

4. Are child support provisions to be designated as such in the Separation Agreement, or are they to be lumped together with the maintenance allowance for the wife? (Tax consequences of this could be severe and should be discussed with the lawyer. Also, commingling child support and spousal maintenance can affect future modification of the awards.)

5. Is there a specific amount allocated to each child?

6. Who claims which child as a dependent for income tax purposes? Under what terms and conditions will the parent claim the children? What is the *value* of this exemption to each parent in after-tax dollars?

7. Are the payments to continue in whole or in part when the children become emancipated? Under what terms and conditions and how?

8. Will support continue through college? Will it include college expenses?

9. Can the primary parent obtain income from employment or some other source without affecting the amount of child support received?

If so, is there to be any limitation?

10. Is the primary parent to receive any supplemental support for such expenses as summer camp, religious training, music lessons, or other special expenses?

11. Who pays for the *ordinary* medical, dental, orthodontic, counseling, and optical expenses for the children?

12. Who pays for the *extraordinary* medical, dental, orthodontic, counseling, optical, and related expenses of the children? Which hospital, optical, orthodontia, dental, medical, surgical, counseling, or psychiatric expenses should be classified as extraordinary? Will this include family counseling expenses?

13. Is there any notice to be given to the non-primary parent before extraordinary medical, dental, orthodontia, counseling or optical expenses are incurred? If so, how much notice?

14. Who chooses the doctor, dentist, or other specialist?

15. Is medical insurance to be maintained? Who will pay for the insurance? What is the minimum extent of coverage to be provided? What evidence of coverage is to be given? (There is new legislation requiring medical insurance coverage.)

16. Are any medical, dental, optical, or related payments to be continued beyond the time a child reaches majority? Will it continue during the time a child attends trade school, college, or professional school?

17. Who pays the trade school or college tuition fees of the children? Who pays for graduate school, professional school, other special school?

18. Who decides what school the children will attend, the location of the school, checks the accreditation of the school?

19. What scholastic performance level must the children maintain?

20. Is there a time limit in which the trade school or college education, graduate school, professional school must be completed?

21. Who pays for room, board, fraternity or sorority, money allowance, vehicle purchase, and other expenses incidental to the children's education?

22. Who pays for travel expenses to and from school? Is there any limit to the number of trips per school year?

23. Must children apply for loans, scholarships, or school employment?

24. Must children carry a full academic program? Are grade records to be made available to the non-primary parent?

25. Is there an effect on support if children have income from employment?

26. May college expenses be paid directly to the children?
27. What is the effect of the child's dropping out of school (leave of absence) and later returning? What about the child's marriage before finishing school?
28. In the case of parents who work for professional services corporations, have all the personal expense deductions (*e.g.* parking, auto, personal legal expenses, *etc.*) been added back into income when calculating *true* net income?

CHAPTER NINE
SELF-HELP

DOING YOUR OWN LEGAL RESEARCH

Most individuals are unable to handle their dissolutions on their own. However, many of my clients have asked whether they could employ me and yet save counsel fees by doing their own legal research or otherwise assist in the preparation of their case. We have encouraged them to do so, not because of cost savings but because they become better informed clients in the process.

In terms of actual costs, a layperson simply cannot expect to match the research skills of a lawyer who has practiced for years in the divorce field. A legal issue that may take me fifteen minutes to research and resolve may take a client a day or more in the law library just to get started. Nonetheless, we honestly believe it is to the client's advantage to be involved in this aspect of the divorce. In fact, we often insist upon it.

A lawyer who guides a client toward the proper research tools performs an invaluable service. A client who reads the myriad of conflicting judicial opinions that the lawyer must deal with has a better appreciation for the adage that lawyering is an art, not a science. Furthermore, by being aware of the legal principles involved, the client becomes better informed about his or her own circumstances. Thus, the client is better able to supply the lawyer with the information needed. I have also observed that the better informed a client is, the more willing he or she is to accept the equivocations and disclaimers the lawyer must give when rendering an opinion on what the court will do in his or her case. Finally, if the matter must go to trial, then the client can anticipate the legal issues involved, apply them to the facts of his or her case, and be an effective witness.

THE LAW LIBRARY

If you want to assist in researching your case and your lawyer agrees, you will need access to a law library. Of course, it is most convenient to start with your own lawyer's resources. Sometimes, however, space or time requirements prohibit use of that law library. With a little effort you can find a law library open to the public. In almost every county there is a law library either in or near the courthouse. Law schools are located in Spokane, Tacoma, and Seattle and they have major collections. If necessary, you can always consult your telephone directory or call the state Attorney General, the clerk of the local court, or the local public library to locate the resources you need.

DIVORCE LAW: STATUTES, CASE LAW, AND CONSTITUTIONS

The laws that affect your particular divorce come from three sources: statutes, case law, and, to a lesser extent, the state and federal constitutions. Statutes are the laws passed by the legislature. Case law consists of the body of law that is created when a case heard by a trial court is appealed and becomes law or precedent when the appellate court decisions are published in case books, which are often referred to as *official reports*. Constitutional law is based upon legal interpretations of both the United States and the Washington State constitutions.

THE RCWA AND THE POCKET PART

Dissolution cases are decided on the basis of (1) statutes promulgated by the legislature; (2) general legal principles; and (3) plain old common sense. Legislative enactments (statutes) are codified by number and then arranged by subject within a multi-volume set of books. In Washington they are found in the *Revised Code of Washington* (RCW) or the *Revised Code of Washington Annotated* (RCWA) Title 26.

The indices for the statutes are located at the end of each set, and sometimes at the conclusion of the dissolution volume as well. Thus, if you have a particular issue you want to research, such as the duty of a mother to provide child support, you would look under *support, child*, and other words that come to mind when checking the indices. You will then be referred to specifically numbered statutes bearing upon the subject. Following each statute in the RCWA will be a summary of court cases interpreting the statutes. These *annotations*, as they are called, are court decisions in which the meaning of the statute has been explained. These court decisions are considered *precedents*, which subsequent courts will attempt to follow.

If some cases in the annotations appear to be inconsistent, it is usually because different facts led the judge to decide the statute did not have the same application as in the other case or cases. Remember, a judge's use of *plain old common sense* is instrumental in deciding individual cases. When you have located the applicable statute, be sure to check the small supplement tucked into a pocket inside the back cover of the RCWA volume. This *pocket part* is periodically replaced to update the divorce volume. It reflects changes in statutes and later court decisions.

CASES: WASHINGTON REPORTS AND WASHINGTON APPELLATE REPORTS

After you have read the statutes, reviewed the annotations, and checked the pocket part for changes in the law or later cases, you will want to make a list of those cases bearing on the issue you are researching. To read these written decisions, you must then turn to the *official reports*. In Washington, you will want *Washington Reports* and *Washington Appellate Reports*.

Finding the decisions you wish to read is simple. The citations in the annotations are nothing more than abbreviated titles of cases. Thus the citation to *Fleege v. Fleege,* 91 Wn.2d 324, means that the case is found in the 91st volume of the second series of *Washington Reports,* beginning at page 324. Be careful to distinguish between the first and second series in *Washington Reports.* The citation 91 Wash. 324 concerns a 1916 case involving a dispute over life insurance coverage — a far cry from 91 Wn.2d 324, which is a key family law case. If you want the second series, look for the 2 on the spine of the book.

READING A CASE

When you have located the case, you will need to become acquainted with its organizational format: (1) first you will see the case number of this court opinion, which enables you to locate the actual court file in the clerk's office; (2) next is the date of the court's decision; (3) before the actual opinion of the court, you will find numbered annotations, a brief history of the case including lower court decisions, and a summary of this court's decision; (4) also listed are the names of legal counsel for both parties. (A few sample pages may be found at the end of this chapter.)

The numbered annotations, called *headnotes,* at the beginning of the report are concise principles of law that the *editor* compiling the volume has gleaned from the court decision. *They are not official statements by the court.* Rather, they are an aid to the reader in spotting issues the court has dealt with in the case. The numbers by the headnotes correspond to specific paragraphs in the body of the opinion, which will allow you to quickly turn to the critical part of the case in which you are interested.

SHEPARDIZING

Every week courts decide cases that limit, modify, or overrule older cases. Therefore, there is always a chance that the case that says everything you want was affected by a recent decision. *Shepard's Citations* is an index devoted to keeping you informed of all recent cases and statutes affecting your case. Basically, *Shepard's* is designed to, but does not always, pick up every subsequent case report that mentions the case or statute you have just read. By following this research trail, you will locate the most current judicial thinking on the case or statute you just read. In the library, you will find that *Shepard's* currently has a hardbound volume for recent cases. More recent cases will be *Shepardized* (and found) in paperbound volumes. The most recent cases will be found in newsprint *slip* volumes. Separate volumes exist for statutory citations.

To ensure that the cases or statutes you have found pertaining to your issues are still good law, you must *Shepardize* those cases or statutes. To do this, you begin with the first volume of *Shepard's* that includes your case or statute and work your way forward to the most recent slip volume. The *Shepard's Citations* will also list legal periodicals and treatises where the name of your reported case or statute was mentioned. By reading the introductory pages of *Shepard's Citations* you may feel comfortable tracking down and researching these subsequent reports. Good lawyers *Shepardize* every case or statute before using it in court and if you are going to do your own legal research you cannot afford to do less! But the process is not easily learned.

OTHER AIDS

In the *Washington Appellate Reports* and the *Washington Reports*, you will find another research aid. This is the West Publishing Company *key-number* system in which each of several hundred legal subjects has a specific number. This number will appear in the headnote of the case and will help you to locate more material on the same subject in other legal publications published by West Publishing Company Other resources for your research include the following:

1. *Legal Treatises.*These are lengthy and often technical treatments of a particular subject by a recognized authority in the field.

2 *Nutshells*. These are short, readable volumes by West Publishing Company on various areas of law from a national perspective. The *Family Law Nutshell* has helped many law students understand family law and it might help you. *Nutshells* are inexpensive to buy and can be found at most law libraries.

3. *Legal Encyclopedias*. These are long, generally thorough sets of books that summarize the state of the law on many subjects, including variations among different states and references to specific cases and other authorities. *American Jurisprudence* (Am.Jur.) and *American Jurisprudence Second* (Am.Jur.2d) are two examples of legal encyclopedias.

4. *Washington Digest*. This contains brief summaries of court decisions organized according to the issues of law involved. This can be very useful in helping you find cases that are similar to your case.

Obviously, doing research is not for everyone. However, the experience is usually well worth the effort.

SHOULD YOU HANDLE YOUR OWN DIVORCE?

There is an old joke about the man who treated himself from the medical articles in *Reader's Digest*. He finally died of a typographical error. In the drafting of legal documents, one word can make an awesome difference in your future lifestyle. For example, substituting the word *dependency* for *majority* in the child support provisions can mean the support obligation will continue right through college.

In a nutshell, I believe that *all clients should work on their own divorce according to their own individual capacity*. Doing your own divorce is like rewiring your home. Some people have the aptitude and patience to read and understand the wiring diagrams and local building codes. They have the manual dexterity to put together hundreds of different colored wires so all the circuits work safely. They also have the courage to work with hazardous electrical circuits. Most of us lack these talents! The purpose of this chapter is to help you do your best with the talents you have, not to enable you to completely do your divorce on your own.

There are several *do-it-yourself* publications available, including a companion publication to this book, *Divorce in Washington — Self-Help*, published by Eagle House Press, Mercer Island, Washington.

Only certain kinds of cases are suited to the *do-it-yourself* approach. I have seen students or young couples recently out of school adapt well to this experience. In cases like these, where both parties agree to the divorce, where there are no minor children involved, and where there is very little or no property to be divided, self-representation is probably feasible. In virtually every other case, some form of legal assistance will be necessary.

Each marital dissolution demands attention to a number of legal issues which, like house wiring, are interconnected and interdependent. You must allow careful consideration for the following: spousal maintenance, parenting plans, child support, life insurance, medical insurance, children's education, debts, hidden assets, social security benefits, taxes, pensions, and wills. The presence of one or more of these issues should cause the do-it-yourselfer to pause and reflect upon whether saving a few dollars now in legal fees is really worth the risk of losing thousands in money or benefits in years to come.

Nonetheless, the advent of our no-fault divorce law and simpler court procedures have made *pro se* (for yourself) divorces easier to obtain. Many divorce kits, books, and secretarial services have appeared on the scene to aid the do-it-yourselfers. They offer assistance for do-it-yourselfers at a fraction of the cost of obtaining legal counsel.

With a *no-fault* divorce law, the spouses no longer need to point the finger of blame to find grounds for divorce. This means that fault finding is no longer a consideration in whether the divorce will be granted by the court. Today, the courts permit evidence of wrongdoing only where it directly affects the future welfare of the children.

No national statistics are available regarding the number of persons who have handled their own divorce without the aid of a lawyer. However, approximately 50% of the divorces in Washington are estimated to have been done without the assistance of a lawyer.

Handling your own divorce may make filling out your own tax return appear easy. Until the substantive and procedural aspects of divorce become less complicated, individuals who represent themselves in divorce actions proceed at their own risk. In King County, Family Law procedures and forms change every few months so *do not completely rely on any published manual.* Go down to your local courthouse and talk to the clerk or bailiff about the latest procedures and forms. They get hundreds of calls daily, so a trip to the courthouse (once you have done all your homework) is well worth the effort.

A SUCCESS STORY

I remember one particular success story. Alan was enrolled in a *Separation and Divorce* class. He chose to represent himself while his wife hired an attorney. He was a very industrious *let's get this show on the road* type of fellow. Alan hired us as an occasional consultant and directed that I not appear in any part of the proceedings. The opposing counsel was impressed with Alan's efficiency. Consequently, his wife's attorney went out of his way to be fair with Alan. In the process, Alan did exceptionally well in the settlement agreement, perhaps better than he would have with more conventional representation.

Some states have simplified the divorce process. California now allows couples who have been married less than two years, with no children, no house, less than $5,000 in personal property, and less than $2,000 of debts to obtain a divorce without a lawyer *or* a court appearance. Alaska has recently published forms and instructions on how to obtain a dissolution decree where there is no disagreement between the spouses concerning property and children. According to these rules, a couple must agree on division of joint and separate property, payment of any alimony, and understand the tax consequences of these agreements. Oregon has a similar law. Efforts to pass similar legislation in Washington continue. Clearly, these circumstances are found in only a small percentage of divorcing couples.

THE SETTLEMENT AGREEMENT

The Dissolution Settlement Agreement, also called the Marital or Property Settlement Agreement, is the foundation of your dissolution proceeding. This agreement must contain provisions for the following issues:

- Property division
- Spousal maintenance
- Parenting plan
- Child support

Please refer to chapters with the above titles for a discussion of these issues. You may wish to do further research on these issues using the legal research techniques outlined in this chapter. There is no such thing as knowing too much about these issues — *especially* if you intend to do your own divorce. Remember, if you have any significant differences over the parenting plan *get the children an advocate.* They should not be penalized for innocent mistakes you have made while doing your own divorce. With that in mind, here are a few guidelines for your work.

KNOW YOUR FORMS: KNOW YOUR COUNTY CLERK

You will need to be familiar with the form of a dissolution agreement. The files of past divorce cases in the County Clerk's office are good references. Review them thoroughly and note how particular problems have been handled. These files are public records and may be checked out and read at the Clerk's office. I recommend that you review between ten and fifteen case files. You will find examples of pleadings, property settlements, parenting plans, and maintenance agreements. By studying the sequence in which the documents were filed at the Clerk's office, you should be able to develop an outline of the procedure to be followed. Although divorce kits will generally outline the necessary procedure, you will no doubt gain some reassurance from reviewing actual, completed cases. Copies of these cases can usually be made at the Clerk's office at nominal cost.

An enforceable workable agreement is the goal of your efforts. Complex state laws affect these issues. The organization and drafting of your dissolution decree plays a major role in how enforceable it will be. Even if both spouses come to an agreement on all the issues, it is advisable to have a lawyer review the agreement before it is signed. The modest fee charged for a review of your own work product can save you hundreds or even thousands of dollars, not to mention emotional grief resulting from a poorly drafted settlement agreement. Sometimes it is advisable to have two agreements, one dealing with the division of property and the other covering only spousal and child support. The existence of two separate agreements may be crucial to a later attempt to modify the spousal support provisions.

This book is not meant to be a do-it-yourself guide. You can, however, obtain help from several other sources. Divorce forms are now available throughout the state. A bookstore, stationery, or office supply store will usually carry a locally written book describing the divorce procedures. Perhaps the book will even offer a set of forms that will get you through the court process. Since the books are written for laypersons, they should not be difficult to use. Divorce forms are sometimes furnished by the County Clerk's office at a nominal charge. *In most courts, the Clerk's office is not allowed to answer inquiries involving the practice of law.* Simple procedural questions, however, such as which spouse's name goes in which blank, will probably be answered.

Please do not forget that your Superior Court Clerk's office is a source of prior divorce cases to aid you in drafting your dissolution decree.

DISSOLUTION: THE BASIC PROCESS

If both spouses have reached an agreement on the above issues, they are ready to proceed with the dissolution. Generally, the order of necessary documents is as follows:

1. Summons

2. Petition for Dissolution, Financial Declaration, Support Schedule

3. Parenting Plan
4. Findings of Fact and Conclusions of Law
5. Decree of Dissolution

If both parties file jointly, the Summons is eliminated. If both spouses are not in agreement with the terms stated in the Petition, more documents than the above will be necessary (for example, a Response and a Counter-Petition). For our purposes, we will assume that the more documents you require, the more you will require the services of an attorney.

A general guideline for dissolution proceedings is as follows:

Day 1	• Summons
	• Petition for Dissolution
	• Motion, Affidavit, or Order to Show Cause (only if temporary relief is necessary)
	• File Parenting Plan
Day 10	• Show Cause hearing (for temporary arrangements if necessary)
Days 20-30	• Response due from spouse
Day after response is received	• File note for trial to obtain position on the Trial Calendar
Day 90 or later	• Findings of Fact and Conclusions of Law, and Decree of Dissolution

SUMMONS AND PETITION

If you are comfortable with the organization of your Settlement Agreement, you are ready to begin the divorce process. The first step is accomplished by simultaneously filing both a Summons and a Petition for Dissolution. The Summons is formalistic and may be copied verbatim from the cases you have read in the Clerk's records. Its function is to alert your spouse that you have initiated dissolution proceedings. The Petition sets out jurisdictional facts such as how long the party initiating the action has been a resident of the state or county; the grounds for the dissolution; the financial circumstances of the spouses; and a *prayer* at the end requesting certain relief. In this instance, *relief* means the financial support (spousal maintenance and child support) that you need as well as any other considerations necessary for your welfare.

Unless a Settlement Agreement has already been signed, the prayer should be for more relief than you expect to finally settle on. You can always bargain away your relief, but the court usually cannot grant more relief than is requested in the Petition. (See Appendix E for a sample Summons and Petition.)

RESPONSE, ANSWER, OR DEFAULT

The other spouse must receive actual copies of the various documents and be given adequate time to respond. In those cases where the other spouse cannot be found and personally served with your paperwork, you should consult specific court rules to determine how to proceed further. These procedures are spelled out in the Washington Court Rules, Civil Rule (CR) 4(d). If no written *Response* or *Answer* is filed by your spouse and served upon you within the time permitted by law (at least twenty days after service of the Petition), the person initiating the divorce is entitled to a default judgment. (See Appendix E for a sample Response.)

TEMPORARY ORDERS: ORDER TO SHOW CAUSE

Perhaps you need to make temporary arrangements for support or use of property pending the final decision of your case. In this event you will next want to file and serve on your spouse a motion for an *Order to Show Cause.* A hearing can be held within ten to twenty days after the Petition is filed and served. Enough time must be allowed for the respondent to hire an attorney if one is desired. Affidavits or Declarations must be filed in support of these Motions for Temporary Arrangements advising the court of the needs and earnings of the spouses. (See Appendix E for a sample Temporary Restraining Order.)

PARENTING PLAN

Chapter 7 details the contents of and filing times for the Parenting Plan. You must file a full Parenting Plan before the divorce becomes final.

DECREE AND FINDINGS OF FACT AND CONCLUSIONS OF LAW

To obtain a *Decree,* you will have to attend a court hearing. This is a less formal proceeding than a regular trial. At the hearing you will present evidence showing the court's jurisdiction, the statutory grounds for divorce, and why you are entitled to the relief desired. A document entitled *Findings of Fact and Conclusions of Law* is true to its name: it contains critical facts concerning the spouses and their circumstances, and the conclusions of law to be drawn from those facts.

At the conclusion of the hearing, a final decree will be entered. This is the *Decree of Dissolution.* It embodies the terms of the marital settlement agreement, or grants the relief warranted by the evidentiary hearing if you have not reached agreement. In Washington, however, the decree is final and the parties are free to remarry immediately. (See Appendix E for a sample Decree and Findings of Fact and Conclusions of Law.)

In summary, if you and your spouse draft a marital settlement agreement, it must address all aspects of parenting and divorce. If you cannot reach an agreement, you are best advised to consult an attorney or a divorce mediator.

Form books can help you to a point. There is no substitute, however, for using your own common sense in drafting or for your thoroughly studying cases filed in your county. If you have arrived at an equitable agreement but you are unsure about specific issues (*e.g.,* tax consequences, inclusion of certain property), you should consult a lawyer. Relying solely upon forms without further research or final consultation with a lawyer is risky business. If, after all the aforementioned considerations, a *pro se* divorce appears right for you, you are definitely entitled to the right of self-representation before the court. Unravelling the mysteries of the law, learning the procedures, and negotiating with your spouse for a fair and equitable result can be a very satisfying experience.

SAMPLE PAGES FROM A CASE LAW BOOK

Following are sample pages from a case law book.

[No. 56584-8. En Banc. May 24, 1990.]

In the Matter of the Marriage of JUDITH ANN
(GRIFFIN) BOOTH, *Respondent, and* GENE
ROSS GRIFFIN, *Appellant.*

[1] **Divorce — Child Support — Standard Worksheet — Deviation — Discretion of Court.** RCW 26.19.020 expressly gives a trial court discretion, in appropriate circumstances, to deviate from the standard amount of child support established by the Washington State Child Support Schedule.

[2] **Appeal — Findings of Fact — Absence of Finding — Resort to Oral Opinion.** In the absence of a written finding of fact, an appellate court may look to the oral opinion to determine the trial court's basis for resolving the issue.

[3] **Divorce — Child Support — Standard Worksheet — Public Policy.** The Legislature's primary concern in providing for the adoption of a statewide child support schedule was the adequacy of child support, rather than equity between custodial and noncustodial parents.

[4] **Divorce — Child Support — Modification — Discretion of Court — Review.** A trial court's modification of a noncustodial parent's child support obligation is reviewed only for an abuse of discretion, *i.e.,* to determine whether the trial court exercised its discretion in an untenable or manifestly unreasonable way.

[5] **Divorce — Attorney Fees — On Appeal — Factors.** In deciding whether to award attorney fees on appeal under RCW 26.09.140, an appellate court will examine the merit of the issues on appeal and the financial resources of the parties.

DURHAM, BRACHTENBACH, ANDERSEN, and GUY, JJ., dissent by separate opinion.

Nature of Action: A divorced parent sought to have the noncustodial parent's child support obligation increased.

Superior Court: The Superior Court for Benton County, No. 82-3-00184-9, Robert S. Day, J., on September 22, 1988, modified the child support obligation to be in accordance with the state child support schedule.

Supreme Court: Holding that the trial court had, and knew that it had, discretion to deviate from the support schedule but that the noncustodial parent's reasons did not warrant deviation from the schedule, the court *affirms* the modification.

Cowan, Walker, Jonson, Moore & Nickola, by *P. Craig Walker,* for appellant.

Timothy W. Mahoney, for respondent.

DOLLIVER, J.—Gene Ross Griffin appeals the modification of an original decree of dissolution. The modification adjusted child support to comply with the Washington State Child Support Schedule, which took effect in July 1988.

A decree of dissolution of marriage was entered on July 19, 1982, dissolving the marriage of Gene and Judith Griffin (now Judith Booth). The decree awarded Mrs. Booth the custody of the two minor children and required Mr. Griffin to pay $280 per month of child support. In 1987 Mr. Griffin voluntarily increased his monthly child support payments to $403. On July 21, 1988, Mrs. Booth filed a petition for modification of the decree under RCW 26.09.170(4). She sought an increased amount of child support based on the Washington State Child Support Schedule Comm'n, Washington State Child Support Schedule (July 1988) (Support Schedule); an order granting her the children's tax exemption; health coverage for the children under Mr. Griffin's policy (this request was subsequently withdrawn); and attorney fees. In response, Mr. Griffin submitted an affidavit indicating his willingness to increase his support payment. He disagreed with the amount of increase and submitted to the court five reasons he felt warranted a deviation from the presumptive amount set forth in the schedule. These reasons were: (a) Mrs. Booth's current unemployment; (b) direct expenditures to children; (c) the remarriage of both parties; (d) the award of the couple's home to Mrs. Booth, thereby saving her housing expenses; and (e) the magnitude of the adjustment from $403 to $848.

The trial court rejected the argument for deviation, stating in its oral opinion:

> And as I read the statute and the guidelines, I don't have any jurisdiction or any authority to do anything but fix the support at guidelines.
>
> . . . .
>
> I'm saying I do not think I can exercise my discretion to lower child support because of high income. . . . If I were exercising my discretion that way I might say, "Well, here's two families that make $91,000 total. This is not enough." I just don't think I can exercise my discretion downward.

On September 22, 1989, the trial court entered its order amending the decree. The relevant portions were as follows:

> (1) Under the State Child support guidelines effective July 1, 1988, this Court has no discretion to make a downward adjustment from scheduled support *based upon the resources available to Petitioner by virtue of her second marriage, or any of the other circumstances outlined in Respondent's affidavit;*
>
> (2) Child support shall be modified to comply with the guidelines established and adopted in the State of Washington and that such amount shall be Four Hundred Twenty Four and no/100 Dollars ($424.00) per month per child starting September 1, 1988.

(Italics ours.)

The trial court also denied attorney fees. Mr. Griffin sought review before the Court of Appeals of the trial court's ruling that it could not deviate from the guidelines based upon the information provided to it in his affidavit. The case was transferred to this court.

Three issues confront us in this case. (1) Under the statute does the trial court have discretion to deviate from the Support Schedule guidelines; (2) was the trial court aware it had the power to deviate from the guidelines; and (3) if the trial court was aware of its power to deviate, were the reasons given by Mr. Griffin adequate?

In considering the first issue we must first examine the statutes dealing with child support which are critical to this case. RCW 26.09.100 authorizes the court to order either or both parents owing a duty of support to any child of the marriage to pay an amount determined pursuant to the schedule adopted under RCW 26.19.040. RCW 26.19.001 explains the Legislature's intent in establishing a statewide child support schedule:

> The legislature intends, in establishing a child support schedule, to insure that child support orders are adequate to meet a child's basic needs and to provide additional child support commensurate with the parents' income, resources, and standard of living. The legislature also intends that the child support obligation should be equitably apportioned between the parents.

On July 1, 1988, RCW 26.19.020 read as follows:

> (1)(a) Except as provided in (b) of this subsection, in any proceeding under this title or Title 13 or 74 RCW in which child support is at issue, *support shall be determined and ordered according to the child support schedule adopted pursuant to RCW 26.19.040.*
>
> . . . .
>
> (2) An order for child support shall be supported by written findings of fact upon which the support determination is based.
>
> . . . .
>
> (5) *Unless* specific reasons for deviation are set forth in the written findings of fact or order and are supported by the evidence, the court or administrative law judge *shall* order each parent to pay the amount of child support determined using the standard calculation.
>
> (6) The court or administrative law judge shall review the worksheets and the order for adequacy of the reasons set forth for any deviation and for the adequacy of the amount of support ordered. Each order shall state the amount of child support calculated using the standard calculation and the amount of child support actually ordered. *Reasons that may support a deviation from the standard calculation include: Possession of wealth, shared living arrangements, extraordinary debts that have not been voluntarily incurred, extraordinarily high income of a child, a significant disparity of the living costs of the parents due to conditions beyond their control, and special needs of disabled children.* A deviation may be supported by tax planning considerations only if the child would not receive a lesser economic benefit. Agreement of the parties, by itself, is not adequate reason for deviation.

(Italics ours.) (In 1989, the Legislature eliminated the term "administrative law judge" from RCW 26.19.020 and substituted the term "the presiding or reviewing officer". *See*

Laws of 1989, ch. 175, § 76, p. 816. RCW 26.19.020 was significantly amended in the 1990 session. *See* Laws of 1990, 1st Ex. Sess., ch. 2, § 19, p. 1754 (effective June 7, 1990). Neither of these amendments, however, affect the outcome of this case.)

These reasons for deviation are also included in the "Standards for the Determination of Child Support and Use of the Schedule", which are made part of the schedule. See Support Schedule, at 3. As evidenced by the word "include" in the statute, the reasons given for deviation from the standard calculation in former RCW 26.19.020(6) are not exclusive.

[1] From reading the plain language of the statute, it is apparent the Legislature intended to allow judicial discretion in appropriate circumstances when calculating child support payments under the schedule.

Case law prior to the enactment of RCW 26.19 also supports a trial court's use of discretion when setting child support. In considering appeals regarding the setting of child support we have relied on the rule that trial court decisions in dissolution proceedings will seldom be changed on appeal. The spouse who challenges such decisions must show the trial court manifestly abused its discretion. When there is no abuse of discretion, we have upheld the trial court. *In re Marriage of Landry,* 103 Wn.2d 807, 699 P.2d 214 (1985). Where there has been an abuse of discretion, we have so held. *Lambert v. Lambert,* 66 Wn.2d 503, 403 P.2d 664 (1965). We hold the trial court had authority to deviate from the schedule.

Next we consider whether the trial court was aware it could deviate from the schedule when reasons for deviation exist. On this issue, we find the record is sparse and unclear. In its order amending the decree, the trial court stated it had no discretion to make a downward adjustment from the Support Schedule "based upon the resources available to Petitioner by virtue of her second marriage, or any of the other circumstances outlined in Respondent's affidavit." When asked by counsel whether he had any discretion, the trial judge replied, "I'm saying I do not think I can exercise my discretion to lower child support because of high income." Even given the paucity and ambiguity of the record we are persuaded, nevertheless, from the record that the trial court was aware it could deviate from the schedule. The language of former RCW 26.19.020 is clear and specific in allowing a deviation from the standard schedule if the "specific reasons for deviation are set forth in the written findings of fact or order and are supported by the evidence". Certainly, the trial court in its oral opinion expressed reservations about the new statute. This was, however, an experienced trial judge, and given the clarity of the statute we have no doubt he understood his authority, under the proper circumstances, to deviate from the standard schedule even though he refused to do so in this instance.

[2] Finally, we must determine whether the reasons given by Mr. Griffin in his affidavit were adequate under former RCW 26.19.020(5) and (6) to warrant deviation. At the outset, we note the trial court made no specific findings of fact regarding any of the five reasons Mr. Griffin provided. The lack of specific findings of fact is not fatal, however. In the absence of a written finding on a particular issue, an appellate court may look to the oral opinion to determine the basis for the trial court's resolution of the issue. *Goodman v. Darden, Doman & Stafford Assocs.*, 100 Wn.2d 476, 670 P.2d 648 (1983).

Based upon the trial court's oral opinion and its order amending the decree, we find the court did consider the reasons given for deviation in Mr. Griffin's affidavit when it decided not to deviate from the Support Schedule.

The first reason given in the affidavit is Mrs. Booth's unemployment. Standard 15 of the guidelines states that "[w]age income shall be imputed for parents who are voluntarily unemployed or voluntarily underemployed." State Register 88–11–004 (1988), Support Schedule, at 4. There is no evidence in the record that her unemployment was voluntary and, thus, it was reasonable for the trial court to conclude her unemployment was not voluntary.

The second reason given is the direct expenditures paid by Mr. Griffin for the children. Standard 10 of the guidelines provides as follows:

> Basic child support shall be allocated between the parents when a child stays overnight with the parent over twenty–five percent (25%) of the year.

Support Schedule, at 4. From this standard, it appears that a legislative decision was made to disallow a reduction in the presumptive level of support based upon overnight stays which amounted to less than 25 percent. The overnight stays of the children with Mr. Griffin were less than 25 percent of the time.

The third reason given is the additional income available to both parties as a result of their remarriage. The court specifically addressed the issue of increased resources resulting from remarriage. It stated that while this might be reason for increasing the level beyond the presumptive level set by the guidelines, it was not a reason to decrease the level of support.

The fourth reason given is the more favorable living arrangements enjoyed by Mrs. Booth due to the property awarded her in the original dissolution decree. Standard 12 of the guidelines lists among the reasons for deviation "a significant disparity in the living costs of the parents due to conditions beyond their control . . .". Support Schedule, at 4. The award of the home to Mrs. Booth was not something beyond the control of the parties but rather was a part of their divorce decree.

[3] The fifth reason given was the magnitude of the increase. The amount, $848, is significant and may well place a burden on Mr. Griffin. However, in adopting the schedule the Legislature considered the needs of the child as well as the equity that should exist between the parents. In the introduction to the Support Schedule, the Commission states:

The 1988 Legislature adopted SHB 1465 which established a
statewide Child Support Schedule. The intention was to insure
child support orders would be adequate to meet a child's basic
needs and to provide additional support commensurate with
the parents' income, resources and standard of living. It was
also intended that child support obligations be equitably
apportioned between the parents.

Support Schedule, at 1. Thus, while it is apparent the Legislature recognized the need for equity in applying the
schedule, its primary concern appears to have been the
adequacy of child support.

[4] In reviewing these reasons given by Mr. Griffin and
the decision made by the trial court to deny deviation from
the Support Schedule, we are unable to find an abuse of
discretion. As we stated in *Landry*:

We once again repeat the rule that trial court decisions in a
dissolution action will seldom be changed upon appeal. Such
decisions are difficult at best. Appellate courts should not
encourage appeals by tinkering with them. The emotional and
financial interests affected by such decisions are best served by
finality.

Landry, at 809. A reviewing court must defer to the sound
discretion of the trial court unless that discretion has been
exercised in an untenable or manifestly unreasonable way.
This is not the case here.

We find that the trial court did review the affidavit presented to it by Mr. Griffin, understood it had the power
under the statute to deviate from the support standards,
but concluded that sufficient reasons for it to deviate did
not exist.

Mrs. Booth claims she is entitled to attorney fees in this
matter. This claim was denied by the trial court. RCW
26.09.140 provides that a court may award attorney fees to
a party after considering the financial resources of both
parties and that an appellate court may order a party to
pay for the cost to the other party of maintaining the
appeal and attorney fees in addition to statutory costs.

[5] In awarding attorney fees on appeal, the court
should examine the arguable merit of the issues on appeal
and the financial resources of the respective parties. *In re*

Marriage of Fernau, 39 Wn. App. 695, 694 P.2d 1092
(1984). The issues here were not frivolous and had arguable
merit. Mr. Griffin and his wife earn $54,200 net income. It
appears from the record that Mrs. Booth and her husband
earn approximately $30,000 net income. Considering the
financial resources of the parties, both are financially able
to pay their attorneys and it would be a hardship to neither
to do so. The trial court did not abuse its discretion and
properly denied the request for attorney fees.

Affirmed.

CALLOW, C.J., and UTTER, DORE, and SMITH, JJ., concur.

DURHAM, J. (concurring in part, dissenting in part)—The
majority correctly interprets the child support guidelines to
allow trial courts the discretion to deviate from the schedule. However, the majority's conclusion that the trial judge
actually exercised that discretion in this case is wrong.
Rather than affirm, I would remand for the trial court to
reconsider its ruling in light of our opinion.

The entire record in this case consists of a 3–page tran-
script of oral argument and a 4–sentence Order Amending
Decree (both attached in full as an appendix). At the hearing, the trial judge began by stating:

> [A]s I read the statute and the guidelines, I don't have any
> jurisdiction or any authority to do anything but fix the support
> at guidelines.

Agreed Report of Proceedings, at 2.

The judge then engages in a short discussion as to why
the lack of discretionary leeway is unfair to trial courts.
Agreed Report of Proceedings, at 3–4. The following collo-
quy then ensues:

> [COUNSEL]: You're saying there is no discretion in this partic-
> ular standard?
> THE COURT: . . . I just don't think I can exercise my discre-
> tion downward.

Agreed Report of Proceedings, at 4.

The trial court's written order is, if anything, even more
clear. Paragraph (1) states:

Under the State Child Support guidelines effective July 1, 1988, *this Court has no discretion* to make a downward adjustment from scheduled support based upon the resources available to Petitioner by virtue of her second marriage, or any of the other circumstances outlined in Respondent's affidavit[.]

(Italics mine.) Clerk's Papers, at 2–3.

The majority gives two reasons why we should ignore this information. First, the majority finds the statute "clear and specific", implying that the trial judge must have also. Majority, at 777. It is only fair, however, to note that we arrived at our conclusion after lengthy briefs from the parties, additional research from our staff, and discussion among ourselves. Here is what the trial judge thought about the clarity of the statute:

THE COURT: I don't think anybody knows what the rule is. . . .

Agreed Report of Proceedings, at 2–3.

Second, the majority notes that the trial judge is experienced and:

given the clarity of the statute we have no doubt he understood his authority, under the proper circumstances, to deviate from the standard schedule even though he refused to do so in this instance.

Majority, at 777. I have not known many experienced trial judges—certainly none as able as Judge Day—who say one thing on the record when they "understand" the opposite to be true. What sort of precedent does this set? Are the plain-worded rulings of trial judges to be contorted, ignored, and psychoanalyzed to fit our results?

Given this record, I am at a loss to understand the majority's reluctance to remand. Although there are no Washington cases directly on point, the law appears to be clear. Failure to exercise discretion because of an erroneous view that the trial court does not have discretion requires the case to be remanded. *Personalized Mktg. Serv., Inc. v. Stotler & Co.*, 447 N.W.2d 447, 450 (Minn. Ct. App. 1989).[1]

---

[1]*See also Lemons v. Old Hickory Coun., Boy Scouts of Am., Inc.*, 322 N.C. 271, 277, 367 S.E.2d 655 (1988) ("When a trial court has failed to exercise its discretion regarding a discretionary matter and has ruled on it under the mistaken

It does not matter that the trial court's result could have been achieved upon the exercise of the withheld discretion. *Sullivan v. Chicago & Northwestern Transp. Co.,* 326 N.W.2d 320, 328 (Iowa 1982). In this case, the trial judge believed he had no discretion to deviate from the child support standards and ruled accordingly. Consequently, this case should be remanded for the trial judge to determine whether, exercising his discretion, a deviation from the child support standards is appropriate.

As to the other issues resolved in the majority opinion, I concur.

BRACHTENBACH, ANDERSEN, and GUY, JJ., concur with DURHAM, J.

---

impression it is required to rule a particular way as a matter of law, its holding must be reversed and the matter remanded for the trial court to exercise its discretion."); 5 Am. Jur. 2d *Appeal and Error* § 773 ("[W]here discretionary power existed in the court below to grant or deny a motion, which it denied on the erroneous assumption that it had no such power, its decision may be reversed and the case remanded to it in order that it may exercise its discretionary power.").

CHAPTER TEN

COHABITATION:
LIVING TOGETHER ARRANGEMENTS

Many people, especially divorce *survivors,* are choosing to live together rather than risk another unsuccessful marriage. Gays and lesbians are not even allowed the protection marriage affords. Living together arrangements are different from marriages in that the state participates neither in the beginning nor in the ending of the relationship. This relationship is often called *cohabitation.* Courts have defined cohabitation as *fellowship* and *the right of each partner to company, cooperation, affection, and aid.* These relationships pose unique legal problems. Traditionally, the courts considered these relationships illegal. Currently, they are struggling to redefine the rights of the two people who venture along this road.

When we were questioned about why we included a chapter on cohabitation in a book on marital dissolutions, we responded that it is becoming a common domestic arrangement that deserves legal recognition. As of 1982, there were an estimated 2,000,000 persons living outside the traditional marriage arrangement. Their legal rights and responsibilities are largely unknown. When they *divorce,* there are few laws to protect them. While the rights of married persons are protected by state law, *cohabitants generally* need written contracts to protect their rights. As more of these couples take their disputes to court for resolution, a body of law has begun to evolve that will protect their rights. Today, most lawyers would agree that love's oral promises are often lost without a good written contract.

LIVING TOGETHER: THE PROS AND THE CONS

Relationships are made more of feelings than of facts, so any decision to marry or live together should be based primarily on the feelings of each party. The protections of marriage are not needed by everyone. However, *no one* should decide against marriage without being well informed of the legal consequences.

145

Marriage laws protect the rights of heterosexual parents regarding access to their children, the rights of children to support from their parents, and the rights of their spouses to be compensated for their financial and emotional investment in their relationship. In addition, married couples are given:

1. Preferential income, gift, and estate tax rates;
2. Social acceptance for themselves and their children;
3. Insurance coverage for the death or injury of the other spouse; and,
4. Homestead rights to protect their home.

Living together provides more freedom and flexibility for the parties to craft the relationship on their own terms. This may require more work than a marriage, but some parties claim that it makes for a more exciting, vital relationship. Living together agreements presume each party has the capacity to bargain with the other over their personal and family needs. Relationships where one party is consistently dominant are not well suited for living together agreements because the legitimate needs of the weaker party will probably not be stated or met. When parties are on equal bargaining terms, the results can be quite satisfying. As one of our clients remarked,

> "It works because we're even and darn careful. I have an income, she has an income, and we both have property and the sort of respect that comes from knowing that each of us can go it alone if we have to. No kids though, as we agreed to get married if it came to kids."

This couple has lived together for almost ten years. They carefully drew up a contract to take care of expenses and incomes, and agreed to renegotiate it every year. In their words,

> "So far it's been great. Sure we've had our fights and arguments, but there's *something about not being legally bound* to stay together that makes this relationship so special. Being able to go anytime gives us the freedom to come home each day because we want to.
>
> "Believe me, we've both thought about leaving lots of times, but we get over the anger. You know, this may sound weird, but being able to think about leaving makes it much easier to choose to stay."

COHABITATION:
PROMISE ME ANYTHING BUT PUT IT IN WRITING

This is blunt advice, but even a formal contract will not dispose of all of the problems involved in cohabitation. The law has been slow to define the rights and responsibilities of cohabitants. It was not many years ago that these relationships were considered unlawful, and several states still make cohabitation a crime. Fortunately, the Washington State Supreme Court has made a major decision providing for legal recognition of certain heterosexual cohabitation relationships in the case of *Lindsey v. Lindsey*.

Nevertheless, you may still need a will, for example, to transfer property to your mate at death (in marriage it goes automatically to the spouse and children if there is no will), as well as a durable power of attorney over each other to make medical decisions and manage property if one of you becomes disabled.

A WARNING

A good cohabitation agreement is extremely important Without it you may be out of luck. For example, in a recent Illinois case, a couple lived together as husband and wife for fifteen years. They had no written agreement. She put him through dental school and her parents loaned them money (believing they were married) for other family costs. During this time they had three children and bought quite a bit of valuable property (all in his name). They parted; the wife sued for her share of fifteen years of work, and the court dismissed her claim on the grounds that the couple lacked a valid marriage. Fortunately, few courts are as unyielding as the Illinois court, but the dangers are still there.

In King County, Rainier Mediation and many others offer services that will help you to draft a cohabitation agreement.

WHAT DO I HAVE WITHOUT AN AGREEMENT?

Until recently, the general rule in Washington law was found in a 1948 case, *Creasman v. Boyle,* which held that

> "Property acquired by a man and woman not married to each other but living together as husband and wife, is not community property and, in the absence of some trust relation, belongs to the one in whose name the title to the property stands."

The thrust of this ruling was that people living together without marriage are treated as strangers who have no claim on each other beyond what they could establish by contract or trust law. The legal maxim for this situation is *Damnum Absque Injuria,* which basically translates as *tough luck, you have an injury that cannot be redressed by a legal action.*

Fortunately for cohabitants, *Creasman* was overruled by our State Supreme Court in *Lindsey v. Lindsey.*

LINDSEY v. LINDSEY: THE BREAKTHROUGH

This case concerned a couple who lived together for almost two years prior to marriage. During this premarital period, the couple logged a large property for $30,000 and built a barn/shop on their farm property. Upon marriage, Mr. Lindsey had extensive properties and Ms. Lindsey had virtually no assets. During marriage, the barn/shop burned down and they received $85,587.37 in insurance proceeds.

Using the *Creasman* presumption, the trial court awarded all of the real property and insurance proceeds to the husband. The Supreme Court reversed this decision, holding that the wife should be compensated for her contribution to building the barn/shop and similarly share in the insurance proceeds. Under this new rule,

> "[T]he courts must examine the [meretricious] relationship and the property accumulations and make a just and equitable disposition of the property."

This rule suggests that each cohabitation relationship will be considered on its own facts. The court may look at the duration and continuity of the relationship, its purpose, whether resources and time were pooled for joint projects, and whether or not a stable and significant relationship existed.

In sum, the *Lindsey* case opens the door for legal protection of cohabitants, *but which specific relationships the* Lindsey *rule will recognize remains an open question.*

The State Supreme Court sent the *Lindsey* case back to the Superior Court to determine Ms. Lindsey's share of the barn proceeds. It should be noted that the Superior Court ultimately awarded Ms. Lindsey approximately $4,000 for her share of the barn.

Another case that may be more powerful than *Lindsey* is *Warden v. Warden.* In that case, the couple had cohabited for nine years, had two children, bought a new home, and held themselves out as man and wife. Upon their separation, the court awarded the woman support for the children and a half interest in their home. The court explicitly extended to cohabitants the community property law that normally applies to legally married persons.

The *Warden* court concluded that

> "We believe that the time has come for the provisions of RCW 26.09.080 to govern the disposition of the property acquired by a man and a woman who have lived together and established a relationship which is tantamount to a marital family except for the legal marriage."

Even if you do not fit within the *Lindsey* or *Warden* criteria, there is still hope in the following doctrines of judicial relief:

1. *Implied partnership/joint venture.* These two concepts are closely related and apply only to business ventures (such as where an unmarried couple bought a tavern in the man's name and both worked to run it together for fifteen years). These doctrines require some very specific facts in order to be used, so don't assume they apply to you until you have consulted a lawyer.

2. *Resulting trust.* Where property was bought in the name of one party with funds from the other party, the court may find that the *owner* is holding the property in trust for the party supplying the funds. Very convincing proof is required here.

3. *Constructive trust.* Here, the party must clearly prove that the other acted in a deceptive or inequitable manner in order to gain relief from the court. The party need not have purchased the property.

4. *Co-tenancy.* If the party can prove he or she helped purchase the property, he or she may be given a share equal to the amount contributed. Maintenance or improvement of the property will not likely count towards the party's share.

These traditional forms of relief illustrate an unfortunate bias in the law that housework doesn't count. Many cohabitants have come to our office for help after being denied their right by the court. Glenna was one of these. She stated at the outset of our interview,

> "Maybe things will change when more men do housework, but right now, all I know is that we lived together for ten years and I put in twelve hours a day keeping house and he put in eight hours a day at work. And look what happens! He got the house and everything because he *earned the money* — I got nothing because all I did was work twelve hours a day for no pay for ten years. I could scream!"

Fortunately, the courts are beginning to respond to Glenna's tragedy. *Lindsey v. Lindsey* and *Warden v. Warden* are the best examples of this.

COMMON LAW MARRIAGE: NOT IN WASHINGTON

A few states have statutes where people living together a certain number of years (*e.g.,* seven years) or under certain conditions will be recognized as married under common law. Washington has a statute prohibiting common law marriages by its residents. However, as of this printing, such marriages are possible only in Alabama, Colorado, Washington, D.C., Georgia, Idaho, Iowa, Kansas, Montana, Ohio, Pennsylvania, Rhode Island, South Carolina, and Texas. If you and your partner lived together in one of these states for a number of years and owned property there, check with a lawyer to see if that state considers you married under common law. If so, Washington may recognize that common law marriage as a valid marriage in Washington. In Washington, your best means of protection is through a contract or other arrangement.

SAFETY FIRST:
ISSUES FOR A LIVING TOGETHER AGREEMENT

A thorough living together agreement is important for most cohabitants and vital for those involving children. Try to draft as much of it as you can on your own. Once you have done so, check with a lawyer who is experienced in this area. Like a medical exam, a small investment now could save you thousands of dollars later. Although each arrangement should reflect the uniqueness of the parties, there are some elements that may be common to most agreements:

1. *Separate property.* What property will be held separately? How will it be managed, and how will it be managed in the event that the owner is incapacitated?

2. *Common property.* What share does each party own of each property? How will purchase costs be shared? How will the payments, maintenance, and other responsibilities be shared? How will properties be divided if the relationship breaks down?

3. *Separate income.* What incomes will be considered separate? How will they be managed by each party and what will be done in the case that either party is temporarily or permanently incapacitated?

4. *Common income.* What specific income or portions of income sources are to be shared? What living expenses and other uses will this shared income be used for and how will such income be managed in the event that one party is disabled?

5. *Children.* What will they be named; who will decide? What provisions will be made for their education? How will paternity be acknowledged? How will they be supported in the event of a breakup or the disability of one of the parents?

6. *Modification, review, and termination of the agreement.* How often will the agreement be updated and how will it be modified? Will parties seek legal advice to ensure that the modifications are valid? What will be the effect if parties decide to marry? When and how can the agreement be terminated?

These are but a few of the concerns that should be addressed in a comprehensive living together agreement. Each couple has unique circumstances that create unique legal problems that should also be addressed. The space limitations of this book do not allow more elaboration at this point, but this chapter plus your own research should allow you to put together a basic agreement that you can then submit to a lawyer for refinement. Remember that doing your own work does more than save you money. It provides you with more confidence to manage your lives together and an agreement that better reflects the uniqueness of your relationship.

YOUR PROPERTY: HOW IT CAN BE OWNED

Generally, the law provides three basic forms of ownership that determine the disposition of property (in the absence of a contract) when the relationship breaks up. These are sole title, tenancy-in-common, and joint tenancy.

Sole title ownership occurs when the title to the property is taken in one name only. When the relationship ends, the property will end up in the possession of the cohabitant whose name is on the title. Even if both cohabitants contributed to the property, either by purchasing it with joint funds or by providing services, the law will rarely protect the non-title holder. However, some courts are beginning to look at the contributions and domestic services rendered by the non-owner in disposing of such property.

Tenancy-in-common (or co-tenancy) describes the situation where property is held by more than one person. Here, each person's name is on the title to the property and cohabitants would have an undivided one-half interest in the property.

Joint tenancy differs from tenancy-in-common in that it includes the right of survivorship. Thus, if one cohabitant dies, the surviving joint tenant gets the property. If there are four joint tenants, the one who lives the longest would get everything.

Thus, tenancy-in-common or joint tenancy are the only means of ensuring that you will get your investment back when the relationship ends. Under this arrangement, each cohabitant is entitled to his or her undivided one-half interest in the property at the end of their relationship. Sole title owners can convert to tenancy-in-common or joint tenancy, but this requires a conveyance (quit claim deed) of the sole owner's interest and a change in the deed. This transaction can create tax consequences, so you should consult a lawyer before attempting it.

INHERITANCE AND YOUR PROPERTY

Persons who live together have no automatic rights of inheritance from their partner's estate. Washington courts have awarded property to the surviving cohabitant where a valid case has been made for an implied partnership or a joint venture. However, these awards are made only in rare circumstances. The best solution at this point in time is to make a will giving specific properties to your cohabitant partner. Remember, if you have significant properties, your wills must be made with extreme care because mistakes and ambiguities invite conflict and court battles between your partner and your relatives. Your partner must live with your will.

Without an adequate will, your relatives may prevent your partner's claim to any of the property you have shared. One couple I knew of had lived together and shared their earnings for forty years when one party died. Neither had written a will, so the surviving partner lost almost everything to his partner's family because title to all the property was in his partner's name. The *Lindsey* and *Warden* cases may be used to prevent such a tragedy from reoccurring, but that question has not been specifically addressed by our State Supreme Court.

CHILDREN: TO ABORT, TO ADOPT, OR TO KEEP

In January 1973, the United States Supreme Court held that the right of privacy included the right of a woman to decide whether or not to terminate her pregnancy. Abortion is legal under certain circumstances.

The United States Supreme Court later held that physicians do not have to perform these abortions, but it did strike down a variety of regulations imposing unreasonable or unduly restrictive licensing regulations on doctors performing abortions in some states. It also held that neither the husband nor the father has a right to withhold consent. Minors, under certain circumstances, have the right to seek abortions without parental consent. The *right to life* debate continues and is beyond the scope of this discussion.

It is, however, an important issue. If abortion is not acceptable, adoption may be the answer. The legal procedure for adoption is not complex. After the birth, the natural mother is required to sign a short form acknowledging that she freely and willingly agrees to turn over the child to an attorney or an agency for adoption. This consent must also be signed by two witnesses. Unlike abortion, the father may withhold his consent and prevent the adoption. A 1972 United States Supreme Court decision held that the interest of a man "in the children he has sired and raised, undeniably warrants deference and... protection." As a consequence, Washington has enacted laws that require the father to be notified of the intended adoption. Washington State retains the power to demonstrate that the natural father is an *inadequate parent* and that his parental rights should be terminated. Evidence of unfitness would include abandonment of the child or failure to support, acknowledge, or care for the child.

Parenthood without marriage creates problems. The first concern is to legally establish paternity. The surest way of taking care of this is for the father to sign the birth certificate and to get a court declaration of paternity.

You also will want to protect your child's rights in case you die. It is especially important for you to name each child in your will and make provisions in that document for their future.

Adoption by cohabitants can be difficult. Cohabitants could encounter greater problems than a single parent. Some caseworkers regard cohabitants as less stable than a single parent. The caseworkers fear the child could be harmed by the breakup of the adoptive parents. Adoption of the natural child of one cohabitant by another cohabitant is not difficult once the absent party's rights are terminated.

A child born of cohabitants is entitled to support from both its parents just as though the child had been born in lawful wedlock. Punishment for nonsupport is similar to that in the marriage situation: the proven father can be sent to jail if he refuses to pay support. When the father has not acknowledged or supported the child, he can be sued to establish paternity and for child support.

In some states there is a statute of limitations concerning paternity suits. The law might provide that unless a suit is brought within three years of the child's birth, it is barred forever. That creates the possibility that cohabitation arrangements that last beyond three years may leave the child with no support rights. *This is not the case in Washington,* but there is still a clear need to establish legal paternity.

Inheritance is resolved according to state laws. In Washington, if the father dies leaving no will, the child will inherit from him. The child will also inherit from the mother.

COHABITATION DURING DIVORCE: THE RISKS

In some states, if you openly live with a person awaiting a divorce, you risk being sued for *alienation of affections.* Washington has done away with the alienation of affections cause of action. Still, persons not yet divorced who live together are, to some extent, compromising the divorce case. Often the other spouse grows hostile and uncooperative when he or she discovers the cohabitation arrangement. That hostility could frustrate the entire divorce negotiation process.

Post-divorce parenting and maintenance provisions can be affected by a cohabitation arrangement. There is a clear trend toward reducing maintenance if the payments are supporting the rent, food, and utilities of a new partner, or if the ex-spouse's financial needs are being partly provided by the person he or she is living with.

CHANGING YOUR NAME: CHANGING YOUR CREDIT

Name changes can be granted to either cohabitant. The only statutory prohibition is that the change of name must not be designed to defraud. You need only go through a simple court procedure. By adopting your mate's name you may find creditors lumping together your credit rating with that of your partner. The *family expense statutes,* which make married spouses liable for family debts, may subject you to the same responsibility for expenses charged by your live-in partner.

Children born of unmarried parents historically were given their mother's surname. Now they may take the father's name as well. This may be accomplished by his written consent, by adoption, or by a paternity suit. Remember, however, that any of those options also gives the father significant rights should the mother later wish to have the child adopted by a third person.

THE DILEMMA OF INSURANCE

Cohabitants have difficulty insuring each other because most insurance companies require that the person buying the policy have an *insurable interest.* Some insurance companies will not allow one cohabitant to insure the life of the other because they have no *interest* in each other. Moreover, it may be difficult for an unmarried individual owning life insurance on his or her own life to name his or her cohabitant as beneficiary upon death. The class of persons you can name as beneficiaries is also limited by law. The *Lindsey* case may limit this problem, but that question has not been fully resolved by the courts or by legislation.

Insurance companies can avoid their obligations by claiming fraud in the application. Thus, if you put down your cohabitant as your *wife* for beneficiary purposes, then the company can claim a breach of contract, alleging that they would have declined to issue the policy if they had known that the beneficiary was not legally your wife. You may have to shop long and hard to find a company that will insure you for the benefit of your cohabitant. Be certain that you are candid with the information you furnish the insurance company lest you lose the entire policy.

The children of these relationships also have problems with insurance. In order to have an insurable *interest* in the life of their father, these children must show that he acknowledged them and that they relied upon him to some extent for support.

Other kinds of insurance policies are also difficult to obtain. Although the usual homeowner's insurance policy has a clause that protects the other residents of the household, this is usually construed to mean members of the insured's immediate family. The same is true of medical and hospitalization insurance. People who live together do not yet have the same *dependency* relationship even though children are certainly dependent upon their father or mother! No marriage may well mean no insurance. As with life insurance, if you lie in order to get coverage for your cohabitant, you may lose your benefits.

SOCIAL SECURITY

One of the few legal benefits of cohabitation is Social Security. Senior singles who have already earned their Social Security benefits can live together and still collect separate checks. If they marry, these double payments end. The law currently allows a wife to receive a percentage of her deceased or divorced husband's Social Security. The spouses must have been married at least nine months for widower's benefits and at least ten years for divorce benefits. Cohabitants cannot collect Social Security from each other. The children of these relationships, however, do derive benefits through both parents. Of course, the deceased worker-father must have been established officially as the father (either by court order or by acknowledgment). In addition, the worker must have been living with the child at the time of death or been contributing to his or her support *and* the child must have been entitled to inherit under the law of the state where they resided.

TAXES: THE EXTRA COST OF COHABITATION

Despite various amendments to the United States Tax Code over the past few years, taxes remain a key concern for most people. This is especially true for cohabitants because they are denied the benefits received by married couples in income, estate, and gift taxes. For example:

1. Cohabitants must file separate returns and are subject to higher tax on their individual incomes than that of married couples with the same joint return.

2. Any payment for companionship from one cohabitant to the other could be taxed as *compensation for services*.

3. Cohabitants must pay gift tax on major gifts given to each other. Gift tax is waived for gifts between married people.

4. Each cohabitant will be taxed for annual gifts to other persons over $10,000. A husband and wife may pool their exemptions so that one or the other may give $20,000 per year without having to pay a gift tax.

5. Upon death of a cohabitant, property passing from one cohabitant to the other is subject to estate tax. Upon death of a spouse, property passes to the other with significant estate tax exemptions.

6. When cohabitants end their relationship they will be subject to income and capital gains tax for dividing their property. When spouses divorce and divide their property evenly they are not subject to income tax.

These are but a few of the areas where cohabitants pay more taxes than married persons. You should consult a tax accountant or a tax lawyer as to whether the convenience of cohabitation is worth these additional costs.

LEGISLATION: A BETTER FUTURE FOR COHABITATION

Clearly, cohabitants cross a mine field of legal problems. The Washington courts have solved some of these problems with the *Lindsey* and *Warden* cases. Further change in this area, however, may require legislation. This legislation should recognize that people, regardless of sex or marital status, have a right to form long-lasting relationships and raise children subject to the protections and controls that this state presently provides to married people. Such legislation must be very carefully drafted and provide protections for *non-marital property,* like those now provided for *community property.*

We recognize and accept that people have a right to believe that living together without marriage may be morally wrong. Our position is simply that while people have a right to make such moral judgments, the state should not legislate such judgments. The state's role is to protect its citizens and we see no reason why the children of a sensitive and productive fifteen-year cohabitation should not deserve the same protection as the children of a fifteen-year marriage.

CHAPTER ELEVEN
THE BASICS OF NEGOTIATION

Nine out of ten divorces in Washington State are settled out of court. Your case is probably going to be negotiated to a settlement unless one or both spouses persist in being unreasonable, spiteful, or determined to prove that he or she alone is "right." This chapter is offered as a primer to help you understand and apply negotiation principles to your own divorce; it is not intended to serve as a handbook to negotiations.

The process of negotiation varies with the couple. In many cases the husband and wife may do much of the bargaining directly, using their lawyers as advisors and draftsmen, or they may leave all face-to-face negotiating to the attorneys. They may also use a mediator to assist them in their own direct negotiations, as described in Chapter 3. For some spouses the bargaining may be completed before the lawsuit for divorce is even started; for others, there is no settlement until they are in the middle of a contested trial after years of fighting. By most odds, however, your case will in some way, at some time, be settled by you and your spouse, rather than by a judge after a trial.

In this chapter you will find basic information about negotiation techniques to aid you in settlement of your divorce case. Divorce negotiations are "in the shadow of the law" in the sense that they are partially shaped by the parties' estimates of what a court will do if no agreement is reached and the case goes to trial. To negotiate effectively, you need information about what a court would likely do if there were a contested trial. Your lawyer will help you make these predictions. Reading this book will give you a general knowledge of the legal principles that Washington courts use in deciding divorce cases. The closer you are able to come in predicting the outcome of your own case, the more you are empowered to participate effectively and creatively in your own negotiations.

The process of negotiation consists of three important phases:

1. The information phase, where you must learn as much about your (and your spouse's) circumstances and objectives as possible;

157

2. The competitive phase, where you try to obtain the very best deal; and

3. The cooperative phase, where you begin to identify your joint interests with your spouse.

GETTING TO KNOW YOUR CASE, GETTING TO KNOW YOUR SPOUSE — THE INFORMATION PHASE

The information phase starts with you learning as much as possible about your case and the law affecting it. To be an effective negotiator, either alone or acting with your attorney, you must have a general grasp of the law and the facts of your case. Reading this book, absorbing the legal principles, and filling out the forms is a good place to start, but you need to delve even deeper into the topic. After all, this is one of the most important transactions of your life so it is well worth your time to learn as much as possible about divorce. A suggested bibliography is found in Appendix B.

At this stage, you need to spend some time with your lawyer analyzing what your spouse's interests and preferences are. Only in that way can you plan your strategy. You must be a psychologist: you need to get behind the stated positions of your spouse to try to understand your spouse's underlying needs and interests. If you know what your spouse really wants to achieve, sometimes you can suggest alternatives that will satisfy both sides sufficiently to produce an accord.

Illustration

Mary Ellen thought Jim did not want to contribute more than 50% toward Justin and Kristin's college education because he feared he would not be able to afford that after the divorce. Jim wanted to pay more, but feared that Mary Ellen's current financial needs would eat up his remaining earnings. Once these fears were aired, Jim and Mary Ellen were able to sit down and discuss a long-term college savings plan to which both parents would contribute after the divorce, in accordance with their respective earnings. Jim did pay more than 50%, but because Mary Ellen would eventually be contributing too, both kids would be assured college educations.

TO THE BARGAINING TABLE — THE COMPETITIVE PHASE AND THE COOPERATIVE PHASE

In the competitive phase, you must learn to articulate your own demands. It will be important in this stage to make "principled" offers and concessions. You must be able to give your spouse sufficient understanding of the reasons underlying your demands. In other words, you must explain to your spouse why you are entitled to the goals you are seeking.

Illustration

Fred announced to Mary's lawyer that he would not consider anything other than a fifty-fifty split of the property. He explained that this was a short-term marriage and the case law he had read backed him up. Mary's lawyer agreed but suggested that the case could be settled if Mary could be assured some short-term rehabilitative maintenance. He explained that Fred earned twice as much as Mary, she needed money to make a substantial deposit on a new apartment, and Fred could afford it. The case settled in twenty minutes, largely because each side understood the other's position and was able to rationally respond to various proposals.

Similarly, if you change your position you should make "principled" concessions. You need to provide your spouse with a rational explanation for why you have modified your position.

Illustration

Assume that while negotiating for the family residence you learn that a judge will probably award your spouse a percentage of the house. You decide to take matters into your own hands by sending a signal that you will accept a lien to your spouse for 10% of the house sale proceeds, explaining to your spouse that you believe there is a good probability that a judge would say he or she is entitled to 10%. This lets your spouse know why the change is being made and helps to keep your spouse on target, namely, that you want the house.

Arguments must be presented objectively. You should never issue threats during negotiations unless you are prepared to carry them out, since failing to do so will undermine your credibility. Instead of making negative threats that suggest what consequences will occur if your spouse will not alter his or her position, you should consider positive promises that indicate your own willingness to change your position simultaneously with your spouse.

Illustration

Mary Ellen wanted to live in the house until Kristin graduated from high school. Instead of remonstrating with Jim and accusing him of trying to throw her and the kids out of the house, she calmly suggested that she would agree to share a percentage of the house sale proceeds, provided the sale occurred after Kristin graduated.

The classic promise "let's split the difference" is often used to conclude a transaction. One side promises to move halfway only if the other spouse will do the same. These affirmative processes are much more effective and less challenging to your opponent.

If you do bargain directly with your spouse you should make it clear that you are reserving the right to check with your lawyer before any tenatative agreement can bind you. The advantage of this "limited authority" approach is that it permits you to obtain a psychological commitment to settlement from your spouse while preserving an "out" for yourself.

If possible, stay away from a "win-lose" situation with your spouse. If you have a spouse who does not evaluate his or her outcome by how well he or she has done but by assessing how poorly you have done, chances are you are not going to succeed in negotiations. This type of spouse is only satisfied if he or she thinks you have been forced to accept a terrible agreement. To get a settlement you may have to give up too much.

Once you have a tentative agreement with your spouse it may be to your advantage to explore alternative trade-offs that might simultaneously enhance the interests of both of you. You could start by preparing alternative "hypothetical" settlements, transferring certain items from the wife's side of the ledger to the husband's and vice versa.

Illustration

You and your spouse have worked out a Parenting Plan which involves your keeping the children with you on Wednesday nights and dropping them off at school Thursday morning. You ask her if she would like to consider altering the weeknight to Tuesdays. (It doesn't matter to you whether you take the kids on Tuesday or Wednesday but you know that she would prefer not to take them to the Boys Club meetings on Tuesdays.) She accepts, expressing appreciation for your thoughtfulness with the implicit promise that she will do you a similar favor later.

Of course, this requires that you and your spouse can act with some candor, indicating whether any of the proposals are preferable to the agreement already achieved. This method does not need to take a lot of time. Sometimes you can increase your personal satisfaction through this technique and you lose little if no mutual gains are achieved. However, remember that in order for this cooperative phase to work, you and your spouse must be willing to say whether alternatives are more or less beneficial to you.

Illustration

In the above example, the negotiations worked because the wife was willing to inform her spouse, after they had already settled on a tentative Parenting Plan, that she really did not relish the idea of taking the kids to Tuesday night Boys Club meetings. She was shy and had difficulty interacting with the other parents at the Boys Club. She preferred to be with the children at home helping them do their homework on Wednesday nights. The parents adjusted the Parenting Plan accordingly.

If you can understand these common negotiating techniques you can certainly plan strategies very effectively. First, you need to enhance your own skills during the information phase. This will increase the likelihood that you will obtain an acceptable agreement during the competitive bargaining phase. Once you have reached a tentative agreement you should try to cooperate with your spouse to see if there are other options mutually satisfactory to both of you in which both of you can maximize the gains obtained.

WHY NEGOTIATIONS FAIL — SIX COMMON REASONS

1. The "Fixed Pie Mentality"

These negotiations fail because each spouse assumes that there is only a fixed amount of pie in what is being negotiated and in order to win something the other must lose. To overcome this negotiation impasse, one or both of the spouses must start looking at acceptable compromises which permit them to expand the size of the pie.

For example, Jane wanted 60% of the property and Jack was not willing to give her more than half. During negotiations, however, both of them learned that Jane really wanted the security of a well-paying job but currently lacked the skills to find that job. So she was holding out for a larger slice of the pie. The solution: Jack offered her more maintenance in exchange for retaining a fifty-fifty split in the property. He told her he would pay her $1,500 per month maintenance and then when she got a job he would not begin reducing the maintenance until six months after she found and kept full-time employment. The initial reductions would only be fifty cents against every dollar she earned until she had stabilized herself in the marketplace. This broke the stalemate. She was willing to give up a larger piece of the pie in order to be assured she had a financial cushion while she was developing her job skills. Jack benefitted because he could get the tax deduction for maintenance payments to Jane while retaining 50% of the property.

Another variation on the win-win alternative to "fixed pie" negotiations: Jane wanted Jack's 50% of the pie to come out of a lien on the family residence years down the road but Jack did not want to be her "banker" that long. There were not enough other assets to balance off the lien so both parties agreed to refinance the house before the divorce was entered. This provided Jack enough cash to look for a place of his own yet permitted Jane to stay in the current residence with a reasonable monthly house payment. Jack was willing to give up a larger balancing lien on the residence to be awarded to Jane in the future in exchange for a fast but smaller cash payment.

Under the settlement, Jane had the cash to give Jack and appreciated not having to make a large balloon payment or having to find financing to pay off his larger lien five years later.

In both these illustrations the husband and wife found a solution to their negotiating needs without taking "a larger percentage of the pie."

2. Buyer's Remorse

This is often observed when one spouse accepts an offer too quickly. The other spouse then feels that it must not have been as good a deal after all, and that the acceptor had better information. This situation can be avoided by acquiring as much knowledge about your facts and the applicable law as possible while obtaining as much information about your spouse's viewpoint as possible. Sometimes this can only be done by developing or borrowing the expertise of others to equalize your negotiating position with a better-informed spouse.

3. Asking for Too Much at the Beginning

It is not uncommon for clients (and sometimes even their lawyers) to commit the fundamental negotiating error of starting out negotiations with extreme and untenable demands, figuring that the case will find a middle ground later. Sometimes however, the spouses (and, yes, even lawyers) get caught up in the struggle, spending large sums on court costs, attorney fees, and generally investing their money and egos too much to back off. As a result, spouses end up taking a hard line. Friends and others may wonder why the conflict keeps escalating, thinking maybe it is the attorney's fault. Sometimes it is the attorneys who have contributed to the conflict. More often, however, it is the spouses themselves.

For example, Betty's lawyer demanded eighteen years of maintenance for his client although she and Dave had only been married six years. Because Dave had plenty of money, Betty's lawyer thoughtlessly assumed Dave would compromise and "split the difference." Instead, Dave became so angry at the opening offer that settlement negotiations broke off and were never resumed. Dave spent the money in court that he would have paid Betty in maintenance trying to prove "that idiot lawyer was dead wrong." The only persons who benefitted from those negotiations were the two lawyers.

4. The Emotional Investment in "Winning"

The emotional investment in winning negotiation comes from our competitive spirit and the images of defeat that follow a person who unilaterally "gives up" or reduces his or her demands. No one wants to come in second. Therefore, it is important that you stop and evaluate the costs and benefits of keeping your present position to ensure that this attitude makes successful negotiating impossible.

For example, Ben knew he could settle his case if he would but agree to a fifty-five/forty-five split, but since he had told his wife Eve on the day he left the house that she would get nothing if she divorced him, he could not budge. The court awarded her the 55% but, again, lawyers had to be hired to litigate what was an obviously negotiable settlement.

5. Pushing Your Spouse into a Corner

Never push your spouse into a corner or otherwise make your spouse feel committed to perpetuating the struggle to the bitter end. Sometimes known as "loss of face," this characteristic can ruin even the best-intentioned negotiations.

For example, in Ben's example above, his "loss of face" could have been avoided. In negotiations, Eve could have suggested that his remark as he left the house was made in the heat of the moment and was understandable at the time. Now that they had both calmed down, she expected both of them to negotiate fairly with the other. This maneuver invites Ben to join Eve in more rational discussions, suggests that she is sharing the fault with him for his heated statement, and clears the table for improved discussions based on "fairness."

6. Your Tolerance for Uncertainty

Lastly, understand your tolerance for uncertainty and risk, as this may affect your success in negotiating. Imagine that you have the choice between a sure $50 and a coin flip which would decide whether you took $100 or nothing. If you have a strong desire to choose the coin flip over a certain $50, you are a risk preferrer in that situation. If you have a strong preference for taking the sure $50, you can be said to be risk adverse. The risk preferrer has an advantage over the risk-adverse spouse in a negotiation because he or she has a greater tolerance for the possibility for losing. The inherent uncertainty in the judicial process gives the risk-preferring spouse an advantage over the risk-adverse spouse. Although your lawyer will give you his or her best estimates of what is likely to happen in a trial, Washington courts have enormous discretion in divorce cases and the judge's decision might be quite different from your lawyer's prediction, for better or for worse. You can avoid that uncertainty by reaching an agreement now. But, a relatively small tolerance for uncertainty may leave you needing an agreement more than your spouse does. If your spouse knows you can't stand uncertainty and risk, he or she may insist on unfair concessions before giving you the certainty you want, that is, by signing the divorce settlement.

CONCLUSION

Finally, there is an old lawyer cliche that a good settlement is one that completely satisfies neither party but each can live with it. If your side wins too much and the opposition gets too little, the whole agreement is more apt to come unhinged and costly litigation may result. Where both sides feel that the terms are fair and reasonable, and were arrived at by give-and-take, there are psychological and moral pressures to abide by the agreement, much in the same way you are honor-bound when you "shake on it."

All negotiations are as different as the persons and the fact situations involved. So do not expect the above illustrations to apply in your case. However, you can do yourself a fundamental service if you study negotiation techniques and acquire the skills to find "fairness" in uncoupling your own marriage.

CHAPTER TWELVE
CONCLUSION

The nature of families and the nature of family law have changed significantly over the past twenty years of the authors' divorce practice. Parenting plans are now common; no-fault divorce is the norm; and the law gives increasing protection to new family forms such as cohabitants, gay families, step-families, and single-parent families. Our law must protect children's best interests regardless of the family form chosen by their parents.

Our goal in writing this book has been to provide the reader with an understandable and relevant manual for humanizing the divorce process. This book would not have been possible without the criticisms and personal stories offered by earlier readers. Future editions will incorporate your suggestions, stories, and concerns. If you have comments, suggestions, or criticisms, please write to us at the following address:

Humane Divorce
c/o John W. Kydd
1616 Bank of California Center
900 Fourth Avenue
Seattle, Washington 98164

With your help, future editions of this book will continue to address legal and procedural questions, and psychological issues critical to families involved in divorce proceedings in Washington.

EPILOGUE

The plain white tablecloth between us mirrored the spring clouds scattering across the sky. Mary Ellen had stopped by for lunch. Three months had passed since her divorce became final. She looked at the worn copy of her book and said,

"Your book is helpful now in a very different way. Nine months ago I was too desperate to figure out where I was on *any* of the stages. I felt like I was drowning in guilt, anger, and confusion, and the only thing that mattered was surviving day-to-day."

She spoke with a tone of certainty and assurance that I had not heard before,

"It's different now.... I know where I am on the psychological stages. I have new men friends and I can feel the lonely and scared part of me really wanting to settle down with one of them and feel *safe*. But my deeper voice says, 'No, this is a time for you to *know yourself* and care for yourself like you never have before ...you can't love another any more than you love yourself.' So, I am going to take some time before my next plunge into a relationship. Right now I am barely to the 'leftovers' stage, and it's been almost a year!

"You know, I am finding more and more in your book. Those damnable checklists for residency, parenting, and support were impossible to do. I thought you were being incredibly picky and a real slave driver for pushing us to confront all of those questions. Now I see that they really were an investment in preventing future problems. There are fewer surprises now for Jim and me, and we can deal better with those surprises that do crop up because of the problems we have already anticipated. The second or third time I read your book, I found all sorts of questions that I need to ask now, but did not notice before.

"The kids are doing well and we've talked about the psychological stages for Jim and me, as well as them, so everyone feels a little more certain about the time it takes to work through something like this. It is funny, now that I am growing, everyone around me seems to be growing too!"

Mary Ellen looked healthier than at any other time I had ever seen her. There was a gleam of certainty in her eyes. She still had much work to do, but she knew that she could do it.

APPENDICES

A. KING COUNTY RESOURCES FOR RECOVERY
B. RECOMMENDED READING ON DIVORCE
C. BILL OF RIGHTS FOR CHILDREN OF DIVORCE
D. KING COUNTY FAMILY COURT SERVICES ACCESS GUIDELINE
E. LEGAL DOCUMENTS FOR DISSOLUTION OF MARRIAGE
   1. Summary for Dissolution of Marriage
   2. Petition for Dissolution
   3. Petitioner's Proposed Parenting Plan
   4. Motion for Temporary Restraining Order and Order to Show Cause
   5. Temporary Restraining Order and Order to Show Cause
   6. Declaration of Petitioner in Support of Temporary Parenting Plan
   7. Declaration of Petitioner in Support of Temporary Restraining Order and Order to Show Cause
   8. Agreed Temporary Restraining Order
   9. Response to Petition for Dissolution of Marriage
   10. Separation Contract
   11. Findings of Fact and Conclusions of Law
   12. Decree of Dissolution
F. SUPERIOR COURTS OF WASHINGTON STATE
G. LAWYER REFERRAL SERVICES IN WASHINGTON
H. DIVIDING UP THE PENSION
I. TAX CONSIDERATION OF DIVORCE
J. WASHINGTON STATE CHILD SUPPORT SCHEDULE WITH WORKSHEETS AND EXAMPLES
K. RESOURCES FOR DOMESTIC VIOLENCE
L. RESOURCES FOR ALCOHOL AND DRUG ABUSE
M. SAMPLE PARENTING PLAN
N. ASSOCIATION OF FAMILY AND CONCILIATION COURTS POLICY RE: AIDS AND FAMILY LAW
O. ORDER FORM FOR ADDITIONAL BOOKS OR FORMS

APPENDIX A
KING COUNTY
RESOURCES FOR RECOVERY

What follows is a partial list of some of the community resources available in King County for individuals going through the divorce procedure. This list is not exhaustive, and we would appreciate being informed of new services or any significant services that we have omitted. In future editions of this book, we hope to expand this appendix to cover resources available throughout the state. In the meantime, if you live outside of King County, we recommend that you consult your local chapter of the United Way, the YWCA, and the YMCA for information about community resources that may be available to you. See also Appendix K, "Resources for Domestic Violence."

Every effort has been made to ensure that the addresses and telephone numbers were correct at press time. However, addresses and telephone numbers do change, and some entities go out of business.

WHERE TO BEGIN

An excellent source of overall information in King County is the Crisis Clinic Community Information Line, which lists almost all public and privately supported human service organizations in the county. This information and referral line is open from 9 a.m. to 5 p.m., Monday through Friday, at 447-3200. This is a toll-free number within King County. In addition, we encourage you to contact your local church and community colleges. To make the best use of your time, try as best you can to clarify the type of resource you need. Try to clarify what specific emotional, financial, and legal resources you need to deal with your problem. Then go look for them!

RESOURCES FOR CRISIS

Although there are a number of specialized crisis lines, the best overall crisis line is the Crisis Clinic at 447-3222. This line is toll-free throughout King County and is open twenty-four hours a day. Other crisis lines are:

Asian Counseling and Referral Center	447-3606
Atlantic Street Center	329-2050
Catholic Community Services	323-6336
Community Psychiatric Clinic	447-3614
Eastside Community Mental Health Center	486-7181
Highline-West Seattle Mental Health Center	932-8285
Lutheran Social Services	365-2700
Mental Health North	365-5550
Redmond Counseling Service	885-1480
Seattle Mental Health Institute	
(Alcohol and Drug Treatment)	281-4300
Seattle Rape Relief	632-7273
(business)	325-5531
Valley City Mental Health Center	854-0760
Youth Eastside Services	454-5502
Youth Service Bureau (King County)	296-5229
Youth Service Bureau (Seattle)	625-4705

LEGAL RESOURCES

Battered Women's Project of the Seattle City Attorney's office (625-2119). This project, along with the abused women's project at Evergreen Legal Services, takes most of the domestic violence cases that go through the court system. Clients are married and unmarried victims of domestic violence. Project staff do crisis intervention, counseling, and provide support throughout the criminal justice procedure.

Evergreen Legal Services (464-1422). Due to recent budget cuts under the present federal administration, Evergreen Legal Services handles very few divorces unless there is domestic violence or the ownership of a home is involved.

Fremont Legal Clinic (632-1285). Every Wednesday evening, volunteer attorneys will provide free, thirty-minute consultations regarding basic areas of the law including divorce. Please be sure to call beforehand for an appointment.

Lawyer Referral and Information Service of the Seattle King County Bar Association (623-2551 and 623-2988) for twenty-four-hour informational tape. This splendid program has trained interviewers who will help people clarify whether legal problems necessitate the hiring of an attorney. If so, you will be referred to an attorney who has experience in your area of interest for a thirty-minute appointment, which will cost $20.

Northwest Women's Law Center (632-8468). This very committed group of individuals provides no direct legal representation, but does provide quite a bit of information and educational material regarding women's legal rights in Washington. Their most recent publication, *Women and the Law in Washington State*, is a very helpful guide. The Law Center maintains a panel of attorneys to which it refers women with family and other legal problems.

Office of Support Enforcement (464-6900). This group can be quite helpful in locating and prosecuting parents who have failed to pay their child support. If necessary, they will bring legal action against your spouse for non-payment of support almost anywhere in the United States. YOU NEED NOT HAVE AN ATTORNEY TO USE THEIR SERVICES.

Tel-Law Program of the Seattle-King County Bar Association (382-0680, 10 a.m. to 5:30 p.m., Monday through Friday). At last count this program had over eighty tapes on a wide range of legal topics, which can be listened to over the phone. If possible, you may wish to send them a self-addressed, stamped envelope to the above program at:

Bank of California Center, Suite 600
Seattle, Washington 98164

Otherwise, call them and ask for the appropriate tape and settle down with note pad in hand.

Washington State Bar Association Legal Department (448-0307, 9 a.m. to 5 p.m., Monday through Friday). Although the legal staff of the Washington State Bar Association cannot give you legal advice, they will help you with *any* complaint you have about an attorney. The legal staff investigates *all* complaints made against lawyers licensed to practice law in Washington. They only prosecute, however, violations of the Code of Professional Responsibility. If you have a question regarding the ethical conduct of an attorney, you should call the Legal Department at 448-0307. They do not handle questions of malpractice or those regarding attorney's fees. If your complaint is about the fees of an attorney, you should call 448-0441 and ask for information about arbitrating an attorney's fee. You will be referred to a fee arbitration panel, where, for a nominal amount, you can have the fees charged by your attorney reviewed by an arbitrator. If you believe your attorney has committed malpractice, you will need the services of another attorney to determine what, if any, liability there may be on the part of your attorney.

RESOURCES FOR WOMEN

Centers for Displaced Homemakers (Seattle, 764-5802; Bellevue, 641-2279). These programs provide significant information and experience for women making the transition from full-time homemaker to wage earner. Free employment classes, support groups, and vocational training are offered at locations throughout the area for minimal fees.

University of Washington Women's Information Center (545-1090, 8 a.m. to 5 p.m., Monday through Friday). The Women's Center publishes a splendid calendar of King County events of interest to women, maintains a large lending library, and will provide you with focused referral to community resources sensitive to the needs of women.

Women's Divorce Cooperative (784-4755, 9 a.m. through 5 p.m., Monday through Friday). This private, non-profit group is run solely by volunteers and focuses on providing women with the information necessary to do their own divorces. The class costs $25 and will provide lawyer referral where necessary.

Women's Therapy Referral Service (587-3854 or 323-9388, 8 a.m. to 5 p.m., Monday through Friday). This group tries to match you with a therapist appropriate to your financial capacity, personality style, therapeutic preference, and your particular emotional issues. They tend to charge a sliding fee for their referral work.

YWCA Women's Resource Centers (447-4882, downtown; 632-4747, University of Washington). Between these two centers, you may find emergency housing, a twenty-four-hour counseling staff, pointed information on employment, community action, and therapy with special expertise for women who have been psychologically or physically abused.

RESOURCES FOR MEN

Men's Counseling Network (329-9919, message phone). This nonprofit organization will help refer you to an appropriate counselor to deal with your particular problem. Services are provided on a sliding scale.

Metro Center YMCA Men's Center (382-5013, 1 p.m. to 5 p.m., Monday through Friday). This program has offered a variety of service to men in the King County area since 1973. Of particular interest is the Men's Divorce Cooperative, which provides low-cost legal advice regarding the process of divorce.

RESOURCES FOR FAMILIES

Atlantic Street Center (329-2050, 9 a.m. to 5 p.m., Monday through Friday). The Center provides counseling and crisis intervention on a sliding scale for families and couples in the Central Area of Seattle.

Dispute Resolution Center of Seattle-King County (329-3944). Free or low-fee mediation for divorce and family conflicts for low income individuals, as well as others.

Divorce Lifeline (624-2959, 8:30 a.m. to 5 p.m., Monday through Friday). This church-sponsored program offers small group classes throughout King County for divorcing parents, teenagers, and youngsters who are involved in a divorce. Their fees are not steep and the staff is well trained in the area of divorce. It is possible for an entire family to go through Divorce Lifeline and the parents could gain the support of their own particular group.

Family Services of King County (447-3883). This service has at least seven locations throughout King County where trained counselors will provide family and couple counseling with special expertise in the area of spouse abuse and incest. Please call for further information about their services.

Lutheran Counseling Network (455-2960, Bellevue office). This nonprofit organization has branches throughout the greater King County area, and provides low-cost individual marital and family counseling regardless of one's faith.

Parents Anonymous (343-2590). This group is associated with the Counsel for Prevention of Child Abuse and Neglect and offers a wealth of information for parents who have abused their children and seek to understand and to remedy this problem.

Parents without Partners (622-8316, answering service). This nation-wide organization has chapters all over King County and provides varied social, educational, and family activities for divorced, never married, or widowed parents.

Rainier Mediation (623-5221). Lawyers and lawyer-therapists specializing in family mediation.

Solo Center (522-7756, 7 p.m. to 11 p.m., daily). This resource center, which is somewhat affiliated with the Unitarian Church, provides a quality support system through information and referral, classes, low-key socializing, and ongoing informal rap groups.

Widowed Information Service for King County (362-0218, north Seattle). This resource center has branches throughout the King County area and will provide services to widowed men and women regarding handling their grief and moving toward a productive recovery from bereavement. Support groups are available for sliding scale fees.

APPENDIX B
RECOMMENDED READING
ON DIVORCE

Alone: Emotional, Legal and Financial Help for the Widowed or Divorced Woman, by Antoniak, Scott, and Worcester. A compassionate guide to a difficult period of life.

The Boy's and Girl's Book about Divorce, by Richard Gardner, M.D. The purpose of this book is to help children get along better with their divorced parents. It was written for children ages eight to thirteen, and is intended for reading by children alone or with a parent. A parent could read it to younger children ages four to seven. Adolescents will also find much of interest to them in this book. Parents often find this book of great help for themselves, because it is written from the side of the child's thoughts and feelings.

The Boy's and Girl's Book About One Parent Families, by Richard Gardner, M.D. This book is a warm guide for children by an excellent author.

Children of Divorce, by J. Louise Despert. This book tells parents in concrete terms how divorce affects children, what to do about it, and where to get help in the doing.

Crazy Time: Surviving Divorce, by Abigail Trafford. A focused effort that examines the emotional conflicts faced by males and females during divorce.

Creative Aggression, by Bach and Wyden. A guide to fair fighting.

Creative Divorce, by Mel Krantzler. The focus of this book is on using the crisis of divorce as an opportunity for the growth and development of men and women.

Crisis Time!, by William A. Nolen, M.D. A warm and fascinating autobiography of a successful surgeon who endured a staggering mid-life crisis. Dr. Nolen attempts to explain the medical basis for the crisis and offers helpful advice.

The Divorced Woman's Handbook, by Jane Wilkie. This book has checklists of things that you must do to make it efficiently through the first year after your divorce.

Don't Say Yes when You Want to Say No (Assertiveness Training Book), by Fensterheim and Baer. An excellent workbook for the intimidated spouse.

Explaining Divorce to Children, edited by Earl A. Grollman. Written for parents and professionals as a guidebook explaining the effects of divorce upon the personality development of a child. This book will teach you how to talk to children about divorce.

Getting Free, by Ginny NiCarthy, M.S.W. The best book we have found for female victims of emotional and physical abuse. Helpful, nonjudgmental, and empowering.

How to Survive the Loss of a Love, by Melba Colgrove, Ph.D., Harold Bloomfield, M.D., and Peter McWilliams. This book provides many hints about ways to allow you to cope with divorce.

The Intimate Enemy, by Bach and Wyden. A readable guide that examines our fears of intimacy and deep relationships.

The Kid's Book of Divorce, written by twenty children of divorced families. This book is a child-to-child guide and should be available from your local library.

Living with Loss, by Dr. Ronald W. Ramsay and Rene Noorberger.

Making Contact, by Virginia Satir. A quasi-academic work on establishing or re-establishing relationships with oneself or others.

Male Mid-Life Crisis, by Nancy Mayer. A focused inquiry into problems faced by fortyish males with helpful suggestions for maintaining relationships while growing.

Marital Separation, by Robert Weiss. A classic sociological work. Heavy reading, but worth the effort.

Mom's House, Dad's House, by Isolina Ricci. This book will help parents to deal with shared custody effectively.

Part-time Father, by Edith Atkin and Estelle Rubin. This book is a guide for the divorced father to help him understand what he will encounter with his chidren, and how to deal with it.

Passages, by Gail Sheehy. A classic on the life phases of people.

P.E.T. Parent Effectiveness Training, by Thomas Gordon. A simple yet profound guide to parent-child communication.

Please Understand Me, by David Kersey and Marilyn Bates. Helps you self-administer the Myers-Briggs Type Indicator Test to determine your personality type.

The Seasons of a Man's Life, by Daniel Levinson. A helpful guide to the life phases faced by men.

Sharing Parenthood after Divorce, by Ciji Ware. An excellent, practical guide to the advantages and disadvantages of shared custody.

Type Talk, by Otto Kroeger and Janet M. Thiersen. A workbook to help you understand how you perceive and relate to others in your life, your loves, and your work.

When Parents Divorce: A New Approach to New Relationships, by Bernard Steinzor. This book will help you deal with the fears and anxieties surrounding the breaking up of a home. Dr. Steinzor shows how today's divorces need no longer be surrounded with hopelessness and a sense of loss — and he means this for both parent and child.

Where is Daddy? The Story of a Divorce, by Beth Goff. Written for young children, ages two to five, this book is a read-aloud with lots of drawings. It tells the story of a little girl and what happened to her when her parents divorced and Daddy wasn't there anymore.

Women and Anxiety, by Helen A. DeRosis, M.D. A quasi-academic study, but worth the effort.

Women in Transition (Feminist Handbook on Separation and Divorce), Women in Transition, Inc. A very encouraging work.

APPENDIX C
BILL OF RIGHTS
FOR CHILDREN OF DIVORCE

1. The right to be treated as important human beings, with unique feelings, ideas, and desires and not as a source of argument between parents.

2. The right to a continuing relationship with both parents and the freedom to receive love from and express love for both.

3. The right to express love and affection for each parent without having to stifle that love because of fear of disapproval by the other parent.

4. The right to know that their parents' decision to divorce is not their responsibility and that they will live with one parent and will visit the other parent.

5. The right to continuing care and guidance from both parents.

6. The right to honest answers to questions about the changing family relationships.

7. The right to know and appreciate what is good in each parent without one parent degrading the other.

8. The right to have a relaxed, secure relationship with both parents without being placed in a position to manipulate one parent against the other.

9. The right to have the residential parent not undermine the nonresidential parent's time with the children by suggesting tempting alternatives or by threatening to withhold the non-residential parent's time as a punishment for the children's wrongdoing.

10. The right to be able to experience regular and consistent time with each parent, and the right to know the reason for a canceled time.

Developed by the staff of Family Court Counseling Service, Dane County, Wisconsin, 1974; modified by the authors.

KING COUNTY FAMILY COURT SERVICES ACCESS GUIDELINES

Family Court Visitation Guidelines were first developed in July 1974 in response to a request by the Family Law Section of the Seattle/King County Bar Association. The guidelines subsequently have been revised to reflect current practice knowledge and research findings about the best interests of children after divorce and/or separation.

The implementation of the Washington State Parenting Act in 1988 creates new models and terminology for divorcing families and family law practitioners. The guidelines reflect these new concepts and seek to guide families in the development of a reasonable and child-centered residential schedule. As policy, the law recognizes the fundamental importance of the parent-child relationship to the welfare of the child and that the relationship between the child and each parent should be fostered unless inconsistent with the child's best interests.

Family Court Services' collective experience tells us that families and their legal advocates need current information which is both focused on the needs of children and relevant to today's families. The guidelines are based on child development theory and on research regarding children of divorce. This guide is offered to help identify the type of residential schedule suited to the needs of each child. The guidelines only provide some of the information that may be needed, but do present some of the possibilities for a schedule. They should not, however, be considered rules, laws, or be used rigidly.

The guidelines which follow focus on the child's needs and abilities as suggested by stages of child development. *However, these suggestions should not be applied without giving due consideration to a range of other factors,* including:

- The existence of conditions which may require restriction of access pursuant to RCW 26.09.191

- The quality of the relationship between the children and each parent as well as the history of parenting

- The ability of the parents to cooperate with each other

- The unique cultural and circumstantial needs of families

THE CHILD'S NEEDS

Some divorced parents are able to flexibly change residential schedules as children grow and their needs change. These families do not need intervention by the legal system or other helping professionals. For other families there will be conflict and these guidelines may be helpful in identifying residential schedules which best suit the needs of each child.

It must be recognized that a child is often influenced by the primary residential parent and/or step-parent. It is essential that these persons support an ongoing relationship with the other parent. Both parents should help the child know that it is normal and healthy to feel positively about both parents and to enjoy time with each.

In understanding the needs of children at different ages it is useful to organize the relevant information into age-related stages. However, it should be emphasized that stage-related plans do not take into account the sometimes significant individual differences between children of the same age. Specific problems and exceptions may require professional consultation. The six developmental stages used here are: infant, toddler, pre-schooler, early elementary, late elementary, and adolescent.

DEVELOPMENTAL ASPECTS

Infants (Birth to Eighteen Months)

(**Birth to Six Months**) For the baby it is essential to have consistency of physical care and sensitive, cooperative interaction between the infant and the care-giver. The pattern of access should not interrupt the ability of the parents to provide smooth child-care routines. Access periods should occur frequently enough to facilitate good bonding between the infant and parents. Daily contact of a few hours in the primary residence of the infant would be the optimal plan with both parents sharing in feeding, bathing, changing, and otherwise caring for the infant as well as playing with the child.

Ideally, both parents are committed to the infant developing a good relationship with both parents. While parental cooperation is important at any age, parental cooperation is the crucial fact affecting what plan can be used during infancy. When parents are unable to restrain themselves from engaging in open conflict, access periods should occur somewhere other than in the home of the residential parent. Special family circumstances may require that access periods occur in a protected setting or in the office of a mental health professional.

During early infancy frequent and predictable contact with the child is best. Unless circumstances allow several contacts a week, time with the child away from the residential parent should be limited to one or two hours.

(Six to Eighteen Months) The forming of secure attachment relationships is the major issue at this age. The most important features of care giving are stability and responsiveness. Young children can quickly lose feelings of attachment to people they do not frequently see.

As for younger infants, the more frequent and stable the pattern of access, the longer it can be. If frequency is less than once or twice a week, access should not be more than one to three hours. Children this age need routine contact with familiar people. Overnights away from the primary care giver should be discouraged unless the instability for the child is outweighed by other factors.

Toddlers (Eighteen Months to Three Years)

Children during this period are developing a sense of separateness from the parents and learning to master limits. The child should be given adequate freedom to explore and permission to resist the parent on unimportant issues, but must be required to obey in areas of safety, self-control, and social interaction.

While frequency and consistency are still important, children of this age can handle a schedule of access which provides less frequent contact. An eighteen-month-old child who is with the other parent only on weekends can handle parts of a day. For older toddlers, when the non-residential parent has been a regular and significant caretaker, an overnight per week is possible once the child has become accustomed to the other parent's surroundings. Weekend long access is still not recommended.

Pre-Schoolers (Three to Five Years)

Pre-school children are developing sex role identification and peer relationships as well as learning to manage their impulses. Parents need to model clear roles and values and to use effective parenting skills.

The level of conflict between parents appears to be more important than the schedule of contact for pre-school children. Almost as important is the predictability of the contact. Frequent contact also is indicated. Sporadic, infrequent access is clearly contra-indicated.

Weekly access consisting of one overnight for younger pre-schoolers and full weekends for older preschoolers throughout the year is recommended. More frequent contact is recommended assuming a low level of conflict between the parents. A few week-long contacts for holidays and summer vacations can be handled well. If practicalities dictate periods longer than a week at a time, the parents should obtain specialized consultation on helping children handle the lengthier time frames.

Early Elementary Age (Five to Nine Years)

For children this age the primary influence of the parents is now shared with teachers, peers, and, often, community contacts. Schedules of access need to take into account various organized activities in which children may be involved.

The recommended schedule is a minimum of two weekends per month, and, assuming the parents get along reasonably well, more frequent access including midweek contacts. At seven to eight years of age children who have contact with the non-residential parent several times a week are most satisfied with the access pattern.

Extended time with the other parent is more feasible at this age because of the child's developed sense of time. Up to six weeks may be appropriate, but should not necessarily be taken all at one time. When the child is staying for long periods with the non-residential parent, contact with the residential parent should be arranged.

Later Elementary Age (Nine to Twelve Years)

The pattern for this age group can be much the same as for ages five to nine. However it should be recognized that children of this age generally need definite involvement in the decisions affecting them. Also, by ages eleven to twelve, their friends and school involvements have increased importance which may lead children to want less contact with the parents and a more flexible schedule of contact.

Adolescents (Twelve or Over)

(Twelve to Fifteen Years) The younger adolescent needs more support and guidance from parents than does the older one. The recommended schedule is much the same as for ages nine to twelve with recognition that the younger adolescent needs to be able to opt out of occasional contacts or vary from the schedule.

(Fifteen to Sixteen Years) The schedule for older adolescents should be mutually established between the teen and the non-residential parent. The schedule for adolescents should take into account that teenagers do not need contact of long duration with either parent, but need to know they can count on both parents. At least brief contact on a weekly or every other week basis is strongly recommended for the teenager and non-residential parent.

It should be noted that there is no legally designated age at which children have the right to decide with whom they live or whether or not they will have time with the other parent. In practice the adolescent's need for autonomy should be balanced against the child's sometimes unfelt need for at least minimal contact with both parents. It should be noted that spending a full weekend with a parent may be experienced by some teenagers as being grounded.

HOLIDAYS

In addition to the suggested routine schedules, provisions are needed for specific holiday access which should be structured according to the family's traditions. Religious or other holidays with significance to the family should be defined and stated in the legal decree. Sharing of time should be the paramount consideration. For example, major holidays such as Thanksgiving, Christmas, and Fourth of July can be alternated. Some parents find it preferable to establish a tradition of Christmas Eve in one home and Christmas Day in the other. Minor holidays which are adjacent to the access weekends can be included in those weekends. School vacations, winter and spring, can be divided between the parents in ways consistent with the children's needs. It should be understood that holidays and special occasions spelled out in a residential schedule take precedence over the routine schedule.

DISTANCE

The residential schedule recommendations will often not be workable when the parents are geographically distant from one another. In those situations, the child's need for a relationship with both parents will have to be met with individualized access programs.

If a pre-school child can separate from the residential parent, extended time with the other parent may be appropriate. When the child reaches school age, consideration may be given to the child spending major portions of school vacations with the non-residential parent.

RESOURCE INFORMATION

The following books are suggested for parents who need more information about developing a plan for their children following separation and divorce:

Interventions for Children of Divorce—Custody, Access, and Psychotherapy, by William F. Hodges.

Mom's House/Dad's House, by Isolina Ricci.

Second Chances—Men, Women, and Children a Decade After Divorce, by Judith S. Wallerstein and Sandra Blakes Lee.

Sharing Parenthood After Divorce, by Ciji Ware.

Sharing the Children: How to Resolve Custody Problems and Get On With Your Life, by Robert E. Adler.

Surviving the Breakup: How Children and Parents Cope With Divorce, by Judith Wallerstein and John B. Kelly.

The Parent's Book About Divorce, by Richard Gardner.

101 Ways to be a Long Distance Super-Dad, by Newman.

APPENDIX E
LEGAL DOCUMENTS FOR DISSOLUTION OF MARRIAGE

IN THE SUPERIOR COURT OF THE STATE OF WASHINGTON
FOR KING COUNTY

In re the Marriage of)	
)	NO. 90-3-00000-0
MARY ELLEN JEFFREY,)	
)	SUMMONS FOR
Petitioner,)	DISSOLUTION
)	OF MARRIAGE
and)	
)	
JAMES L. JEFFREY,)	
)	
Respondent.)	
_____)	

TO THE RESPONDENT, **JAMES L. JEFFREY**: The Petitioner has started an action in the above court requesting that your marriage be dissolved. Additional requests, if any, are stated in the petition, a copy of which is attached to this summons.

You must respond to this summons and petition by serving a copy of your written response on the person signing this summons. If you do not serve your written response within 20 days after the date this summons was served on you, exclusive of the day of service, the court may enter an order of default against you, and at the end of 90 days after service and filing, the court may, without further notice to you, enter a decree dissolving your marriage and approving or providing for other relief requested in the petition. If you serve a notice of appearance on the undersigned person, you are entitled to notice before an order of default or a decree may be entered.

You may demand that the petitioner file this action with the court. If you do so, the demand must be in writing and must be served upon the person signing this summons. Within 14 days after you serve the demand, the petitioner must file this action with the court, or the service on you of this summons and petition will be void.

If you wish to seek the advice of an attorney in this matter, you should do so promptly so that your written response, if any, may be served on time.

One method of serving a copy of your response on the petitioner is to send it by certified mail with return receipt requested.

This summons is issued pursuant to rule 4.1 of the Superior Court Civil Rules of the State of Washington.

DATED: this 10th day of January, 1990.

_____
Attorneys for Petitioner

SERVE A COPY OF YOUR
RESPONSE ON:

Name of Attorney
Street Address
City, Washington

IN THE SUPERIOR COURT OF THE STATE OF WASHINGTON
FOR KING COUNTY

In re the Marriage of	)
	) NO. 90-3-00000-0
MARY ELLEN JEFFREY,	)
	) PETITION FOR
Petitioner,	) DISSOLUTION OF MARRIAGE
	) (RCW 26.09.020)
and	)
	)
JAMES L. JEFFREY,	)
	)
Respondent.	)
_____	)

COMES NOW the Petitioner, being represented by her attorney, Lowell K. Halverson, and petitions this Court for a Decree of Dissolution of Marriage, and states as follows:

I. BASIS

This is a petition for the dissolution of a marriage which is irretrievably broken.

II. PARTIES

2.1 Wife: The last known residence of the wife is: 9102 90th Place Southeast, Mercer Island, Washington 98040.

2.2 Husband: The last known residence of the husband is: 4466 West Mercer Way, Mercer Island, Washington 98040.

2.3 Neither party is in the military service of the United States.

III. MARRIAGE

3.1 Date. We were married on August 20, 1974, at Seattle, Washington.

3.2 Registration. Our marriage was registered in King County, Washington.

IV. SEPARATION

We were separated on August 16, 1989.

V. DEPENDENT CHILDREN

5.1 The names and birthdates of our dependent children are: Justin David Jeffrey, born May 1, 1977; and Kristin Jeffrey, born December 2, 1980.

5.2 Pregnancy. The wife is not now pregnant.

VI. ARRANGEMENTS REGARDING PARENTING AND VISITATION

6.1 Attached hereto and incorporated herein by this reference as if fully set forth is Petitioner's Proposed Parenting Plan under RCW 26.09.070.

VII. CHILD SUPPORT

7.1 Respondent should pay Petitioner child support in accordance with the Washington State Child Support Schedule.

VIII. MAINTENANCE

8.1 We have not made arrangements as to maintenance of spouse.

IX. PROPERTY

9.1 There is community and separate property to be disposed of which has not been accomplished by an agreement.

PETITION FOR DISSOLUTION OF MARRIAGE - Page 1 of 3

X. LIABILITIES

10.1 The discharge of any liabilities owing has not been provided for by agreement.

XI.
STATEMENT IN ACCORDANCE WITH
UNIFORM CHILD CUSTODY JURISDICTION ACT

11.1 I am a party in this action, requesting custody of the children.

11.2 The present address of the children is:

Child's Name	Address	Currently Residing With
Justin	9102 90th Place S.E. Mercer Island, WA 98040	mother
Kristin	9102 90th Place S.E. Mercer Island, WA 98040	mother

3. The above-named children have lived at the following places during the past five years:

Child's Name	Address	With Whom	Current Address of Person Child Was Living With
Justin	9102 90th Pl. S.E. M. I., WA 98040	mother	same
Kristin	9102 90th Pl. S.E. M. I., WA 98040	mother	same

4. I have not participated as a party, witness, or in any other capacity, in any other court case concerning the custody of the above-named children in this or any other state;

5. I have no information of any custody proceeding concerning the children in a court of this or any other state;

6. I do not know of any person not a party to this proceeding who has physical custody of the children or claims to have custody or visitation rights with respect to the children.

7. I acknowledge that if the declaration as to paragraphs 4, 5 or 6 is in the affirmative, I shall be required to give additional information under oath as required by the court. I further acknowledge that I have a continuing duty to inform the court of any custody proceeding concerning the children in this or any other state of which I obtain information.

XII. RELIEF SOUGHT

The court is requested to grant the following relief:

12.1 Enter a Decree of Dissolution.

12.2 Provide child support for the children of the marriage in accordance with the Washington State Child Support Schedule.

12.3 Provide reasonable maintenance for Petitioner.

12.4 Approve the Proposed Parenting Plan submitted by the Petitioner (attached) unless a Parenting Plan is agreed to by both parties.

12.5 Approve Separation Contract.

12.6 Dispose of property and liabilities.

12.7 Change name of wife to Mary Ellen _____.

12.8 Award litigation costs including reasonable attorney fees to attorney for Petitioner.

12.9 Other just and equitable relief.

    DATED: this 10th day of January, 1990.

_____

Attorneys for Petitioner

State of Washington   )

                           : ss.

County of King   )

    Mary Ellen Jeffrey, being first duly sworn upon oath, deposes and says:

    That I have read the foregoing Petition for Dissolution of Marriage, know the contents thereof and believe the same to be true.

    Any notices may be made on the undersigned at: 3030 Island Crest Way, Mercer Island, Washington 98040.

_____

Mary Ellen Jeffrey

    SUBSCRIBED AND SWORN TO before me this 10th day of January, 1990.

_____

NOTARY PUBLIC in and for the State
of Washington, residing at

_____

My commission expires _____

IN THE SUPERIOR COURT OF THE STATE OF WASHINGTON
FOR KING COUNTY

In re the Marriage of	)	
	)	NO. 90-3-00000-0
MARY ELLEN JEFFREY,	)	
	)	PETITIONER'S PROPOSED
Petitioner,	)	PARENTING PLAN
	)	
and	)	
	)	
JAMES L. JEFFREY,	)	
	)	
Respondent.	)	
	)	

We, the parents of Justin and Kristin, enter into this Agreement in order to better meet our parental responsibilities and to safeguard our children's future development. We both recognize that Justin and Kristin wish to love and respect both of us, regardless of our marital status or our place of residence, and that Justin's and Kristin's welfare can best be served by our mutual cooperation as partners in parenting and by each of us providing a home in which the children are loved and to which each child belongs: their mother's house and their father's house.

I. DECISION MAKING

A. General. Each parent desires to remain responsible and active in Justin's and Kristin's growth and development consistent with the best interest of the children. The parents will make a mutual effort to maintain an open, on-going communication concerning the development, needs and interests of the children and will discuss together any major decisions which have to be made about or for the children.

1. Each parent shall have an equal say in all major decisions. In the event of an irreconcilable conflict, the matter shall be submitted to mediation and, if necessary, arbitration or final disposition on the Family Law Motion Calender, in accordance with paragraph XI below.

2. The residential parent shall have authority to make day-to-day decisions affecting the children's welfare; HOWEVER, major decisions concerning the children's welfare shall not be made without agreement by both parents.

3. Major Decisions. Major decisions are as follows:

1. Non-emergency medical and/or dental care and providers thereof.
2. Change of school not mandated by authorities.
3. Moving the children more than ten (10) miles from their present residence.
4. Choice of care providers.

Before any of the three following events may occur prior to the children's eighteenth (18th) birthday, parents must consent, in writing, to their:

1. Acquisition of a driver's license.
2. Marrying.
3. Entry into any type of military service.

In the event of disagreement each parent has temporary veto power with reference to these three (3) decisions until referral to mediation or Court.

Each parent shall have equal and independent authority to confer with school, day care and other programs with regard to the children's progress and each shall have free access to school, day care and other records. Each parent shall have authority to give parental consent or permission as may be required concerning school, day care or other programs for the children while the children are in his or her custody.

Each parent agrees to honor one another's parenting style, privacy, and authority. Neither will interfere in the parenting style of the other, nor will either parent make plans and arrangements that would impinge upon the other parent's authority or time with the children without the express agreement of the other parent. Each parent agrees to encourage the children to discuss his or her grievance with a parent directly with the parent in question. It is the intent of both parents to encourage a direct child-parent bond.

   C. Education.

1. The children shall attend the school mutually agreed upon by the parents, recognizing that the decisions should be made in the best interest of the children's education needs, rather than the needs of the parents.

2. All schools, health care providers and counselors shall be selected by the parents jointly. In the event the parents cannot agree to the selection of a school, the children shall be maintained in the present school, pending mediation and/or further order of the court.

3. Each parent is to provide the other parent promptly upon receipt with information concerning the well-being of the children, including, but not limited to, copies of report cards, school meeting notices, vacation schedules, class programs, requests for conferences, results of standardized or diagnostic tests, notices of activities involving the diagnostic tests, notices of activities involving the children, samples of school work, order forms for school pictures, all communications from health care providers, the names, addresses and telephone numbers of all schools, health care providers, regular day care providers, and counselors.

   D. Health Care.

1. Each parent shall be empowered to obtain emergency health care for the children without the consent of the other parent. Each parent is to notify the other parent as soon as reasonably possible of any illness requiring medical attention, or any emergency involving the children.

2. Each parent shall have equal and independent authority to provide routine and emergency medical and dental services of the children while the children are in his or her care and residence.

3. Major decisions regarding non-routine, non-emergency medical care must be made jointly by the parents.

E. Religious Upbringing.

1. Each parent shall have an equal right to include the children in his or her religious activities and expressions. The children shall have the right to make their own religious choice as they mature.

F. Revisions in Plan.

1. Both parents acknowledge that as the children grow and change, revisions may be required in the Plan and, though unable to predict such revisions, agree to remain flexible with respect to access, parental responsibility, etc. Both parents agree that adjustments shall be made without showing substantial change in circumstances.

II. RESIDENTIAL ARRANGEMENTS

A. School Year Schedules. From one week prior to the commencement of the child's school year through the Saturday following its conclusion, the following shall be the children's residential arrangements:

The children shall reside with father on the first, third, and fifth weekends of each month from 5:30 p.m. Friday evening through 8:00 p.m. Sunday evening, and with the other parent the remainder of the time. The weekends shall be extended if they include a holiday.

B. Summer Schedule. The residential arrangements of the children during the summer of the year shall be as follows:

The children shall reside with the father for six uninterrupted weeks during the summer school vacation. Proposed dates should be submitted by the father prior to April 15 each year.

C. Holidays. The children's holiday time shall be allocated as follows:

1. During odd-numbered years, the children shall reside with the father on President's Day, Fourth of July and Thanksgiving.

2. During even-numbered years, the children shall reside with the mother on President's Day, Fourth of July and Thanksgiving.

3. During even-numbered years, the children shall reside with the father on Memorial Day, Labor Day, Veteran's Day, and Easter.

4. During odd-numbered years, the children shall reside with the mother on Memorial Day, Labor Day, Veteran's Day, and Easter.

5. The parent having the children for the weekend immediately before or after a national holiday shall have the weekend time expanded to include such holiday.

6. Thanksgiving shall be defined as beginning at 5:00 p.m., Wednesday preceding Thanksgiving until 7:00 p.m., Sunday following Thanksgiving.

III. BIRTHDAYS AND SPECIAL FAMILY DAYS

A. The children shall celebrate their birthdays with their mother in even-numbered years, and with their father in odd-numbered years.

B. The non-residential parent shall be allowed to spend some time with the child to celebrate the children's birthdays, within a week of that birthday.

C. The mother shall have the children every year for Mother's Day and the father shall have the children every year for Father's Day from 9:00 a.m. to 6:00 p.m.

IV. VACATIONS, CHRISTMAS/WINTER AND SPRING BREAK

A. The children shall spend a portion of the Christmas school holiday from the first day of school vacation until 10 a.m. Christmas Day with the father in even-numbered years, and with the mother in odd-numbered years.

B. The children shall spend every other Spring vacation as defined by the school schedule, with the father.

V. PARENT'S VACATIONS

A. In addition to the other arrangements, each parent shall have the children for vacation purposes during that parent's scheduled vacation from work for up to two weeks each year provided that 30 days notice is given to the other parent and provided that such vacation time does not conflict with the children's school schedule. Each parent shall endeavor to arrange their vacation during the summer months, if possible.

VI. TELEPHONE ACCESS

A. The children shall have liberal telephone privileges with the parent with whom they are not then residing without interference of the residential parent.

VII. PARTICIPATION IN CHILDREN'S EVENTS

A. Children shall be accompanied by the parent with whom they are residing at the time of a given social event. The other parent shall not be limited from attendance at that event, providing said attendance by the non-residential parent is not disruptive to the other participants.

B. Each parent shall be responsible for keeping themselves advised of school, athletic, and social events in which the children participate. Both parents may participate in school activities for the children such as open house, attendance at an athletic event, etc.

VIII. REMOVAL OF CHILDREN FROM STATE

A. A parent shall not remove the residence of the children from the State of Washington except by the advance written approval of the other parent or by court order entered after notice of hearing having been given to the other parent.

IX. TRANSPORTATION

A. Responsibility for providing transportation shall be divided between the parents. Each parent shall be responsible for providing transportation to his or her home.

B. The children shall be picked up and returned at the designated times. Should a delay become necessary, the receiving parent shall be notified immediately.

C. The father shall be responsible for all transportation in connection with his exercise of visitation. Both parents shall share responsibility for transportation to and from the children's games, practices, and cultural enrichment activities.

X. OTHER

A. It is the responsibility of the parent scheduled to have the children to arrange suitable alternative care if necessary and pay for needed care.

B. Each parent shall notify the other parent at least 48 hours in advance if he/she is unable to exercise the regular schedule.

XI. DISPUTE RESOLUTION

A. Any decision concerning the children shall be made only after consideration is given to the needs, feelings, and desires of the children.

B. In the event that there are difficulties or differences of opinion between the parents regarding provisions for the children, the matter shall be referred to a private mediator chosen by the parties.

C. Notice. Parents shall notify the other in writing of a request for mediation and mediation shall commence within 10 days thereafter.

D. Writing. If an agreement is reached through mediation, it shall be reduced to writing and shall become part of the Parenting Plan.

E. In the event the parties are unable to agree on a private mediator, the matter shall be referred to the King County Family Law Motion Calendar for designation of a mediator. Should mediation not be successful in resolving the dispute, the same may be referred to the King County Superior Court Family Law Motion Calendar for final resolution.

F. In undertaking this dispute resolution process, the parents agree:

1. That preference shall be given to carrying out the parenting plan;

2. That the parents shall use the designated process to resolve the disputes relating to implementation of the plan, except those related to financial support, unless an emergency exists;

3. If the court finds that a parent has used or frustrated the dispute resolution process without good reason, the court shall award attorneys' fees and financial sanctions to the prevailing party; and

4. The parents have the right of review from the dispute resolution process to the superior court.

XII. RESIDENTIAL DESIGNATION (JURISDICTIONAL ONLY)

A. The following designations shall not affect either parent's rights or responsibilities under this Plan:

1. The children's residence for the purposes of jurisdiction, venue and child support only is that of the mother.

2. The children's custodian for the sole purpose of compliance with all other state and federal laws is the mother.

XIII. FINANCIAL SUPPORT

A. Major Expenses. Prior to either parent obligating any parent for major expenses on behalf of the children, such as orthodontia expenses, private educational expenses, tutoring, or other expenses in excess of the day-to-day standard expenses for public school children, the parents shall in good faith attempt to amicably reach an agreement on the subject.

B. Health Care Insurance; Uninsured Expense. Both parents shall continue to carry all health care insurance as may be available through their respective employment, provided that the employer or other organization pays part or all of the premium. Mother shall pay 30% and father shall pay 70% of all uninsured medical, dental, optical, and orthodontic expenses for the children. The parents shall cooperate in the prompt processing of all insurance claims and reimburse the other for all out of pocket expenditures.

C. <u>Duration of Support.</u> Child support for each child shall continue until such child is 18 years old, or graduates from high school, whichever occurs later, provided that support continues through September of the year of graduation if the child is enrolled for college. In no event shall support continue past the child's 19th birthday.

D. <u>Support Amount.</u> Based upon the present financial circumstances and joint parenting arrangements of the parents, the father shall pay to the mother the sum of $1,375 per month as child support for the two children, payable on or before the fifth (5th) day of each month. The monthly support provided herein shall be adjusted beginning March 1, 1991 and each successive year on March 1 based upon both parents' earned income from all sources and utilizing the Washington State Child Support Schedule, as now or hereafter amended.

E. <u>Dispute Resolution.</u> Disputes in applying the Schedule or any other financial matters affecting the children shall be mediated or referred to court for final resolution, in accordance with paragraph XI above.

F. <u>Life Insurance as Security.</u> The father shall maintain a policy of decreasing term life insurance on his life payable for the benefit of the children in the initial face amount of $100,000 during the time that he is still obligated to pay support. In the event there is insufficient life insurance (less social benefits or other entitlements payable for the children due to the father's death) to support his obligations, the mother shall have a continuing claim against the father's estate, which shall survive his death and which shall be treated with the same statutory priority as an Award of Homestead.

G. <u>Exemptions.</u> So long as he is current in his support obligation the father shall be entitled to claim the younger child as an exemption for IRS reporting purposes and the mother shall execute appropriate forms for this purpose. So long as there is a continuing support obligation, the parents shall exchange authenticated copies of tax returns upon request.

H. <u>College Expense.</u> Each parent shall contribute to the children's post-secondary educational expenses taking into consideration the income and expenses and other resources of each parent at the time and the ability of the children to obtain loans and scholarships and to work part-time. In no event shall a parent's obligation exceed that for a student attending the University of Washington full-time; nor shall the obligation extend beyond the child's 23rd birthday. Both parents agree that the Court shall retain jurisdiction for the purpose of adjudicating the parents' college expense obligation if they are unable to agree.

XIV. PAYMENT OF SUPPORT

Family:

Mother:	Father:
Mary Ellen Jeffrey	James L. Jeffrey
9102 90th Place Southeast	4466 West Mercer Way
Mercer Island, WA 98040	Mercer Island, WA 98040
Child: Justin	d.o.b. 5/1/77, age 12
Child: Kristin	d.o.b. 12/2/80, age 9

PETITIONER'S PROPOSED PARENTING PLAN - Page 6 of 8

Social Security Numbers:

Mother: 532-38-0955 Father: 501-55-4682

Justin: 599-33-0324 Kristin: 501-22-2441

Employer Address:

Mother: Father:

Bank of California Jeffrey Limited

Bank of California Center 4466 West Mercer Way

Seattle, WA 98105 Mercer Island, WA 98040

Monthly Net Income:

Mother: $ 0 Father: $ 4,224

Parent Who Will Pay Support: father

Parent Who Will Receive Support: mother

Monthly Support Amount to be paid: $1,375

Payment Due Date: the 15th day of each month

Basic child support payment shall be paid directly to the mother.

Other payments (such as child care costs) shall be made directly to the mother.

NOTICE: Both parents are shall maintain any health insurance on their minor children herein which is available through a present or future employer or other organization provided that the employer pays part or all of the premium.

NOTICE: If a support payment is more than fifteen (15) days past due in an amount equal to or greater than the support payable for one month, a Notice of Payroll Deduction may be issued or other withholding action under RCW Chapters 26.18 or 74.20A without prior notice to the person who is obligated to pay support.

NOTICE: Each parent listed above shall promptly notify the Washington State Support Registry of any changes of address of themselves or their employment.

XV. COMPLIANCE WITH THE PLAN

A. If a parent fails to comply with a provision of this Plan the other parent's obligations under the Plan are not affected.

B. If a support payment as provided for is more than 15 days past due in an amount equal to or greater than the support payable for one month, the person entitled to receive support may seek a mandatory wage assignment without prior notice to the person who is obligated to pay support.

C. Violation of Restraining Orders set forth in this Plan or Order may constitute a civil contempt and/or a criminal misdemeanor.

XVI. ACKNOWLEDGEMENTS

Both parents acknowledge by their signatures below that they are in agreement and have a copy of this plan.

DATED: this 10th day of January, 1990.

_____	_____
Mary Ellen Jeffrey,	James L. Jeffrey,
Petitioner	Respondent

IN THE SUPERIOR COURT OF THE STATE OF WASHINGTON
FOR KING COUNTY

In re the Marriage of	)	
	)	NO. 90-3-00000-0
MARY ELLEN JEFFREY,	)	
	)	MOTION FOR TEMPORARY
Petitioner,	)	RESTRAINING ORDER
	)	AND ORDER TO SHOW CAUSE
and	)	
	)	(Clerk's Action Required)
JAMES L. JEFFREY,	)	
	)	
Respondent.	)	
	)	

RELIEF REQUESTED

Petitioner respectfully moves the Court for an Order restraining both parties from:

(1) Selling, transferring, giving away, mortgaging, secreting, encumbering, destroying, damaging or in any manner disposing of any of the property of either party;

(2) Withdrawing any monies from any savings account, cashing in any securities, selling or assigning any negotiable instruments or contracts;

(3) Withdrawing any monies from any checking account, except in the ordinary course of business or for the necessities of life;

(4) Dissipating any of the community funds and from incurring any obligations except in the ordinary course of business;

(5) Canceling, surrendering, borrowing on or impairing in any manner any insurance policy, pension or retirement plan owned by these parties or either of them;

(6) Canceling, impairing or changing the medical and/or dental or life insurance coverage presently in effect for the benefit of these parties and any dependent children of these parties;

(7) Removing any furniture, furnishings, or other items from the family home, other than Respondent's clothing and personal effects, without an Order of the Court;

(8) Harassing, bothering or molesting the other party, pending the hearing of this Motion;

(9) Telephoning or appearing in person at the other parties' place of employment;

(10) Entering the safety deposit box of either or both parties except by mutual consent; and

(11) Incurring any debt unless the incurring party assumes sole responsibility therefore.

and, further, for an Order requiring the Respondent to appear and show cause, if any he has, why:

(1) The restraining orders set out above should not remain in full force and effect pending termination of this action;

(2) He should not be required to pay maintenance to Petitioner in the amount of $1000 per month retroactive to January 1, 1990;

(3) He should not be required to pay child support to Petitioner in accordance with the Washington State Child Support Schedule retroactive to January 1, 1990;

(4) Based upon the separation on August 16, 1989, Petitioner should not be confirmed in exclusive possession and control of the family home; and

(5) The temporary parenting arrangements of the parties should not be as set forth in the attached parenting plan of Petitioner pending further order of this Court; and

(6) He should not be required to pay $1000 to Petitioner's attorney as temporary attorney fees and costs.

STATEMENT OF FACTS

Petitioner seeks to maintain and protect the status quo until a court hearing with both parties in attendance may be had.

STATEMENT OF ISSUES

This motion does not present an issue of law before the court, but depends upon the court's discretion to protect the status quo.

EVIDENCE RELIED UPON

The evidence relied upon is set out in the declaration of Petitioner.

AUTHORITY

This motion is made pursuant to CR 7 and CR 65.

Petitioner moves that the temporary restraining orders requested above be entered without the giving of security in accordance with the provisions of C.R. 65(c) for the reason that irreparable injury may result unless the restraining order is entered immediately, as set forth in the declaration filed herewith.

THIS MOTION is based on the files and records herein and on the declaration filed herewith.

DATED: this 10th day of January, 1990.

_____
Attorneys for Petitioner

IN THE SUPERIOR COURT OF THE STATE OF WASHINGTON
FOR KING COUNTY

In re the Marriage of	)	
	)	NO. 90-3-00000-0
MARY ELLEN JEFFREY,	)	
	)	TEMPORARY RESTRAINING
Petitioner,	)	ORDER AND ORDER TO
	)	SHOW CAUSE
and	)	
	)	
JAMES L. JEFFREY,	)	
	)	
Respondent.	)	
	)	

Upon the Motion and Declaration of Petitioner, and for good cause shown, it is hereby ORDERED that both parties be and are hereby restrained from:

(1) Selling, transferring, giving away, mortgaging, secreting, encumbering, destroying, damaging or in any manner disposing of any of the property of either party;

(2) Withdrawing any monies from any savings account, cashing on any securities, selling, or assigning any negotiable instruments or contracts;

(3) Withdrawing any monies from any checking account, except in the ordinary course of business or for the necessities of life;

(4) Dissipating any of the community funds and from incurring any obligations except in the ordinary course of business;

(5) Canceling, surrendering, borrowing on or impairing in any manner any insurance policy, pension or retirement plan owned by these parties or either of them;

(6) Canceling, impairing or changing the medical and/or dental or life insurance coverage presently in effect for the benefit of these parties and any dependent children of these parties;

(7) Removing any furniture, furnishings, or other items from the family home, other than respondent's clothing and personal effects, without an Order of the Court;

(8) Harassing, bothering or molesting the other party, pending the hearing of this motion;

(9) Telephoning or appearing in person at the other parties' place of employment;

(10) Entering the safety deposit box of either or both parties except by mutual consent; and

(11) Incurring any debt unless the incurring party assumes sole responsibility therefore.

NOTICE: VIOLATION OF THE TERMS OF THE RESTRAINING ORDER SET OUT ABOVE CAN BE A CRIMINAL OFFENSE. PUNISHABLE IN ACCORDANCE WITH SECTION 26.09 OF THE REVISED CODE OF WASHINGTON.
and it is further

ORDERED that pursuant to RCW 26.09.060(6), the Clerk of the court shall forward a copy of this temporary restraining order on or before the next judicial day to the King County Sheriff's Office and said law enforcement agency shall forthwith enter the order for one year into their computer based law enforcement information system;
and it is further

ORDERED that respondent be, and is hereby ordered to appear personally or by attorney before the Family Law Motion Judge/Court Commissioner, Room W-291, of the King County Courthouse, Third and James, Seattle, Washington, at 9:30 a.m. on the 25th day of January, 1990, then and there to show cause, if any there be, why

(1) The restraining orders set out above should not remain in full force and effect pending termination of this action;

(2) He should not be required to pay maintenance to Petitioner in the amount of $1,000 per month retroactive to January 1, 1990;

(3) He should not be required to pay child support to Petitioner in accordance with the Washington State Child Support Schedule retroactive to January 1, 1990;

(4) Based upon the separation on August 16, 1989, Petitioner should not be confirmed in exclusive possession and control of the family home;

(5) The temporary parenting arrangements of the parties should not be as set forth in the attached parenting plan of Petitioner pending further order of this Court; and

(6) He should not be required to pay $1,000 to Petitioner's attorney as temporary attorney fees and costs.

and it is further

ORDERED that this temporary restraining order issue to prevent the occurrence of irreparable injury and damage; and that it be effective for a period longer than fourteen days in order to assure proper service and a suitable period for the responding party to prepare his answer; and that the restraining order shall issue without the giving of security by the applicant in with the provisions of C.R. 65(c); it is further

ORDERED that service of this Restraining Order and Order to Show Cause may be effectuated as follows: if the party is represented by an attorney, by service of a conformed copy upon said attorney. If said party has not appeared through an attorney, then by service upon him of a conformed copy hereof.

If you fail to appear in person and/or by an attorney and answer this application, the relief as described in the Motion may be granted.

DONE IN OPEN COURT this 10th day of January, 1990.

_____
JUDGE/COURT COMMISSIONER

Presented by:

_____
Attorneys for Petitioner

IN THE SUPERIOR COURT OF THE STATE OF WASHINGTON
FOR KING COUNTY

In re the Marriage of)	NO. 90-3-00000-0
)	
MARY ELLEN JEFFREY,)	DECLARATION OF PETITIONER
)	IN SUPPORT OF TEMPORARY
Petitioner,)	PARENTING PLAN
)	
and)	
)	
JAMES L. JEFFREY,)	
)	
Respondent.)	
)	

I, MARY ELLEN JEFFREY, certify under penalty of perjury under the laws of the State of Washington that the following is true and correct.

1. I am the Petitioner in the above-captioned case and have personal knowledge of the facts set forth herein, and am competent to testify to the same.

2. The following statement is true and correct to my knowledge and belief.

3. The name, address, and length of residence with the person or persons with whom the children have lived for the preceding twelve months is:

The children have resided with Mary Ellen and James L. Jeffrey at 9102 90th Place Southeast, Mercer Island, Washington 98040 for the preceding twelve months.

4. The performance by each parent during the last twelve months of the parenting functions relating to the daily needs of the children:

I have performed most of the parenting functions relating to the daily needs of the children for the past twelve months. Since my husband works, he does not have as much time as I do to tend to the children's needs.

5. The parents' work and child-care schedules for the preceding twelve months:

My husband works all day and often brings work home with him at night. I do not work therefore I have provided the bulk of the child-care for the preceding twelve months.

6. The parents' current work and child-care schedules:

I do not work and I continue to provide most of the child-care. My husband works a lot and he spends time with the children when he has time.

7. Any of the circumstances set forth in RCW 26.09.191 that are likely to pose a serious risk to the children and that warrant limitation on the award to a parent of temporary residence or time with the children pending entry of a permanent parenting plan:

None.

DATED: this 10th day of January, 1990.

_____
Mary Ellen Jeffrey

DECLARATION OF PETITIONER IN SUPPORT OF
TEMPORARY PARENTING PLAN - Page 1 of 1

IN THE SUPERIOR COURT OF THE STATE OF WASHINGTON
FOR KING COUNTY

In re the Marriage of	)	
	)	NO. 90-3-00000-0
MARY ELLEN JEFFREY,	)	
	)	DECLARATION OF PETITIONER
Petitioner,	)	IN SUPPORT OF TEMPORARY
	)	RESTRAINING ORDER AND
and	)	ORDER TO SHOW CAUSE
	)	
JAMES L. JEFFREY,	)	
	)	
Respondent.	)	
_____	)	

I, MARY ELLEN JEFFREY, certify under penalty of perjury under the laws of the State of Washington that the following is true and correct.

1.   I am the Petitioner in the above-captioned case and have personal knowledge of the facts set forth herein, and am competent to testify to the same.

2.   The following statement is true and correct to my knowledge and belief.

3.   *The children and I need support from my husband in order to live day to day.* We have no independent source of income. At the signing of this statement, I have $212.57 in my checking account. That will barely pay for our food bills for two weeks. We have no money left over for gas, utilities, monthly bills, or emergencies. The children and I need a minimum of $2,180 a month temporary support for just our food, children's clothing and expenses, and utilities. I ask that my husband continue to pay for our mortgage, insurance, credit card charges and any doctor bills that the children and I might incur.

4.   *My husband brings home over $4,200 per month.* I don't have an income because it was always understood that my place was in the home raising the children and making life comfortable for the family. Therefore, I have no money and no means to earn any. At the same time, my husband controls over $7,000 in our savings and $27,000 in stocks. He knows what it costs to maintain the house, feed and clothe the children, and pay for all of their activities. He should be responsible for supporting those costs until I am trained and able to find suitable employment.

5.   *There is too much conflict in the family home if my husband lives there with us.* Therefore, he should be required to stay away from our home unless he is visiting the children.

6.   *I have no independent money to pay my attorney,* so it is necessary for my husband to pay temporary attorney fees for me.

DATED: this 10th day of January, 1990 in Seattle, Washington.

_____
Mary Ellen Jeffrey

DECLARATION OF PETITIONER IN SUPPORT OF
TEMPORARY ORDER AND RESTRAINING ORDERS - Page 1 of 1

IN THE SUPERIOR COURT OF THE STATE OF WASHINGTON
FOR KING COUNTY

In re the Marriage of	)	
	)	NO. 90-3-00000-0
MARY ELLEN JEFFREY,	)	
	)	AGREED TEMPORARY
Petitioner,	)	RESTRAINING
	)	ORDERS
and	)	
	)	
JAMES L. JEFFREY,	)	
	)	
Respondent.	)	
	)	

THIS MATTER having come on for hearing before the undersigned Judge/Court Commissioner; Petitioner appearing through her attorney, Lowell K. Halverson; and Respondent appearing pro se; the court having reviewed the files and records herein and the Declaration of Petitioner and deeming itself fully advised in the premises; now, therefore, it is hereby

ORDERED, ADJUDGED AND DECREED as follows:

A.   Both parties be and are hereby restrained from:

(1) Selling, transferring, giving away, mortgaging, secreting, encumbering, destroying, damaging or in any manner disposing of any of the property of either party;

(2) Withdrawing any monies from any savings account, cashing on any securities, selling, or assigning any negotiable instruments or contracts;

(3) Withdrawing any monies from any checking account, except in the ordinary course of business or for the necessities of life;

(4) Dissipating any of the community funds and from incurring any obligations except in the ordinary course of business;

(5) Canceling, surrendering, borrowing on or impairing in any manner any insurance policy, pension or retirement plan owned by these parties or either of them;

(6) Canceling, impairing or changing the medical and/or dental or life insurance coverage presently in effect for the benefit of these parties and any dependent children of these parties;

(7) Removing any furniture, furnishings, or other items from the family home, other than respondent's clothing and personal effects, without an Order of the Court;

(8) Harassing, bothering or molesting the other party;

(9) Telephoning or appearing in person at the other party's place of employment;

(10) Entering the safety deposit box of either or both parties except by mutual consent; and

(11) Incurring any debt unless the incurring party assumes sole responsibility therefore.

NOTICE: VIOLATION OF THE TERMS OF THE RESTRAINING ORDER SET OUT ABOVE CAN BE A CRIMINAL OFFENSE, PUNISHABLE IN ACCORDANCE WITH SECTION 26.09 OF THE REVISED CODE OF WASHINGTON.

B. Pursuant to RCW 26.09.060(6), the Clerk of the court shall forward a copy of this temporary restraining order on or before the next judicial day to the King County Sheriff's Office and said law enforcement agency shall forthwith enter the order for one year into their computer based law enforcement information system.

Petitioner's Birthdate:	7/7/44
Respondent's Birthdate:	9/6/43
Petitioner's Address:	9102 90th Place S.E.
	Mercer Island, WA 98040
Respondent's Address:	4466 West Mercer Way
	Mercer Island, WA 98040
Petitioner's Physical Description:	Petitioner is 5'3" tall with brown hair and brown eyes and weighs approximately 110 lbs.
Respondent's Physical Description:	Respondent is 5'10" tall with black hair and brown eyes and weighs approximately 165 lbs.

C. Petitioner is hereby granted the sole right of occupancy and possession of the family residence pending further order of this Court.

D. The Respondent shall pay the sum of $1,000 as child support per month, retroactive to January 1, 1990 and the 1st day of each month thereafter. The reason for deviation from the Washington State Child Support Schedule relates to tax savings by both parties, as specified in item No. 12 of "Standards for the Determination of Child Support and Use of the Schedule," Washington State Child Support Schedule.

E. The Respondent shall pay the sum of $1,000 as spousal maintenance per month retroactive to January 1, 1990 and the 1st day of each month thereafter. The Respondent shall have no obligation or liability to make any such payment for any period after the death of the Petitioner, and there is no liability provided for herein for the Respondent to make any payment as a substitute for such payments after the death of the Petitioner.

F. The temporary parenting arrangements of the parties shall be as set forth in the attached parenting plan until further order of this Court.

G. The parties shall meet the following mandatory provisions required by the State Support Registry Act 26.23:

(1) Payment of support set forth above shall be paid through:

> Washington State Support Registry
> P.O. Box 9009
> Olympia, Washington 98504

(2) The above mandatory wage assignment complies with RCW 26.18;

(3) The Petitioner's monthly net income is $0. The Respondent's monthly net income is $4,224;

AGREED TEMPORARY RESTRAINING ORDERS - Page 2 of 3

(4) The support amount as set forth above is a sum certain;

(5) The social security number and residence address of the Petitioner is 9102 90th Place Southeast, Mercer Island, Washington, 98040; 532-38-0955;

(6) The social security number and residence address of the Respondent is 4466 West Mercer Way, Mercer Island, Washington, 98040; 501-55-4682;

(7) The names, dates of birth and social security numbers, if applicable, of the parties' dependent children are as follows: Justin, d.o.b. 5/1/77, age 12, 599-33-0324; and Kristin, d.o.b. 12/2/80, age 9, 501-22-2441;

(8) If a support payment is more than fifteen (15) days past due in an amount equal to or greater than the support payable for one month, a Notice of Payroll Deduction may be issued or other withholding action under RCW Chapters 26.18 or 74.20A without prior notice to the person who is obligated to pay support and/or this Order may be submitted to the Washington State Support Registry (P.O. Box 9009, Olympia, Washington 98504) for enforcement. Any receipt of a Support Order by the Washington State Support Registry on behalf of the Petitioner who at the time of submission to the Washington State Support Registry is not a recipient of public assistance shall be deemed to be a request for Support Enforcement Services under RCW 74.20A.040; and

(9) Each parent listed above shall promptly notify the Washington State Support Registry of any changes of address of themselves or their employment.

NOTICE: VIOLATION OF THE TERMS OF THIS ORDER CAN BE A CRIMINAL OFFENSE PUNISHABLE IN ACCORDANCE WITH SECTION 26.09 REVISED CODE OF WASHINGTON.

SO ORDERED: this 23rd day of January, 1990.

_____
Judge/Court Commissioner

Presented by:

_____
Attorneys for Petitioner

Approved for entry;
Notice of Presentation waived:

_____
James L. Jeffrey, Respondent
Pro se

IN THE SUPERIOR COURT OF THE STATE OF WASHINGTON
FOR KING COUNTY

In re the Marriage of	)	
	)	NO. 90-3-00000-0
MARY ELLEN JEFFREY,	)	
	)	RESPONSE TO PETITION FOR
Petitioner,	)	DISSOLUTION OF MARRIAGE
	)	
and	)	
	)	
JAMES L. JEFFREY,	)	
	)	
Respondent.	)	
	)	

COMES NOW the Respondent, JAMES L. JEFFREY, and responds to the Petition for Dissolution of Marriage herein as follows:

I.

Responding to Paragraphs I, II, III, IV, and V, Respondent admits the same.

II.

Responding to Paragraph VI, Respondent admits the same except that Respondent alleges that the children should reside with him and the Petitioner should be granted the residential time granted to him in her proposed parenting plan.

III.

Responding to Paragraphs VII, VIII, IX, X, and XI, Respondent admits the same.

IV.

Responding to Paragraph XII, Respondent admits the same with the exception of 12.4 (see II above) and 12.8, Respondent denies the same. Petitioner should be responsible for litigation costs and attorney fees on her behalf.

V.

WHEREFORE, having answered the Petition in full, the Respondent requests the Court to grant the following relief:

1. A Decree of Dissolution of Marriage be entered herein.

2. Provide child support for the children of the marriage in accordance with the Washington State Child Support Schedule.

3. That Respondent be given residential care of the children of this marriage.

4. That the community and separate property of the parties be equitably divided between them.

5. That the community and separate debts of the parties be equitably divided.

6. Each party be responsible for their own debts incurred since the date of separation; and hold the other party harmless therefrom and should indemnify the other party should either be required thereon.

7. That the court approve such written separation agreement that the parties may enter into.

8. That each party be responsible for their own litigation costs including reasonable attorney fees in connection with this matter.

9. For other just and equitable relief as the court may deem necessary.

DATED: this 12th day of February, 1990.

_____

James L. Jeffrey, Respondent

Pro se

State of Washington   )

                              : ss.

County of King   )

James L. Jeffrey, being first duly sworn upon oath, deposes and states:

I am the Respondent in the above entitled action. I have read the foregoing RESPONSE TO PETITION FOR DISSOLUTION OF MARRIAGE, know the contents thereof and believe the same to be true.

SUBSCRIBED AND SWORN TO before me this 12th day of February, 1990.

_____

NOTARY PUBLIC in and for the State

of Washington, residing at

_____.

My commission expires _____.

IN THE SUPERIOR COURT OF THE STATE OF WASHINGTON
FOR KING COUNTY

In re the Marriage of	)	
	)	NO. 90-3-00000-0
MARY ELLEN JEFFREY,	)	
	)	
Petitioner,	)	SEPARATION CONTRACT
	)	
and	)	
	)	
JAMES L. JEFFREY,	)	
	)	
Respondent.	)	
	)	

I. INTRODUCTION

THIS SEPARATION CONTRACT, entered into on the date below stated by and between Mary Ellen Jeffrey, hereinafter called "Wife", and James L. Jeffrey, hereinafter called "Husband", is made and entered into in order to promote the amicable settlement of disputes attendant upon their separation and the filing of a petition for dissolution of their marriage.

II. RECITALS

2.1 <u>Marriage</u>. Husband and Wife were married on August 20, 1974 in Seattle, Washington.

2.2 <u>Pending Action</u>. The parties have filed a Petition for Dissolution, dated January 10, 1990, in the Superior Court of the State of Washington for King County.

2.3 <u>Residences</u>. Wife currently resides at: 9102 90th Place Southeast, Mercer Island, Washington 98040. Husband currently resides at: 4466 West Mercer Way, Mercer Island, Washington 98040.

2.4 <u>Separation</u>. The parties separated on August 16, 1989.

2.5 <u>Children</u>. The parties have the following children born of this marriage: Justin David Jeffrey, born May 1, 1977; and Kristin Jeffrey, born December 2, 1980.

2.6 <u>Wife</u>. Wife is not now pregnant.

2.7 Neither party is a member of the United States Armed Services.

2.8 <u>Full Settlement</u>. These parties are now desirous of making a full and final settlement of their marital and property rights, and obligations, by means of this document and without court intervention.

2.9 <u>Full Disclosure</u>. Each party has fully disclosed to the other all properties he or she owns, and all income he or she derives therefrom, and from all other sources and all claims, liens or encumbrances affecting such property and income, and entering into this Contract. The parties have attempted to divide their properties in such a manner that after deducting all liabilities each will receive a fair and equitable share of property or cash.

2.10 <u>Incorporation into Decree</u>. The parties are not contracting to dissolve their marriage but agree if a Decree of Dissolution is obtained, this Separation Contract shall be incorporated in said Decree of Dissolution and given full force and effect thereby. It is understood and agreed by the parties that this Contract shall be final and binding upon the execution by both parties, whether or not a Decree of Dissolution is obtained.

2.11 <u>Mutual Promises</u>. In consideration of the mutual promises and covenants of the parties and in consideration of the mutual benefits to be derived by them, the parties hereby agree, covenant and promise as follows.

III. WAIVERS

3.1 <u>Release of Claims</u>. Except as otherwise authorized by this Contract, each of the parties hereby covenants to make no claim upon the property or earnings assigned herein to the other party by way of marital community interest therein, and hereby releases any and all rights or interest in any real or personal property not assigned to him or her herein, or acquired by the other party after the date of separation of the parties as set forth herein. Both parties agree that neither will assert any claim or demand of any kind against the other, except as expressly recognized herein.

3.2 <u>Inheritance</u>. Each party hereto does hereby waive any and all right to inherit the estate of the other at his or her death, or take property from the other by devise or bequest (unless under a will <u>subsequent</u> to the effective date hereof), or to claim any family allowance or probate homestead, or to act as administrator or administratrix of the other (except as nominee of another person legally entitled to said right), or to act as executor or executrix under the will of the other (unless under a will executed <u>subsequent</u> to the effective date hereof). All previous wills, contracts, or community property agreements are hereby revoked.

3.3 <u>Fairly Negotiated</u>. The parties acknowledge that they are making this agreement of their free will and volition and that no coercion, force, pressure or undue influence whatsoever has been employed against either of them in negotiations leading to the execution of this Contract.

3.4 <u>Court Approval</u>. It is the intent of the parties that the court approve this Separation Contract as fair and equitable at the time it was entered into and thus enforceable. Either party may apply to the Superior Court of the State of Washington for a decree dissolving the marriage and granting all relief provided for in this agreement. The parties are executing this Contract and each voluntarily consents to the jurisdiction of the Superior Court of the State of Washington for King County to award all such relief and ratify all rights and obligations set forth in this Contract.

3.5 <u>Benefit of Counsel</u>. The parties agree that each has been represented in negotiations and in the preparation of this Contract by counsel of his or her own choosing, or has had the opportunity to have this Contract reviewed by independent counsel. The parties have read this Contract and fully understand it.

_____   _____
Mary Ellen Jeffrey, date   James L. Jeffrey, date

IV. STATUS OF CONTRACT

4.1 Notwithstanding that the provisions of this Contract may be included and merged into a Decree of Dissolution, if one is obtained, it is also the intention of the parties that this Contract retains its status independently as a Contract between the parties, each spouse to enforce his or her rights as they arise from this Contract by contract law, as well as those remedies available for the enforcement of judgments and dissolution law, specifically including the use of the contempt power of the court, in the event a Decree of Dissolution is granted. It is understood and agreed by the parties that this Contract shall be final and binding upon execution by both parties, whether or not a Decree of Dissolution is obtained. This Contract may be terminated and modified only by a written document so reflecting, signed by the parties.

4.2 Entire Contract. This Contract represents the entire agreement of the parties with regard to the subject matter hereof. All agreements, covenants, representations and warranties, express or implied, oral or written, of the parties with regard to the subject matter hereof are contained herein. No other agreements, covenants, representations or warranties, express or implied, oral or written, have been made by either party to the other with respect to the subject matter of this Contract. All prior and contemporaneous conversations, negotiations, possible and alleged agreements and representations, covenants and warranties with respect to the subject matter hereof are waived, merged herein and superseded hereby.

4.3 Interpretation. No provision of this Contract shall be interpreted for or against any party because that party or that party's legal representative drafted this Contract.

V. PROCEDURAL AGREEMENTS

5.1 Partial Invalidity. In the event that any portion of this Contract shall be declared invalid by any court of competent jurisdiction, those parts not at issue shall still be of full force and effect.

5.2 Findings and Decree. This Separation Contract may be embodied in the Findings and Decree of Dissolution as provided in RCW 26.09.070, enacted by Laws 1973, First Extraordinary Session, Chapter 157, Section 7. Findings of Fact, Conclusions of Law, and Decree shall be subject to approval as to form by both parties' attorneys which approval shall not be unreasonably withheld.

VI. DIVISION AND DISTRIBUTION OF PROPERTY AND LIABILITIES

6.1 Property Disposition. All of the property of the parties is set forth in Exhibits "H" and "W" attached hereto and by this reference incorporated herein. The property described in Exhibit "W" shall be the sole and separate property of Wife, and the property described in Exhibit "H" shall be the sole and separate property of Husband. Each party does hereby convey and quit claim his or her interest therein, if any, to the party to whom it is awarded, subject to all taxes, outstanding mortgages, obligations, encumbrances, reservations, liens and restrictions of record, unless otherwise provided herein; and except as set forth otherwise in this Contract, the party to whom the property is awarded shall assume, pay and hold the other party harmless therefrom.

6.2 After Acquired Property. From and after the date of separation, any property of the parties acquired by either and not specifically herein mentioned shall be the separate property of the party acquiring or having possession of said property, provided the source for said acquired asset shall have been the separate credit, monies accumulated hereafter, or an asset or derivative thereof herein awarded.

6.3 <u>Earnings after Separation</u>. From and after the date of separation, any earnings of the parties hereto are and shall be the sole and separate property of the party earning the same.

6.4 <u>Outstanding Community Obligations</u>. All of the outstanding community obligations of the parties are set forth in Exhibit "O" attached hereto and by this reference incorporated herein. The parties shall pay the outstanding community obligations as set forth in that Exhibit "O".

6.5 <u>Warranty of Wife</u>. Wife hereby warrants to husband that she has not incurred and she hereby covenants that she will not in the future incur any liabilities or obligations for which the husband is or may be liable except as have been expressly set forth herein; wife hereby covenants and agrees that if any claim, action or proceeding shall hereafter be brought seeking to hold husband liable on account of any such debt, liability, act or omission of wife, she will, at her sole expense, defend husband against any such claim or demand, whether or not well-founded and that she will hold him harmless therefrom.

6.6 <u>Warranty of Husband</u>. Husband hereby warrants to wife that he has not incurred and he hereby covenants that he will not in the future incur any liabilities or obligations for which the wife is or may be liable except as have been expressly set forth herein; husband hereby covenants and agrees that if any claim, action or proceeding shall hereafter be brought seeking to hold wife liable on account of any such debt, liability, act or omission of husband, he will, at his sole expense, defend wife against any such claim or demand, whether or not well-founded and that he will hold her harmless therefrom.

6.7 <u>Other Property</u>. To the extent not otherwise awarded herein, the following shall be awarded as stated:

(a) Separate (as distinguished from community) personal and real property to the party who originally acquired such separate property.

(b) Legal rights of action to the party through whom derived.

(c) Rights and benefits to the party through whom directly or indirectly derived as a result of his or her past or present employment, union affiliation, United States or other citizenship and/or residence within a state, all of which include but are not limited to:

> Various forms of insurance, rights of social security payments, welfare payments, unemployment compensation payments, disability payments, medicare and medicaid, educational benefits and grants, interests in health or welfare plans and profit-sharing plans, and all other legislated or contractual benefits, provided, that marriage to the party through whose activity said benefits have been derived shall not be in an indirect basis for an award of that benefit.

6.8 <u>Fair Division</u>. The division of the property as set forth in this document is fair, just and equitable.

VII. PARENTING PLAN

We, the parents of Justin and Kristin, enter into this Agreement in order to better meet our parental responsibilities and to safeguard our children's future development. We both recognize that Justin and Kristin wish to love and respect both of us, regardless of our marital status or our place of residence, and that Justin's and Kristin's welfare can best be served by our mutual cooperation as partners in parenting and by each of us providing a home in which the children are loved and to which each child belongs: their mother's house and their father's house.

7.1 Decision Making.

A. General. Each parent desires to remain responsible and active in Justin's and Kristin's growth and development consistent with the best interest of the children. The parents will make a mutual effort to maintain an open, on-going communication concerning the development, needs and interests of the children and will discuss together any major decisions which have to be made about or for the children.

1. Each parent shall have an equal say in all major decisions. In the event of an irreconcilable conflict, the matter shall be submitted to mediation and, if necessary, arbitration or final disposition on the Family Law Motion Calender, in accordance with paragraph 7.11 below.

2. The residential parent shall have authority to make day-to-day decisions affecting the children's welfare; HOWEVER, major decisions concerning the children's welfare shall not be made without agreement by both parents.

B. Major Decisions. Major decisions are as follows:

1. Non-emergency medical and/or dental care and providers thereof.

2. Change of school not mandated by authorities.

3. Moving the children more than ten (10) miles from their present residence.

4. Choice of care providers.

Before any of the three following events may occur prior to the children's eighteenth (18th) birthday, parents must consent, in writing, to their:

1. Acquisition of a driver's license.

2. Marrying.

3. Entry into any type of military service.

In the event of disagreement each parent has temporary veto power with reference to these three (3) decisions until referral to mediation or Court.

Each parent shall have equal and independent authority to confer with school, day care and other programs with regard to the children's progress and each shall have free access to school, day care and other records. Each parent shall have authority to give parental consent or permission as may be required concerning school, day care or other programs for the children while the children are in his or her custody.

Each parent agrees to honor one another's parenting style, privacy, and authority. Neither will interfere in the parenting style of the other, nor will either parent make plans and arrangements that would impinge upon the other parent's authority or time with the children without the express agreement of the other parent. Each parent agrees to encourage the children to discuss his or her grievance with a parent directly with the parent in question. It is the intent of both parents to encourage a direct child-parent bond.

SEPARATION CONTRACT - Page 5 of 17

C. Education.

1. The children shall attend the school mutually agreed upon by the parents, recognizing that the decisions should be made in the best interest of the children's education needs, rather than the needs of the parents.

2. All schools, health care providers and counselors shall be selected by the parents jointly. In the event the parents cannot agree to the selection of a school, the children shall be maintained in the present school, pending mediation and/or further order of the court.

3. Each parent is to provide the other parent promptly upon receipt with information concerning the well-being of the children, including, but not limited to, copies of report cards, school meeting notices, vacation schedules, class programs, requests for conferences, results of standardized or diagnostic tests, notices of activities involving the diagnostic tests, notices of activities involving the children, samples of school work, order forms for school pictures, all communications from health care providers, the names, addresses and telephone numbers of all schools, health care providers, regular day care providers, and counselors.

D. Health Care.

1. Each parent shall be empowered to obtain emergency health care for the children without the consent of the other parent. Each parent is to notify the other parent as soon as reasonably possible of any illness requiring medical attention, or any emergency involving the children.

2. Each parent shall have equal and independent authority to provide routine and emergency medical and dental services of the children while the children are in his or her care and residence.

3. Major decisions regarding non-routine, non-emergency medical care must be made jointly by the parents.

E. Religious Upbringing.

1. Each parent shall have an equal right to include the children in his or her religious activities and expressions. The children shall have the right to make their own religious choice as they mature.

F. Revisions in Plan.

1. Both parents acknowledge that as the children grow and change, revisions may be required in the Plan and, though unable to predict such revisions, agree to remain flexible with respect to access, parental responsibility, etc. Both parents agree that adjustments shall be made without showing substantial change in circumstances.

7.2 Residential Arrangements.

A. School Year Schedule. From one week prior to the commencement of the child's school year through the Saturday following its conclusion, the following shall be the children's residential arrangements:

The children shall reside with father on the first, third, and fifth weekends of each month from 5:30 p.m. Friday evening through 8:00 p.m. Sunday evening, and with the other parent the remainder of the time. The weekends shall be extended if they include a holiday.

B. Summer Schedule. The residential arrangements of the children during the summer of the year shall be as follows:

The children shall reside with the father for six uninterrupted weeks during the summer school vacation. Proposed dates should be submitted by the father prior to April 15 each year.

C. Holidays. The children's holiday time shall be allocated as follows:

1. During odd-numbered years, the children shall reside with the father on President's Day, Fourth of July and Thanksgiving.

2. During even-numbered years, the children shall reside with the mother on President's Day, Fourth of July and Thanksgiving.

3. During even-numbered years, the children shall reside with the father on Memorial Day, Labor Day, Veteran's Day, and Easter.

4. During odd-numbered years, the children shall reside with the mother on Memorial Day, Labor Day, Veteran's Day, and Easter.

5. The parent having the children for the weekend immediately before or after a national holiday shall have the weekend time expanded to include such holiday.

6. Thanksgiving shall be defined as beginning at 5:00 p.m., Wednesday preceding Thanksgiving until 7:00 p.m., Sunday following Thanksgiving.

7.3 Birthdays and Special Family Days.

A. The children shall celebrate their birthdays with their mother in even-numbered years, and with their father in odd-numbered years.

B. The non-residential parent shall be allowed to spend some time with the child to celebrate the children's birthdays, within a week of that birthday.

C. The mother shall have the children every year for Mother's Day and the father shall have the children every year for Father's Day from 9:00 a.m. to 6:00 p.m.

7.4 Vacations, Christmas/Winter and Spring Break.

A. The children shall spend a portion of the Christmas school holiday from the first day of school vacation until 10 a.m. Christmas Day with the father in even-numbered years, and with the mother in odd-numbered years.

B. The children shall spend every other Spring vacation as defined by the school schedule, with the father.

7.5 Parent's Vacations.

A. In addition to the other arrangements, each parent shall have the children for vacation purposes during that parent's scheduled vacation from work for up to two weeks each year provided that 30 days' notice is given to the other parent and provided that such vacation time does not conflict with the children's school schedule. Each parent shall endeavor to arrange their vacation during the summer months, if possible.

7.6 Telephone Access.

A. The children shall have liberal telephone privileges with the parent with whom they are not then residing without interference of the residential parent.

7.7 Participation in Children's Events.

A. Children shall be accompanied by the parent with whom they are residing at the time of a given social event. The other parent shall not be limited from attendance at that event, providing said attendance by the non-residential parent is not disruptive to the other participants.

B. Each parent shall be responsible for keeping themselves advised of school, athletic, and social events in which the children participate. Both parents may participate in school activities for the children such as open house, attendance at an athletic event, etc.

7.8 Removal of Children From State.

A. A parent shall not remove the residence of the children from the State of Washington except by the advance written approval of the other parent or by court order entered after notice of hearing having been given to the other parent.

7.9 Transportation.

A. Responsibility for providing transportation shall be divided between the parents. Each parent shall be responsible for providing transportation to his or her home.

B. The children shall be picked up and returned at the designated times. Should a delay become necessary, the receiving parent shall be notified immediately.

C. The father shall be responsible for all transportation in connection with his exercise of visitation. Both parents shall share responsibility for transportation to and from the children's games, practices, and cultural enrichment activities.

7.10 Other.

A. It is the responsibility of the parent scheduled to have the children to arrange suitable alternative care if necessary and pay for needed care.

B. Each parent shall notify the other parent at least 48 hours in advance if he/she is unable to exercise the regular schedule.

7.11 Dispute Resolution.

A. Any decision concerning the children shall be made only after consideration is given to the needs, feelings, and desires of the children.

B. In the event that there are difficulties or differences of opinion between the parents regarding provisions for the children, the matter shall be referred to a private mediator chosen by the parties.

C. Notice. Parents shall notify the other in writing of a request for mediation and mediation shall commence within 10 days thereafter.

D. Writing. If an agreement is reached through mediation, it shall be reduced to writing and shall become part of the Parenting Plan.

E. In the event the parties are unable to agree on a private mediator, the matter shall be referred to the King County Family Law Motion Calendar for designation of a mediator. Should mediation not be successful in resolving the dispute, the same may be referred to the King County Superior Court Family Law Motion Calendar for final resolution.

F. In undertaking this dispute resolution process, the parents agree:

1. That preference shall be given to carrying out the parenting plan;

2. That the parents shall use the designated process to resolve the disputes relating to implementation of the plan, except those related to financial support, unless an emergency exists;

3. If the court finds that a parent has used or frustrated the dispute resolution process without good reason, the court shall award attorneys' fees and financial sanctions to the prevailing party; and

4. The parents have the right of review from the dispute resolution process to the superior court.

SEPARATION CONTRACE - Page 8 of 17

7.12 <u>Residential Designation (Jurisdictional Only)</u>.

A. The following designations shall not affect either parent's rights or responsibilities under this Plan:

1. The children's residence for the purposes of jurisdiction, venue and child support only is that of the mother.

2. The children's custodian for the sole purpose of compliance with all other state and federal laws is the mother.

7.13 <u>Financial Support</u>.

A. <u>Major Expenses</u>. Prior to either parent obligating any parent for major expenses on behalf of the children, such as orthodontia expenses, private educational expenses, tutoring, or other expenses in excess of the day-to-day standard expenses for public school children, the parents shall in good faith attempt to amicably reach an agreement on the subject.

B. <u>Health Care Insurance; Uninsured Expense</u>. Both parents shall continue to carry all health care insurance as may be available through their respective employment, provided that the employer or other organization pays part or all of the premium. Mother shall pay 30% and father shall pay 70% of all uninsured medical, dental, optical, and orthodontic expenses for the children. The parents shall cooperate in the prompt processing of all insurance claims and reimburse the other for all out of pocket expenditures

C. <u>Duration of Support</u>. Child support for each child shall continue until such child is 18 years old, or graduates from high school, whichever occurs later, provided that support continues through September of the year of graduation if the child is enrolled for college. In no event shall support continue past the child's 19th birthday.

D. <u>Support Amount</u>. Based upon the present financial circumstances and joint parenting arrangements of the parents, the father shall pay to the mother the sum of $1,475 per month as child support for the two children, payable on or before the fifth (5th) day of each month. The monthly support provided herein shall be adjusted beginning June 1, 1991 and each successive year on June 1 based upon both parent's earned income from all sources and utilizing the Washington State Child Support Schedule, as now or hereafter amended.

E. <u>Dispute Resolution</u>. Disputes in applying the Schedule or any other financial matters affecting the children shall be mediated or referred to court for final resolution, in accordance with paragraph 7.11 above.

F. <u>Life Insurance as Security</u>. The father shall maintain a policy of decreasing term life insurance on his life payable for the benefit of the children in the initial face amount of $100,000 during the time that he is still obligated to pay support. In the event there is insufficient life insurance (less social benefits or other entitlements payable for the children due to the father's death), to support his obligations, the mother shall have a continuing claim against the father's estate, which shall survive his death and which shall be treated with the same statutory priority as an Award of Homestead.

G. <u>Exemptions</u>. So long as he is current in his support obligation the father shall be entitled to claim the younger child as an exemption for IRS reporting purposes and the mother shall execute appropriate forms for this purpose. So long as there is a continuing support obligation, the parents shall exchange authenticated copies of tax returns upon request.

SEPARATION CONTRACT - Page 9 of 17

H. <u>College Expense</u>. Each parent shall contribute to the children's post-secondary educational expenses taking into consideration the income and expenses and other resources of each parent at the time and the ability of the children to obtain loans and scholarships and to work part-time. In no event shall a parent's obligation exceed that for a student attending the University of Washington full-time; nor shall the obligation extend beyond the child's 23rd birthday. Both parents agree that the Court shall retain jurisdiction for the purpose of adjudicating the parents' college expense obligation if they are unable to agree.

7.14 <u>Payment of Support.</u>

Family:

Mother:	Father:
Mary Ellen Jeffrey	James L. Jeffrey
9102 90th Place Southeast	4466 West Mercer Way
Mercer Island, WA 98040	Mercer Island, WA 98040

Child: Justin	d.o.b. 5/1/77, age 13
Child: Kristin	d.o.b. 12/2/80, age 9

Social Security Numbers:

Mother: 532-38-0955	Father: 501-55-4682
Justin: 599-33-0324	Kristin: 501-22-2441

Employer Address:

Mother:	Father:
Bank of California	Jeffrey Limited
Bank of California Center	4466 West Mercer Way
Seattle, WA 98105	Mercer Island, WA 98040

Monthly Net Income:

Mother: $ 0	Father: $ 4,224

Parent Who Will Pay Support: father

Parent Who Will Receive Support: mother

Monthly Support Amount to be paid: $1,475

Payment Due Date: the 15th day of each month

Basic child support payment shall be paid through:
>   a. Washington State Support Registry
>   P.O. Box 9009
>   Olympia, Washington 98504

SEPARATION CONTRACT - Page 10 of 17

Other payments (such as child care costs) shall be made directly to the mother.

NOTICE: Both parents are shall maintain any health insurance on their minor children herein which is available through a present or future employer or other organization provided that the employer pays part or all of the premium.

NOTICE: If a support payment is more than fifteen (15) days past due in an amount equal to or greater than the support payable for one month, a Notice of Payroll Deduction may be issued or other withholding action under RCW Chapters 26.18 or 74.20A without prior notice to the person who is obligated to pay support.

NOTICE: Each parent listed above shall promptly notify the Washington State Support Registry of any changes of address of themselves or their employment.

DOCUMENT EXCHANGE: Failure to provide information as required by said Schedule, or timely compliance, i.e., an interchange of six wage stubs for the immediate six (6) prior pay periods, and a complete copy of the prior years income tax return, shall cause the Court to assess terms of not less than $250.00 against the violating party. Such information shall be exchanged not later than May 1, 1991 and May 1st of each and every year thereafter.

7.15 Compliance With The Plan.

A. If a parent fails to comply with a provision of this Plan the other parent's obligations under the Plan are not affected.

B. If a support payment as provided for is more than 15 days past due in an amount equal to or greater than the support payable for one month, the person entitled to receive support may seek a mandatory wage assignment without prior notice to the person who is obligated to pay support.

C. Violation of Restraining Orders set forth in this Plan or Order may constitute a civil contempt and/or a criminal misdemeanor.

7.16 Acknowledgements.

Both parents acknowledge by their signatures below that they are in agreement and have a copy of this plan.

DATED: this 27th day of June, 1990.

_____   _____
Mary Ellen Jeffrey,   James L. Jeffrey,
Petitioner   Respondent

VIII. SPOUSAL MAINTENANCE

8.1 Commencing June 1, 1990 and continuing through May 31, 1991, Husband shall pay spousal maintenance to Wife in the sum of $1,000 per month.

8.2 Except as hereinafter stated the maintenance obligation shall be non-modifiable except upon the death of either spouse or Wife's remarriage.

8.3 Husband shall have no obligation or liability to make any such payment for any period after the death of Wife, and there is no liability provided for herein for Husband to make any payment as a substitute for such payments after the death of Wife.

IX. TAX LIABILITIES

9.1 Income Tax. The parties shall file separately and each shall be fully liable for his or her own taxes commencing 1990 and all subsequent years.

SEPARATION CONTRACT - Page 11 o f 17

Each of the parties shall assume and pay any and all tax on any income received by said party subsequent to December 31, 1990, and each of the parties shall pay and be responsible for any tax incident to any asset awarded to said party. Likewise, each of the parties shall be entitled to all income tax deductions incident to any property awarded to that party.

The parties acknowledge that Section 1041 of the Internal Revenue Code of 1954, as amended, applies to all transfers of property other than cash, under this agreement. Each party will report the transfers and treat the property for federal tax purposes consistently with the treatment provided in Section 1041. Each party agrees to provide the other party with any requested information necessary for complete and accurate tax reporting about the property, such as adjusted basis and depreciation information.

9.2 <u>Spousal Maintenance</u>. Wife shall include all spousal maintenance payments in her taxable income. Husband shall be entitled to deduct said payments from his gross income for tax reporting purposes.

9.3 <u>Adjustment of Tax Effects of Recomputation</u>. In the event the wife files a petition to modify maintenance and as a result of such petition the maintenance award is modified causing an excess amount under Section 71(f) of the Internal Revenue Code of 1954, as amended, the parties agree that the wife shall pay as follows: In any taxable year in which there is an excess amount requiring the husband to include such excess amount in gross income and allowing the wife to deduct such excess amount, the wife shall pay the husband an amount equal to the reduction in the wife's federal income tax liability in the applicable taxable year attributable to the Section 71(f) deduction. The payment from the wife to the husband shall be equal to the wife's total tax liability without the Section 71(f) deduction in excess of her total tax liability with the Section 71(f) deduction.

Any payment by the wife to the husband under this clause is designated as not includible in the gross income of the husband under Section 71(b)(1)(B) and not allowable as a deduction to the wife under Section 215 of the Internal Revenue Code of 1954, as amended. The parties agree to treat the payment for federal income tax purposes consistently with this designation.

9.4 <u>Income Tax Exemption</u>. So long as Husband pays Wife the child support in accordance with the provisions of the agreement and is not in default thereof, Husband shall be allowed the claim the children as excmptions for federal income tax purposes. Wife shall execute and provide Husband each year the form required by the IRS to allow the non-residential parent to claim the children as exemptions.

9.5 <u>Dependents</u>. Wife shall claim the children as dependents for the purposes of her taking the head of household status.

9.6 <u>Necessary Documents</u>. Each party shall sign any and all necessary documents to allow complete access to the IRS files for the years covered by this Contract.

X. DISPUTE RESOLUTION

10.1 In the event that the parties alone cannot resolve a conflict, they agree to seek appropriate competent assistance from a professional person skilled in the area of resolution of the problems of families prior to either party's seeking relief from the court.

XI. CHANGE OF NAME

11.1 Wife shall change her name to Mary Ellen _____.

XII. ATTORNEY FEES

12.1 Each party shall pay his or her own attorney fees and courts costs incurred in connection with this action.

XIII. CONTINUING RESTRAINING ORDERS

Each party shall be restrained from:

13.1 Harassing, maligning, threatening, or disturbing the peace of each other.

13.2 Harassing, disturbing, or discussing this case with either party's employer, employees, or co-employees except through their respective attorneys; coming to the place of employment of either party.

13.3 Opening each other's mail.

13.4 Coming to each other's residence without prior approval and arrangement with the other.

13.5 Interfering in any way with the other's personal, business, or financial affairs, directly or indirectly.

13.6 Removing the residence of the children from the State of Washington except by the advanced written approval of the other parent or by court order, with proper and timely notice of hearing being given to the other parent, as set forth in Paragraph 7.8 above.

XIV. EFFECTIVE DATE

14.1 This Contract shall be effective upon execution, and both parties agree to request that any court which hears the petition for dissolution of the marriage between the parties shall ratify and confirm the same in all respects, and incorporate it in the Decree of Dissolution.

XV. AGREEMENT EFFECTIVE AFTER DEATH

15.1 Should the death of either party to this agreement occur following execution of this agreement, the distribution of property agreed upon, the allocation of debts agreed upon, and other obligations agreed upon, shall nonetheless be valid and shall be enforceable against the estate of either party insofar as applicable law permits.

XVI. EXECUTION OF INSTRUMENTS

16.1 The parties shall execute any documents (including without limitation trust revocation and distribution documents, quit claim deeds and stock transfer documents) necessary to complete and effectively carry out the terms of this Contract. In the event that legal descriptions are insufficient, each party agrees properly to execute new documents as may be required to effectuate the terms of this Contract.

XVII. LEGAL DESCRIPTIONS

17.1 In the event that any legal descriptions are not attached to this agreement at the time the agreement is executed, or if the legal description is incorrect, the parties expressly authorize their attorneys to attach exhibits with legal descriptions and to correct any incorrect descriptions which may now or later be attached, subject to the approval of both parties' attorneys, which approval shall not be unreasonably withheld.

XVIII. APPLICABLE LAW

18.1 The parties do hereby stipulate that interpretation of this document may be made by any court of competent jurisdiction which may be called upon to interpret it and in so doing said court shall apply the substantive law and law of modification of the State of Washington.

DATED: this 27th day of June, 1990.

_____

Mary Ellen Jeffrey

DATED: this 27th day of June, 1990.

_____

James L. Jeffrey

STATE OF WASHINGTON   )
)   : ss.
COUNTY OF KING   )

On this day personally appeared before me Mary Ellen Jeffrey, to me known to be the individual described in and who executed the within and foregoing instrument, and acknowledged that she signed the same as her free and voluntary act and deed, for the uses and purposes therein mentioned.

GIVEN unto my hand and official seal this 27th day of June, 1990.

                                              _____

                                              NOTARY PUBLIC in and for the State of Washington, residing at

                                              _____.

                                              My commission expires _____.

STATE OF WASHINGTON   )
)   : ss.
COUNTY OF KING   )

On this day personally appeared before me James L. Jeffrey, to me known to be the individual described in and who executed the within and foregoing instrument, and acknowledged that he signed the same as his free and voluntary act and deed, for the uses and purposes therein mentioned.

GIVEN unto my hand and official seal this 27th day of June, 1990.

                                              _____

                                              NOTARY PUBLIC in and for the State of Washington, residing at

                                              _____.

                                              My commission expires _____.

EXHIBIT "O"

to

SEPARATION CONTRACT

<u>OBLIGATIONS</u>

Each party shall assume and pay any obligations incurred by him or her since the date of their separation and hold the other harmless therefrom.

Outstanding community obligations shall be paid as follows:

A.   Wife shall assume the following obligations:
   1.   Balance owed on Master Charge;
   2.   Balance owed to Pande Cameron; and
   3. $600 balance on dining room table and chairs.

B.   Husband shall assume the following obligations:
   1.   Balance owed on VISA Card;
   2.   Balance owed to Dr. Trevor;
   3. $300 owed on bunkbed/desk; and
   4.   Balance owed to Nordstrom's.

EXHIBIT "H"

to

SEPARATION CONTRACT

PROPERTY AWARDED TO HUSBAND

Husband shall be awarded as his sole and separate property, free and clear of any claims of Wife, and Wife hereby conveys, quit claims and relinquishes and releases unto Husband all of her right, title and interest in and to the following:

1. 1973 Ranger Sailboat.
2. One-third interest in duplex at 110 Riverton Drive (see attached legal description).
3. One-third interest in condominium at 1411 Mirror Lake.
4. One-third interest in 12 acres undeveloped land (see attached legal description).
5. $3,300 from joint savings account.
6. Pool table.
7. T.V. in recreation room.
8. Tent.
9. 500 shares of Celanese stock.
10. Penn Mutual Life insurance policy #7654012.
11. Profit sharing plan.
12. Diamond ring inherited from grandmother.

EXHIBIT "W"

to

SEPARATION CONTRACT

<u>PROPERTY AWARDED TO WIFE</u>

Wife shall be awarded as her sole and separate property, free and clear of any claims of Husband, and Husband hereby conveys, quit claims and relinquishes and releases unto Wife all of his right, title and interest in and to the following:

1. The family residence (see attached legal description).
2. All household furniture.
3. 1987 Honda automobile, license number _____.
4. Antique Persian rug.
5. All household items in Wife's possession.
6. Tennis Club membership.
7. $4,000 from joint savings account.
8. Personal jewelry.
9. Penn Mutual Life Insurance Policy #6542301.

IN THE SUPERIOR COURT OF THE STATE OF WASHINGTON
FOR KING COUNTY

In re the Marriage of	)
	) NO. 90-3-00000-0
MARY ELLEN JEFFREY,	)
	) FINDINGS OF FACT AND
Petitioner,	) CONCLUSIONS OF LAW
	)
and	)
	)
JAMES L. JEFFREY,	)
	)
Respondent.	)
	)

THIS MATTER came on regularly before the undersigned Judge/Court Commissioner of the above-entitled court on the date below stated, upon a Petition for Dissolution of Marriage sought by Petitioner. The Petitioner appeared in person and through counsel, Lowell K. Halverson, whereupon the court considered the sworn testimony in support of the petition and the records and files herein, and being fully advised in the premises, finds that

I. FINDINGS OF FACT

1.1 Petitioner's residence address is 9102 90th Place Southeast, Mercer Island, Washington 98040.

1.2 Respondent's residence address is 4466 West Mercer Way, Mercer Island, Washington 98040.

II. JURISDICTION

The court has jurisdiction over the parties hereto and of the subject matter herein.

III.

More than 90 days have elapsed from the filing of the Petition and service of process.

IV.

The marriage of the parties on the 20th day of August, 1974, at Seattle, Washington is irretrievably broken.

V.

Petitioner and Respondent entered into a written Separation Contract on the 27th day of June, 1990. Said Contract was fair at the time of execution.

VI.

The following are the names and birthdates of the dependent children of this marriage: Justin D. Jeffrey, born May 1, 1977; and Kristin Jeffrey, born December 2, 1980.

VII.

The wife is not pregnant.

VIII.

Neither party is a member of the United States Military Service.

FINDINGS OF FACT AND CONCLUSIONS OF LAW - Page 1 of 2

IX.

A Decree of Dissolution of Marriage should be entered herein upon the provisions for the same as set forth in the written Separation Contract, which has been filed herein and is hereby approved and confirmed as being full, fair and equitable. Under the terms of the Contract

A. The property described in the Separation Contract awarded to Petitioner should be confirmed.

B. The property described in the Separation Contract awarded to Respondent should be confirmed.

C. The debts and obligations provided for in the Separation Contract should be awarded in accordance with the provisions of said Contract.

D. The arrangements with regard to the support and maintenance of the wife should be confirmed.

E. The arrangements with regard to child support in the Separation Contract are in compliance with Laws of 1988, Ch. 275, Section 5 and should be confirmed. Attached hereto and incorporated herein are the Washington State Child Support Schedule Worksheets which show all income and resources of each parent's household.

BASED UPON THE FOREGOING Findings of Fact the court now makes the following

CONCLUSIONS OF LAW

1. That this court has jurisdiction over the parties hereto and over the subject matter herein.

2. That a Decree of Dissolution of Marriage should be entered herein fully, finally and forever dissolving the bonds of matrimony heretofore existing between the parties.

3. That such Decree of Dissolution of Marriage should provide for the maintenance of the wife, division of the parties' properties and debts and obligations, and provide for the children of the marriage, all in accordance with the preceding Findings of Fact.

DONE IN OPEN COURT this 11th day of July, 1990.

_____
JUDGE/COURT COMMISSIONER

Presented by: Approved for entry:

_____   _____
Attorneys for Petitioner   Mary Ellen Jeffrey,
                                     Petitioner

Approved for entry;
Notice of Presentation waived:

_____
James L. Jeffrey, Respondent
Pro se
FINDINGS OF FACT AND CONCLUSIONS OF LAW - Page 2 of 2

IN THE SUPERIOR COURT OF THE STATE OF WASHINGTON
FOR KING COUNTY

In re the Marriage of	)
	) NO. 90-3-00000-0
MARY ELLEN JEFFREY,	)
	) DECREE OF DISSOLUTION
Petitioner,	) OF MARRIAGE
	)
and	)
	)
JAMES L. JEFFREY,	)
	)
Respondent.	)
	)

THIS MATTER having come on duly and regularly before the undersigned Court Commissioner, Mary Ellen Jeffrey, Petitioner, appearing in person and through her attorney Lowell K. Halverson, and James L. Jeffrey, Respondent, Pro se, having waived notice of presentation, the parties having endorsed their approval hereon for the entry of this Decree, testimony having been taken, and the Court having entered written Findings of Fact and Conclusions of Law,

NOW THEREFORE IT IS HEREBY ORDERED, ADJUDGED AND DECREED as follows:

1. The marriage of the parties on the 20th day of August, 1974, at Seattle, King County, Washington is hereby dissolved.

2. Each party is awarded that property and those obligations as set forth in the Separation Contract the terms of which are hereby confirmed and incorporated herein by this reference.

3. The Parenting Plan of the parties as more fully set forth in the Separation Contract is confirmed.

4. The arrangements as to maintenance of the Petitioner as more fully set forth in the Separation Contract are confirmed.

5. Each party shall pay his/her own attorney fees and costs.

DATED: this 11th day of July, 1990.

_____
JUDGE/COURT COMMISSIONER

Presented by: Approved for entry:

_____   _____
Attorneys for Petitioner   Mary Ellen Jeffrey,
                                          Petitioner

Approved as to form;
Notice of Presentation Waived:

_____
James L. Jeffrey, Respondent
Pro se

DECREE OF DISSOLUTION OF MARRIAGE - Page 1 of 1

Worksheet A
Computation of the Child Support Obligation

Mother _Mary Ellen_   Father _James_

County _KING_   Superior Court Case Number _90-3-00000-0_

Children and Ages:	_Justin, 12; Kristin, 9._		

Part I: Basic Support Obligation (See Instructions)

		Father	Mother
1. Monthly Gross Income			
a. Wages, Salaries, and Tips		$ _5036.67_	$ —
b. Interest and Dividend Income		$ —	$ —
c. Business Income		$ —	$ —
d. Other Income		$ —	$ —
e. Total Gross Income (add lines 1a through 1d)		$ _5036.67_	$ —
2. Monthly Deductions from Gross Income			
a. Income Taxes		$ _511.83_	$ —
b. FICA/Self-Employment Taxes		$ _300.42_	$ —
c. *Mandatory* Union/Professional Dues		$ —	$ —
d. *Mandatory* Pension Plan Payments		$ —	$ —
e. Non-recurring Income		$ —	$ —
f. Total Deductions from Gross Income (add lines 2a through 2e)		$ _812.25_	$ —
3. Monthly Net Income (line 1e minus line 2f)		$ _4224.42_	$ —
4. Combined Monthly Net Income (add father's and mother's monthly net incomes from line 3)		$ _4224.42_	
5. Basic Child Support Obligation (enter total amount in box ⟶) Child #1 _Justin_ – $_815_ Child #3 _____ Child #2 _Kristin_ – $_660_ Child #4		$ _1475.00_	
6. Proportional Share of Income (each parent's net income from line 3 divided by line 4)		_1.00_	_0.00_
7. Each Parent's Basic Child Support Obligation (multiply each number on line 6 by line 5)		$ _1475.00_	$ —

Part II: Health Care, Day Care, and Special Child Rearing Expenses (See Instructions)

		Father	Mother
8. Health Care Expenses			
a. Monthly Health Insurance Premiums		$ —	$ —
b. Uninsured Monthly Health Care Expenses		$ —	$ _67.50_
c. Total Monthly Health Care Expenses (line 8a plus line 8b)		$ —	$ _67.50_
d. Combined Monthly Health Care Expenses (Add father's and mother's monthly health care expenses from line 8c)		$ _67.50_	
e. Maximum Ordinary Monthly Health Care		$ _73.75_	
f. Extraordinary Monthly Health Care Costs (line 8d minus line 8e, if "0" or negative, enter "0")		$ _0_	

Continued on Back of Form

Part II: Health Care, Day Care, and Special Child Rearing Expenses (cont.)				
9. Day Care and Special Expenses		Father		Mother
a. Day Care Expenses	$		$	
b. Education Expenses	$		$	
c. Long Distance Transportation Expenses	$		$	
d. Other Special Expenses (list below)	$		$	
	$		$	
	$		$	
	$		$	
	$		$	
e. Total Day Care and Special Expenses (add lines 9a through 9d)	$		$	
10. Combined Monthly Total of Day Care and Special Expenses (add father's and mother's total day care and special expenses from line 9e)		$		
11. Total Extraordinary Health Care, Day Care, and Special Expenses (line 8f plus line 10)		$		
12. Each Parent's Obligation for Extraordinary Health Care, Day Care, and Special Expenses (multiply each number on line 6 by line 11)	$		$	
Part III: Total Child Support Obligation				
13. Total Support Obligation (line 7 plus line 12)	$ 1475.00		$	
Part IV: Child Support Credits (See instructions)				
14. Child Support Credits				
a. Monthly Health Care Expenses Credit	$		$ 67.50	
b. Day Care and Special Expenses Credit	$		$	
c. Other Ordinary Expense Credit (list below, expenses must have court approval)				
	$		$	
d. Residential Schedule Credit (from worksheet B, lines 27 and 28)	$		$	
e. Total Support Credits (add lines 14a through 14d)	$		$ 67.50	
Part V: Net Support Obligation and Transfer Payment (See Instructions)				
15. Net Support Obligation (line 13 minus line 14e)	$ 1,475.00		$ -67.50	

Continue to Worksheet C

WSCSS/07-01-89

Worksheet B
Residential Schedule Adjustment

Mother _Mary Ellen_   Father _James_

County _KING_   Superior Court Case Number _90-3-00000-0_

Complete Worksheet B if a residential schedule credit is allowable and desired pursuant to Standard #10 and the instructions.				
16. List Children (first name only)	Justin	Kristin		
17. Basic Support Obligation Per Child (from worksheet A, line 5 - individual amounts)	$ 815.00	$ 660.00	$	$
18. Ordinary Expenses Per Child				
a. Total Monthly Health Care Expenses	$ 33.75	$ 33.75	$	$
b. Maximum Ordinary Monthly Health Care	$ 40.75	$ 33.00	$	$
c. Ordinary Health Care Amount (lesser amount of 18a or 18b)	$ 33.75	$ 33.00	$	$
d. Other Ordinary Expenses	$ —	$ —	$	$
e. Total Ordinary Expenses Per Child (line 18c plus line 18d)	$ 33.75	$ 33.00	$	$
19. Adjusted Basic Support (line 17 minus line 18e)	$781.25	$627.00	$	$
20. Overnights with Father	89	89		
21. Proportional Overnights with Father (divide each entry on line 20 by 365)	0.24	0.24	.	.
22. Overnights with Mother	276	276		
23. Proportional Overnights with Mother (divide each entry on line 22 by 365)	0.76	0.76	.	.
24. Father's Credit Proportion (for each child subtract .25 from the entry on line 21 and multiply the resulting amount times 2) Note: For answers less than 0 enter "0" For answers greater than 1.0 enter "1.0" For answers between 0 and 1 enter exact amount	0.0	0.0	.	.
25. Mother's Credit Proportion (for each child subtract .25 from the entry on line 23 and multiply the resulting amount times 2) Note: For answers less than 0 enter "0" For answers greater than 1.0 enter "1.0" For answers between 0 and 1 enter exact amount	1.00	1.00	.	.
26. Father's Residential Schedule Credits (for each child multiply the entry on line 24 times the entry on line 19)	$ —	$ —	$	$
27. Mother's Residential Schedule Credits (for each child multiply the entry on line 25 times the entry on line 19)	$ 781.25	$ 627.00	$	$
Return to Worksheet A, line 14d				

This worksheet has been certified by the State of Washington Office of the Administrator for the Courts.
Photocopying of the worksheet is permitted.

WSCSS/07-01-89

Worksheet C
Additional Factors for Consideration

Mother __Mary Ellen__ Father __James__

County __KING__ Superior Court Case Number __90-3-00000-0__

	Father's Household	Mother's Household
This worksheet must be completed regardless of whether or not a deviation is being requested. Pursuant to RCW 26.19.020 the resources and income of each parent's household must be considered.		
28. List the estimated present value of all major household assets. (if there is a new marraige, include assets held in the new household)		
a. Real Estate	$ 91,000	$ 175,000
b. Stocks and Bonds	$ 27,750	$
c. Vehicles	$ 10,500	$ 4,800
d. Boats	$ 14,000	$
e. Pensions/IRAs/Bank Accounts	$ 29,240	$ 4,000
f. Cash	$ 50	$ 30
g. Insurance Plans	$ 50,000	$ 100,000
h. Other	$	$
29. List liens against assets owned by the household and/or any extraordinary debt.		
a. Real Estate	$ 13,000	$ 38,000
b. Vehicles	$	$ 1,200
c. Boat	$ 2,000	$
d.	$	$
e.	$	$
30. List the monthly household income not attributable to these proceedings.		
a. Income of new spouse	$	$
b. Income of other adults in household	$	$
c. Child support received from another relationship	$	$
d. Extraordinary income of children	$	$
e. Income from any assistance programs (i.e., AFDC, SSI, Food Stamps, etc.)	$	$
f. Maintenance received from another relationship	$	$
g. Other (describe)	$	$
31. Monthly child support paid for other children	$	$
32. Maintenance Paid for Prior Relationships	$	$
33. Children not of this relationship living in the household (first names and ages)	a.	a.
	b.	b.
	c.	c.
	d.	d.
34. New spouse's name.	$	$
35. Names of other adults living in the household.	$	$
Continued on Back of Form		

36. Use this section to list any other factors that should be considered in determining the child support obligation. (for nonparental custody proceedings, see instructions)

Signature and Dates

I declare, under penalty of perjury under the laws of the State of Washington, the information contained in Worksheet A, Worksheet B, and Worksheet C is complete, true, and correct.

Mother's Signature	Father's Signature
Date City	Date City

This worksheet has been certified by the State of Washington Office of the Administrator for the Courts. Photocopying of the worksheet is permitted.

WSCSS/07-01-89

APPENDIX F
SUPERIOR COURTS OF WASHINGTON STATE

County	Address	City	ZIP
Adams	Courthouse	Ritzville	99169
Asotin	P.O. Box 159	Asotin	99402
Benton	P.O. Box 1000	Prosser	99350
Chelan	P.O. Box 3025	Wenatchee	98801
Clallam	223 E. Fourth	Port Angeles	98362
Clark	P.O. Box 5000	Vancouver	98668
Columbia	341 E. Main	Dayton	99328
Cowlitz	Hall of Justice	Kelso	98626
Douglas	P.O. Box 516	Waterville	98858
Ferry	P.O. Box 302	Republic	99166
Franklin	P.O. Box 214	Pasco	99301
Garfield	P.O. Box 915	Pomeroy	99347
Grant	P.O. Box 37	Ephrata	98823
Grays Harbor	P.O. Box 647	Montesano	98563
Island	P.O. Box 668	Coupeville	98239
Jefferson	Courthouse	Port Townsend	98368
King	516 Third Ave.	Seattle	98104
Kitsap	614 Division	Port Orchard	98366
Kittitas	5th & Main	Ellensburg	98926
Klickitat	205 S. Columbus	Goldendale	98620

County	Address	City	ZIP
Lewis	P.O. Box 357	Chehalis	98532
Lincoln	450 Logan	Davenport	99122
Mason	P.O. Box 340	Shelton	98584
Okanogan	P.O. Box 112	Okanogan	98840
Pacific	P.O. Box 67	South Bend	98586
Pend Oreille	Hall of Justice	Newport	99156
Pierce	930 Tacoma Ave. S.	Tacoma	98402
San Juan	P.O. Box 127	Friday Harbor	98250
Skagit	P.O. Box 837	Mount Vernon	98273
Skamania	P.O. Box 269	Stevenson	98648
Snohomish	County Courthouse	Everett	98201
Spokane	P.O. Box 470	Spokane	99201
Stevens	215 S. Oak	Colville	99114
Thurston	2000 Lakeridge Dr. S.W.	Olympia	98501
Wahkiakum	P.O. Box 116	Cathlamet	98612
Walla Walla	P.O. Box 836	Walla Walla	99362
Whatcom	311 Grand Ave.	Bellingham	98225
Whitman	P.O. Box 679	Colfax	99111
Yakima	N. Second & E. B Sts.	Yakima	98901

APPENDIX G
LAWYER REFERRAL SERVICES IN WASHINGTON

1. King County 1-206-623-2551

2. Lewis County 1-206-748-9121

3. Pierce County 1-206-383-3432

4. Spokane County 1-509-456-6032

5. People residing in all other counties may call the Washington State Bar Association Lawyer Referral Service toll-free number: 1-800-552-0787.

APPENDIX H
DIVIDING UP THE PENSION

Two typical pension provisions are provided below. One deals with a private company pension and the other deals with a military pension. The language to be used in a pension provision of a Decree of Dissolution varies from company to company, as well as with the governmental agency involved. **You must check with the pension provider to be certain the language you decide to use in your Decree of Dissolution conforms to the pension provider's requirements.**

1. PRIVATE COMPANY PENSION

(Wife)/(Husband) shall have an interest in (Husband's)/(Wife's) monthly retirement benefits under the Company Employee Retirement Plan, equal to fifty percent (50%) of the following formula: the total number of (husband's)/(wife's) years of service with the Company during the marriage prior to dissolution shall be the numerator of the fraction; the denominator shall be the (husband's)/(wife's) total number of years of service with the Company at the time of (his)/(her) retirement. The total monthly benefit shall be multiplied by the foregoing fraction to determine the community interest. (Wife)/(Husband) shall be entitled to receive fifty percent (50%) of the community interest. The Plan shall pay directly to (Wife)/(Husband) (her)/(his) interest in the (Husband's)/(Wife's) benefits, when they become payable, subject to the terms of the Plan. When (Husband)/(Wife) retires, (Wife)/(Husband) shall notify the Plan of the calculations of (her)/(his) interest, (her)/(his) social security number, and (her)/(his) mailing address and the Plan shall be under no obligation to pay (Wife)/(Husband) until so notified. Payments to (Wife)/(Husband) shall terminate immediately upon the earlier) of (Wife's)/(Husband's) death or (Husband's)/(Wife's) death.

2. MILITARY BRANCH PENSION

(Husband)/(Wife) shall receive monthly retirement benefits from the Military Branch Pension commencing at age _____ (19__). (Husband)/(Wife) shall direct the Military Branch Retirement Benefits Department to divide the monthly benefits equally between the parties giving fifty (50%) of the benefit after taxes to (Wife)/(Husband), but excluding any deductions in the event (Husband)/(Wife) has a new spouse. (Wife's)/(Husband's) fifty percent (50%) shall be increased by the annual cost of living allowance. The Department shall be further directed to mail fifty percent (50%) of the monthly benefits to (Wife)/(Husband) and fifty percent (50%) of the monthly benefits to (Husband)(Wife).

The Military Branch Retirement Benefits Department shall be directed to deduct taxes in an equal amount from each party. In the event that the Department is unable to deduct taxes from (Wife's)/(Husband's) fifty percent (50%) interest, then (Wife)/(Husband) shall reimburse (Husband)/(Wife) for (her)/(his) fair share of the tax liability, which shall be calculated at (Husband's)/(Wife's) effective tax rate.

(Husband)/(Wife) shall elect to provide an SBP/RCSBP annuity for (Wife)/(Husband) pursuant to 10 U.S.C. §1448(b)(2), and (Husband)/(Wife) shall complete and mail to the Military Branch Retirement Benefits Department any and all forms necessary to enact the election. (Husband)/(Wife) shall provide the Department with a written statement, signed by (him)/(her) and (Wife)/(Husband), setting forth that this election is made pursuant to a written agreement entered into voluntarily as part of a proceeding of divorce and that it has been incorporated in, or ratified by, a court order.

APPENDIX I
TAX CONSIDERATIONS OF DIVORCE

The 1984 Tax Reform Act dramatically revised the impact of federal income tax on divorcing couples. Highlights of the Act are summarized below. The reader is warned, however, that these tax laws are complex and are frequently modified. A tax consultant, accountant, or attorney must be consulted before you irrevocably sign any agreement containing tax consequences.

1. **Property transfers between spouses.** Transfers of property, including installment obligations, are no longer potentially taxable events. Instead, the transferee spouse takes the property subject to the same tax attributes as the property had during the marriage. Although no gain (or loss) is recognized when the transfer occurs, the transferee will be solely responsible for the tax consequences on a subsequent sale of the asset.

Thus, if the transferee spouse gets the family home, he or she will be responsible for all the gain on its subsequent sale, even if the other spouse is to share in the proceeds of its sale. One way to avoid this anomaly would be to require both spouses to retain an ownership interest in the house after the divorce so that each will be taxed on a portion of the gain when the house is ultimately sold. Another way to avoid this effect is to make an adjustment in the value of the house to reflect later tax consequences before agreeing to share the sale proceeds with the transferor spouse.

2. **Exemption.** Divorcing couples with dependent children may agree who will get the tax exemption. Absent an agreement or provision in the decree, the primary residential parent will get the exemption unless he or she signs a written declaration to the contrary, which is then filed with the nonprimary parent's income tax return.

3. **Child-care expenses.** Only the parent who has custody of the child for a majority of the tax year may claim the 20% to 30% tax credit for child-care expenses.

4. Health insurance. The cost of employer-paid health insurance for dependent children is still excludable from a parent's income even if that parent does not have custody.

5. Taxpayer filing status during separation. Married persons who file separate returns pay taxes at much higher rates than single taxpayers or couples filing joint returns. If legally separated or divorced before the end of the taxable year, however, the taxpayer may file as a single person. Married persons who are living separate and apart, but are not legally separated, can still file a joint return. In addition, a married parent who is not yet legally separated or divorced can get favorable head of household status provided that he or she maintained a household that was used as the principal abode of the child for more than one-half of the taxable year.

6. Complex alimony rule. Alimony payments continue to be deductible by the payor spouse and includable in the income of the payee spouse. The Internal Revenue Service has, however, introduced new requirements designed to prevent alimony payments from being used as a means of transferring property between spouses at lower income tax rates.

To be deductible by the payor spouse, alimony:

A. Must be made in cash (non-cash transfers are ineffective);

B. Must cease on the death of the payee and the written agreement or decree must state that there is no liability to continue payments beyond the death of the payee;

C. Cannot be reduced upon any contingency relating to the children; and,

D. Payments in excess of $15,000 per year will be allowable only if the excess payments continue for at least three years. Even then, annual payments which decrease significantly in the second and third year are subject to "recapture" in the third year. Recapture rules apply if either (1) alimony payments in the second year exceed payments in the third year by more than $15,000 *or* (2) if payments in the first year exceed the average payments in the second and third year by more than $15,000, reduced by any year two recapture tax.

The parties can still agree on whether alimony payments are to be deductible by the payor or includable in the income of the payee.

The payor spouse faces a $50 penalty if he or she fails to provide the Internal Revenue Service with the social security number of the payee spouse.

7. Impact of taxes on parents with joint custody. Unless there is an agreement between the parents (with appropriate provisions in the decree of dissolution), only the parent who has custody of the child for the majority of the tax year can claim the dependency exemption, head of household status, or child-care credit.

Caution

These tax rules are complex. They will probably be changed or modified in the near future. Do not make the mistake of substituting your own judgment for that of a professional who has been trained in taxation and who can advise you on the current tax consequences of your separation or divorce agreement.

APPENDIX J
WASHINGTON STATE CHILD SUPPORT SCHEDULE

Including:
- **Standards for Setting Support**
- **Economic Table**
- **Instructions**
- **Worksheets**

Effective Date: July 1, 1990
Washington State Child Support Schedule Commission

AUTHORS' WARNING: The Schedule is subject to significant change. Please check with the Clerk of your local Superior Court to be certain your Schedules are current

TABLE OF CONTENTS

Page

INTRODUCTION

The 1988 Legislature adopted SHB 1465 establishing a statewide Child Support Schedule with the intention of ensuring adequate child support orders to meet a child's basic needs and to provide additional support commensurate with the parents' income, resources, and standard of living. It was also intended that child support obligations be equitably apportioned between the parents. The Child Support Schedule was revised in 1989 pursuant to the November 1, 1988, Washington State Child Support Commission Report to the Legislature and again in 1990 pursuant to HB2888. This 1990 version of the Washington State Child Support Schedule incorporates these changes.

This Child Support Schedule is comprised of:

(1) The *Standards for the Determination of Child Support* adopted by RCW 26.19.010 and .040.

(2) The *Economic Table,* which sets forth the basic child support obligation to be shared by the parents in proportion to their incomes. The Economic Table developed by the Commission is based on the 1972-73 Consumer Expenditure Survey as updated and revised by the federal government. It states ordinary child-rearing expenditures based on the age of a child, number of children in a family, and the net income of the parents. Because the Table is income based, cost-of-living differences between areas of the state are indirectly taken into account.

(3) The *Worksheets* and *Instructions* provide for the calculation of each parent's share of the support obligation. The Instructions should be read carefully while completing the worksheets

Worksheet A contains five parts. Part I provides the determination and allocation of the basic child support obligation. Included in the Table's basic support amount are *ordinary expenses* that are common to all children. These expenses are generally assumed to be paid according to the child's residential schedule. If an ordinary expense is assigned to one parent regardless of the residential schedule, a child support credit is provided for that parent in Part IV. Part II of the worksheet addresses the issues of health care and special child-rearing expenses. While the amounts listed on the economic table cover ordinary health care expenses, extraordinary health care expenses as well as other special child-rearing expenses (*e.g.* day care) are not included. These expenses as well as expenses that far exceed an average for an income group are added to the basic support obligation. Part III calculates the total support obligation. Part IV provides for child support credits and Part V determines the actual amount of money to be transferred from one parent to the other parent for the support of the child(ren).

Worksheet B is used to determine a residential schedule credit adjustment. This worksheet needs to be completed only if a residential schedule credit is desired.

Worksheet C provides additional factors for consideration when support is being determined and is required to be completed in each proceeding. Pursuant to RCW 26.19.020, all income and resources of each household must be disclosed and considered by the court or administrative law judge.

Pursuant to RCW 26.19, all income and resources of each household must be disclosed and considered by the court. This worksheet also provides the basis for determining when a deviation from the standard calculation is appropriate.

Also included with the Child Support Schedule is a **CHILD SUPPORT ORDER SUMMARY REPORT FORM.** *Purusant to HB 2888 this form is required to be completed and filed with the county clerk in any proceeding where child support is established or modified.*

RCW 26.19 requires that the Child Support Worksheets are to be completed under penalty of perjury, that the court is not to accept incomplete worksheets or worksheets that vary from the worksheets developed by the Office of the Administrator for the Courts. A copy of the Child Support Schedule and Summary Report Form may be obtained from the Office of the Administrator for the Courts, 1206 S. Quince, Olympia, Wa., 98504.

STANDARDS FOR THE DETERMINATION OF CHILD SUPPORT AND USE OF THE SCHEDULE

1. The Washington Child Support Schedule shall be applied as follows:
   a. In each county of the state;
   b. In judicial and administrative proceedings;
   c. In all proceedings in which child support is determined or modified;
   d. For setting temporary and permanent support; and
   e. For adjusting support orders instead of using a cost-of-living or escalation provision.

2. The parents' obligation for support shall be based on their combined net income, resources and special child-rearing costs.

3. Monthly gross income shall include income from any source: salaries, wages, commissions, deferred compensation, bonuses, overtime, dividends, interest, trust income, severance pay, annuities, capital gains, social security benefits, workers compensation, unemployment, disability insurance benefits, gifts and prizes. AFDC, SSI, General Assistance, and Food Stamps shall be disclosed but shall not be included in gross income or be a reason to deviate from the schedule. Spousal maintenance or child support received from other relationships shall be disclosed and considered under Standards 12 and 13, but shall not be included in gross income.

4. Allowable deductions from gross income are income taxes, FICA, state industrial insurance, mandatory pension plan payments, and mandatory union/professional dues. Payment of child support or maintenance involving other relationships shall be disclosed and considered under Standards 12 and 13, but shall not be included as a deduction from gross income.

   For self-employed persons, normal business expenses and self-employment taxes may be deducted. Justification shall be required for any business expense deduction about which there is disagreement.

   Non-recurring overtime/bonus income may be separately identified and allowed as a discretionary deduction from gross income.

5. Tax returns for the preceding three years and current paystubs shall be provided to verify income and deductions. Other sufficient verification shall

be required for income and deductions which do not appear on tax returns or paystubs.

In the absence of information to the contrary, a parent's income shall be based on the median income of year-round full-time workers as derived from the United States Bureau of Census, Current Population Reports. (See Instructions, Part I.)

6. The basic child support obligation derived from the economic table shall be allocated between the parents based on each parent's share of the combined monthly net income.

7. Ordinary health care expenses are included in the economic table. Monthly health care expenses that exceed five percent of the basic support obligation shall be considered extraordinary health care expenses. Extraordinary helath care expenses shall be shared by the parents in the same proportion as the basic child support obligation.

Day care and special child-rearing expenses such as tuition and long-distance transportation costs to and from the parents for visitation purposes are not included in the economic table. These expenses shall be shared by the parents in the same proportion as the basic child support obligation.

The court may exercise its discretion to determine the necessity for and reasonableness of all amounts ordered in excess of the basic child support obligation.

8. When combined monthly net income is less than $600, a support order not less than $25 per month per child shall be entered.

When combined monthly net income exceeds $7,000, child support shall not be set at a level lower than that amount from the table, but the court has discretion to establish support at higher levels upon written finding of fact.

9. Neither parent's child support obligation shall exceed fifty percent (50%) of net earnings unless good cause is shown. Good cause could include possession of substantial wealth, children with day-care expenses, special medical, educational, or psychological needs, and larger families.

10. Basic child support shall be allocated between the parents when a child stays overnight with the parent over twenty-five percent (25%) of the year. When this adjustment is sought, and the parents are not in agreement, the parent seeking the adjustment shall provide evidence to demonstrate the parents' actual past involvement with the child. However, the support payment should not be reduced if there will be insufficient funds available to meet the basic needs of the child in the house receiving the support, or if the child is receiving AFDC payments.

11. The presumptive amount of support shall be determined according to the schedule. Deviations must be explained in writing and supported by evidence. When reasons exist for deviation, discretion shall be exercised in considering the extent to which the factors would affect the support obligation.

12. Reasons for deviation may include the possession of wealth, shared living arrangement, extraordinary debt not voluntarily incurred, extraordinary high income of a child, a significant disparity in the living costs of the parents due to conditions beyond their control, special needs of disabled

children, and tax planning. The transfer payment amount may deviate if tax planning results in greater benefit to the child.

13. When there are children from other relationships, the schedule shall be applied to the mother, father and children of the relationship being considered. Deviations from the amount of support derived from this application may be based upon all the circumstances of both households. All income, resources, and support obligations paid and received shall be disclosed and considered. Support obligations include children in the home and children outside of the home.

14. The schedule shall be advisory and not mandatory for post-secondary educational support.

15. Wage income shall be imputed for parents who are voluntarily unemployed or voluntarily underemployed. A parent will not be deemed underemployed as long as that parent is gainfully employed on a full-time basis. Income shall not be imputed for an unemployable parent.

16. All income and resources of each parent's household shall be disclosed and considered by the court. The worksheets shall be completed under penalty of perjury and filed in every proceeding in which child support is determined. The court shall not accept incomplete worksheets or worksheets that vary from the worksheets developed by the Office of the Administrator for the Courts.

INSTRUCTIONS FOR WORKSHEET A:
COMPUTATION OF THE CHILD SUPPORT OBLIGATION

Fill in the names and ages of the child(ren) whose support is at issue. Do not include children of other relationships.

PART I: BASIC SUPPORT OBLIGATION
MONTHLY GROSS INCOME

Monthly gross income is defined by Standard #3.

Enter only the income of the parents of the children whose support is at issue. Do not include wages and salaries of any other person. Income of other members of the household is to be listed on Worksheet C. If the income of a parent is unknown, see the instructions for **Unknown Income.**

Pursuant to Standard #5, tax returns for the preceding three years are required for income verification purposes.

Monthly Average of Income:
* *If income varies during the year, divide the annual total of the income by 12.*
* *If paid weekly, multiply the weekly income by 52 and divide by 12.*
* *If paid every other week, multiply the two-week income by 26 and divide by 12.*
* *If paid twice a month (bi-monthly), multiply the bi-monthly income by 24 and divide by 12.*

LINE 1a, *Wages, Salaries, and Tips:* Enter the average monthly total of all wages, salaries, commissions and tips. Wages and salaries include bonus and overtime pay. *(If a parent is not working full time see the instructions for Imputed Income.)*

LINE 1b, *Interest and Dividend Income:* Enter the average monthly total of dividends and interest income.

LINE 1c, *Business Income:* Enter the average monthly income from self-employment after normal business expenses have been deducted. *(If, after normal business expenses have been deducted, business income is negative, enter 0. Pursuant to Standard #4, justification shall be required for any business expense deduction about which there is a disagreement.)*

LINE 1d, *Other Income:* Enter the average monthly total of other income. Other income includes, but is not limited to, deferred compensation, trust income, severance pay, annuities, capital gains, social security benefits, workers compensation, unemployment, disability insurance benefits, gifts, prizes, self-employment retirement plans, matching stock options and savings plans.

LINE 1e, *Total Monthly Gross Income:* Add the monthly income amounts for each parent (lines 1a through 1d) and enter the totals on line 1e.

Income Exclusions: Not included as gross income are maintenance awarded for any relationship, child support received for children of another relationship, educational grants or loans, or any benefits received from the following public assistance programs: Aid to Families with Dependent Children (AFDC), Supplemental Social Security (SSI), Food Stamps, and General Assistance. Pursuant to Standard #3, excluded income must be disclosed and listed on Worksheet C.

Imputed Income: Pursuant to Standard #15, the court has discretion in determining whether income is to be imputed. A parent who is working full time is not considered underemployed.

If income is imputed because a parent is voluntarily unemployed or underemployed, the past earnings or earnings potential of the parent should be considered in determining the amount of income imputed to that parent. This amount should be entered on line 1a as wages, salaries, and tips with the notation "imputed" added on that line.

Examples of voluntary unemployment may include a parent who quits a job or refuses to work in order to impact a child support obligation or a parent who is remarried or is cohabitating and not working.

Unknown Income: The following table shall be used to determine a parent's income only if there is no other information from which a parent's income can be determined or estimated. Examples of information from which income can be determined or estimated include: tax returns, paystubs, and information about the parent's standard of living, or earning ability. (See Standard #5.)

Approximate Median Net Monthly Income		
MALE	age	FEMALE
$ 678	15-19	$ 650
$ 988	20-24	$ 876
$1567	25-34	$1177
$1938	35-44	$1325
$2049	45-54	$1276
$1949	55-65	$1190
U.S. Bureau of the Census,		
Statistical Abstract of the United States: 1989		

[Net income has been determined by subtracting FICA (7.51 percent) and the tax liability for a single person (one withholding allowance).]

MONTHLY DEDUCTIONS FROM GROSS INCOME

Allowable monthly deductions from gross income are defined in Standard #4.

Pursuant to Standard #5, verification of all claimed deductions is required.

Monthly Average of Deductions: If a deduction is annual or varies during the year, divide the annual total of the deduction by 12 to determine a monthly amount.

LINE 2a, *Income Taxes: Enter the monthly amount actually owed for state and federal income taxes.* **Do not include the income taxes paid on non-recurring income amounts entered on line 2e.** *(The amount of income tax withheld on a paycheck may not be the actual amount of income tax owed due to tax refund, etc. It is appropriate to consider tax returns from prior years as indicating the actual amount of income tax owed if income has not changed.)*

LINE 2b, *FICA/Self Employment Taxes, State Industrial Insurance Deductions:* Enter the total monthly amount of FICA/Self-Employment taxes owed and state industrial insurance deductions.

LINE 2c, *Mandatory Union/Professional Dues:* Enter the monthly cost of mandatory union or professional dues.

LINE 2d, *Mandatory Pension Plan Payments:* Enter the monthly cost of mandatory pension plan payments.

LINE 2e, *Non-recurring Income:* Enter income from lines 1a through 1d that is not a regular, anticipated part of annual income. *(An example would be a one time special bonus. This deduction is discretionary with the court.)*

LINE 2f, *Total Deductions From Gross Income:* Add the monthly deductions for each parent (lines 2a through 2e) and enter the totals on line 2f.

LINE 3, *Monthly Net Income:* For each parent subtract total deductions (line 2f) from total monthly gross income (line 1e) and enter these amounts on line 3.

LINE 4, *Combined Monthly Net Income:* Add the parents' monthly net income (line 3) and enter the total on line 4.

LINE 5, *Basic Child Support Obligation:* In the work area provided on line 5 enter the basic support obligation amounts determined for each child. Add these amounts together and enter the total in the box on line 5. *(To determine a per child basic support obligation see the following economic table instructions.)*

ECONOMIC TABLE INSTRUCTIONS

The Economic Table is located in this Appendix, following the Child Support Order Summary Report.

To use the Economic Table to determine an individual support amount for each child:

- Locate in the left-hand column the monthly net income amount closest to the amount entered on line 4 of Worksheet A. *(Round up when the combined monthly net income falls halfway between the two amounts in the left hand column.)*

- Locate on the top row the family size for the number of children for whom child support is being determined. *(When determining family size for the required worksheet, do not include children from other relationships.)*

- Circle the two numbers in the columns listed below the family size that are across from the net income amount. The amount in the "A" column is the basic support amount for a child up to age 12. The amount in the "B" column is the basic support amount for a child 12 years of age or older.

LINE 6, *Proportional Share of Income:* Divide the monthly net income for each parent (line 3) by the combined monthly net income (line 4) and enter these percentages (*e.g.* 0.67) on line 6. *(The entries on line 6 when added together should equal 1.00.)*

LINE 7, *Each Parent's Basic Child Support Obligation:* Multiply the *total* basic child support obligation (amount in box on line 5) by the income share proportion for each parent (line 6) and enter these amounts on line 7. *(The amounts entered on line 7 added together should equal the amount entered on line 5.)*

PART II: HEALTH CARE, DAY CARE, AND SPECIAL CHILD-REARING EXPENSES

Pursuant to Standard #7, discretion may be exercised to determine the reasonableness and necessity of extraordinary and special expenses.

Unknown Expenses: *Pursuant to Standard #7, if the amount of a health care, day care, or* **approved** *special child rearing expense is unknown, the expense shall be apportioned between the parents by the same percentage as the basic child support obligation (line 6). If an expense is to be apportioned in this manner, enter the notation "apportioned" on the appropriate line of the worksheet for that expense. In addition, the court order should also reflect that the particular expenses designated are to be apportioned in the same percentage as the basic child support obligation.*

Monthly Average of Expenses: *If a health care, day care, or special child rearing expense is annual or varies during the year, divide the annual total of the expense by 12 to determine a monthly amount.*

HEALTH CARE EXPENSES

(The following allocation of ordinary and extraordinary health care expenses may not apply if the combined monthly net income exceeds $2,500 and an alternative economic table has been adopted in the county where the action is filed.)

LINE 8a. *Monthly Health Insurance Premiums Paid For Child(ren):* List the monthly amount paid by each parent for health care insurance for the child(ren) of the relationship. *(When determining an insurance premium amount do not include the portion of the premium paid by an employer or other third party and/ or the portion of the premium that covers the parent or other household members.)*

LINE 8b, *Uninsured Monthly Health Care Expenses Paid For Child(ren):* List the monthly amount paid by each parent for the health care expenses of the children of the relationship not reimbursed by insurance.

LINE 8c, *Total Monthly Health Care Expenses:* For each parent add the health insurance premium payments (line 8a) to the uninsured health care payments (line 8b) and enter these amounts on line 8c.

LINE 8d, *Combined Monthly Health Care Expenses:* Add the parents' total health care payments (line 8c) and enter this amount on line 8d.

LINE 8e, *Maximum Ordinary Monthly Health Care:* Enter the *greater* amount of either:

- 5 percent of the basic support obligation (line 5 x .05); or,
- $20 times the number of children whose names are listed at the top of Worksheet A.

LINE 8f, *Extraordinary Monthly Health Care Expenses:* Subtract the maximum monthly health care deduction (line 8e) from the combined monthly health care payments (line 8d) and enter this amount on line 8f. *(If the resulting answer is "0" or a negative number, enter a "0".)*

The court order should reflect that reasonable health care costs not listed should be apportioned by the same percentage as the basic child support obligation (line 6) once the annual amount for the maximum ordinary health care (line 8e x 12) has been reached.

DAY CARE AND SPECIAL CHILD REARING EXPENSES

LINE 9a, *Day Care Expenses:* Enter average monthly day care costs.

LINE 9b, *Education Expenses:* Enter the average monthly costs of tuition and other related educational expenses.

LINE 9c, *Long distance Transportation Expenses:* Enter the average monthly costs of long distance travel incurred pursuant to the residential or visitation schedule.

LINE 9d, *Other Special Expenses:* Identify any other special expenses and enter the average monthly cost of each.

LINE 9e, *Total Day Care and Special Expenses:* Add the monthly expenses for each parent (lines 9a through 9d) and enter these totals on line 9e.

LINE 10, *Combined Monthly Total of Day Care and Special Expenses:* Add the parents' total expenses (line 9e) and enter this total on line 10.

LINE 11, *Total Extraordinary Health Care, Day Care, and Special Expenses:* Add the extraordinary health care payments (line 8f) to the combined monthly total of day care and special expenses (line 10) and enter this amount on line 11.

LINE 12, *Each Parent's Obligation For Extraordinary Health Care, Day Care, and Special Expenses:* Multiply the total extraordinary health care, day care, and special expense amount (line 11) by the income proportion for each parent (line 6) and enter these amounts on line 12.

PART III: TOTAL CHILD SUPPORT OBLIGATION

LINE 13, *Total Support Obligation:* For each parent add the basic child support obligation (line 7) to the obligation for extraordinary health care, day care, and special expenses (line 12). Enter these amounts on line 13.

PART IV: CHILD SUPPORT CREDITS

LINE 14a, *Monthly Health Care Expenses Credit:* Enter the total monthly health care expenses amounts from line 8c for each parent.

LINE 14b, *Day Care and Special Expenses Credit:* Enter the total day care and special expenses amounts from line 9e for each parent.

LINE 14c, *Other Ordinary Expense Credit:* If approval of another ordinary expense credit is being requested, in the space provided, specify the expense and enter the average monthly cost in the column of the parent to receive the credit. *(It is generally assumed that ordinary expenses are paid in accordance with the child's residence. If payment of a specific ordinary expense does not follow this assumption, the parent paying for this expense may request approval of an ordinary expense credit. This credit is discretionary with the court.)*

LINE 14d, *Residential Schedule Credit:* For *father's* residential schedule credit enter the amount listed on Worksheet B, line 26. FoR *mother's* residential schedule credit enter the amount listed on Worksheet B, line 27. *(Worksheet B is required to be completed if a residential schedule credit is being claimed.)*

LINE 14e, *Total Support Credits:* For each parent add the entries on lines 14a through 14d and enter the totals on line 14e.

PART V: NET SUPPORT OBLIGATION AND TRANSFER PAYMENT

LINE 15, *Net Support Obligation:* For each parent, subtract the total support credits (line 14e) from the total support obligation (line 13) and enter the resulting amounts on line 15.

Transfer Payment: Pursuant to the following directions, circle the amount entered on line 15 that will be the transfer payment amount.

• If no residential schedule credit has been claimed on line 14d the transfer payment is the amount entered on line 15 in the column of the parent with whom the child(ren) will reside for less than 25 percent of the time. That parent should transfer that amount to the other parent for the support of the child(ren).

• If a residential schedule credit is claimed on line 14d, the transfer payment is the positive amount entered on line 15. The parent with the positive amount should transfer that amount to the other parent for the support of the child(ren). *(If a residential schedule credit is claimed the amounts entered on line 15 should be exactly the opposite of each other. For example, if one parent's amount is $500, the other parent's amount should be minus $500.)*

CONTINUE TO WORKSHEET C.

INSTRUCTIONS FOR WORKSHEET B: RESIDENTIAL SCHEDULE ADJUSTMENT

This worksheet should be completed if any child listed on Worksheet A spends more than 25 percent of the year (91 nights) with each parent and a residential schedule credit is desired, or if more than one child is listed on Worksheet A and one or more of the children will spend more than 75 percent of the year with one parent and the other child or children will spend 75 percent of the year with the other parent (a situation formerly identified as "split custody").

Separate calculations must be performed for each of the children.

LINE 16, *List Children:* List each child's name. *(List only the names of the children entered at the top of Worksheet A.)*

LINE 17, *Basic Support Obligation:* For each child enter the basic support amount listed in the work space on Worksheet A, line 5.

ORDINARY EXPENSES *PER CHILD*

LINE 18a, *Total Monthly Health Care Expenses:* Enter the *per child* monthly amount paid by the parents for health care insurance and uninsured medical expenses. *(To determine a **per child** health insurance premium amount, if unknown, divide the entry on line 8a by the number of children. Then add the resulting amounts to each child's portion of uninsured health care expenses (line 8b) to determine the per child total monthly health care expenses. The total of all amounts entered on line 18a should equal the amount entered on Worksheet A, line 8d.)*

LINE 18b, *Maximum Ordinary Monthly Health Care:* For each child enter the *greater* amount of either:
- 5 percent of the basic support obligation (line 18 x .05); or,
- $20

LINE 18c, *Ordinary Health Care Amount:* For each child enter the *lesser* amount of either total monthly health care expenses (line 18a) or maximum ordinary monthly health care (line 18b).

LINE 18d, *Other Ordinary Expenses:* For each child enter the monthly amount paid by the parents for other ordinary expenses. *(The total of all amounts entered on line 18d should equal the total of the amounts entered on Worksheet A, line 14c.)*

LINE 18e, *Total Ordinary Expenses:* For each child add the ordinary health care amount (line 18c) to other ordinary expenses (line 18d) and enter this amount on line 18e.

LINE 19, *Adjusted Basic Support:* For each child subtract total ordinary expenses (line 18e) from the basic support amount (line 17) and enter this amount on line 19.

LINES 20 and 22, *Overnights with Father and Mother:* Enter the number of overnights per year each child will be spending with each parent. *(For each child, the overnights with father plus the overnights with mother should equal 365.)*

LINES 21 and 23, *Proportional Overnights with Father and Mother:* Divide each parent's overnights (lines 20 and 22) by 365 and enter the resulting percentages *(e.g, 0.50)* on lines 21 (father's) and 23 (mother's). *(For each child, father's proportional overnights plus mother's proportional overnights should total 1.00.)*

LINES 24 and 25, *Credit Proportions for Father and Mother:* Instructions appear on the worksheet. *(The credit proportion calculations incorporate the 25 percent threshold required pursuant to Standard #10 and adjust the support such that a 50-50 sharing of residential time between the parents results in a 50-50 sharing of the basic support monies contributed by both.)*

LINE 26, *Father's Residential Schedule Credits:* For each child, multiply father's credit proportion line (line 24) by the adjusted basic support (line 19) and enter this amount on line 26.

LINE 27, *Mother's Residential Schedule Credits:* For each child multiply mother's credit proportion (line 25) by the adjusted basic support (line 19) and enter this amount on line 27.

RETURN TO WORKSHEET A, LINE 14d.

INSTRUCTIONS FOR WORKSHEET C:
ADDITIONAL FACTORS FOR CONSIDERATION

This worksheet must be completed whether or not a deviation is requested.

Enter on this worksheet information about assets (line 28a through 28h), debts (line 29), and other relationships (lines 30 through 35). Pursuant to RCW 26.19, all income and resources of each parent's household shall be disclosed. This information may also be used as a basis for a deviation from a standard calculation support amount. *(RCW 26.19.010(7) defines "standard calculation" as "the amount of child support which is owed as determined from the worksheets before any deviation is considered.")*

Reasons for deviations may be found in Standards 9 through 13.

If a deviation is made, the child support order must include the support obligation of each parent prior to deviation, the support obligation of each parent after deviation, and the reason for deviation.

Maintenance Considerations: *If maintenance is being paid or received because of another relationship, information about that other relationship may be reviewed and maintenance may be considered as representing child support, wealth (pay-off of assets in the prior relationship), support for a dependent ex-spouse, or a combination of the above.*

Children From Other Relationships: *When there are children from other relationships, the schedule shall first be applied to the mother, father and children of the relationship being considered on Worksheets A and B. Discretion may then be used to deviate from that amount of support by considering the information on Worksheet C. Deviations may be based on all the circumstances of both households. All income, resource and support obligations paid and received shall be disclosed and considered. Support obligations include children in the home and children outside the home.*

No one formula for determining the deviation is suitable for all the varying family situations. The Commission adopted the following principles for the situation involving children from other relationships:

• *Each child has an equal right to share in a parent's income and the schedule should avoid creating economic disincentives for remarriage.*

• *The actual amount of support ordered for each child of a parent may vary, however, because of the financial situation of the other parent of the child.*

• *An approach of directly counting the income of a new spouse may act as a disincentive for remarriage for either parent. The approach for deviation must treat both parents in the same way, either including or excluding the income of new spouses and the needs of other children.*

If a deviation is made because of children of other relationships, the method used to compute the amount of each parent's support obligation should be described.

Nonparental Custody Cases: When the children do not reside with either parent, the household income and resources of the children's custodian(s) should be listed on line 36.

CHILD SUPPORT ORDER SUMMARY REPORT

Father's Name: _____   Mother's Name: _____

Cause Number: _____   Court: _____

Date of Order: _____

1. Type of Order (check one):   ___ Judicial   ___ Administrative

2. Was the order for child support (check one): __original order for support __order modifying support

3. Number of children of the parties: ____

4. List each child's age:

    Child 1 ____   Child 2 ____   Child 3 ____   Child 4 ____

    Child 5 ____   Child 6 ____   Child 7 ____   Child 8 ____

5. Combined monthly net income of the parties, from Worksheet A, Line 4: $____

6. Father's monthly net income, as determined by the court from Worksheet A, Line 3: $____

7. Mother's monthly net income, as determined by the court from Worksheet A, Line 3: $____

8. List the basic child support obligation for each child (individual amounts), from
   Worksheet A, Line 5:

    Child 1 ____   Child 2 ____   Child 3 ____   Child 4 ____

    Child 5 ____   Child 6 ____   Child 7 ____   Child 8 ____

                                              Total: $____

9. Did the court deviate from any of the amounts set forth in Worksheet A, Line 5?

   ___ No   ___ Yes

10. If the court deviated, what were reasons stated by the court for the deviation?

_____

_____

_____

11. If the court deviated, list the amount of child support (after the deviation) for each child:

    Child 1 ____   Child 2 ____   Child 3 ____   Child 4 ____

    Child 5 ____   Child 6 ____   Child 7 ____   Child 8 ____

                                              Total: $____

12. Amount awarded for daycare, if any: $____

13. Other extraordinary amounts awarded, if any: Purpose: _____   Award: $____

                                            Purpose: _____   Award: $____

                                            Purpose: _____   Award: $____

14. Amounts awarded for postsecondary education, if any: $____

15. Total amount of support ordered: $____

16. Amount of transfer payment ordered: $____

17. Which parent was ordered to make the transfer payment?   ___father   ___mother

Answer the remaining questions only if this was an order modifying support.

18. Total amount of support in the previous order? $____

19. Percentage change: Question 15 divided by Question 18 = ___%

20. If modification was greater than 30% change (that is, if question 19=130 or more),
   was the change phased in?   ___yes   ___no

Economic Table
Monthly Basic Support Obligation *Per Child*

(This table shall be used in all administrative proceedings. Check with the Superior Court Clerk where the case is filed to see if an alternative economic table is being used in that county.)

Key: A=Age 10-11; B=Age 12-18

Combined Monthly Net Income Income	One Child Family Schedule		Two Children Family Schedule		Three Children Family Schedule		Four Children Family Schedule		Five Children Family Schedule	
	A	B	A	B	A	B	A	B	A	B
0										
10										
200										
300				For income less than $600, see Standard No. 8						
400										
500										
600	133	164	103	127	86	106	73	90	63	78
700	155	191	120	148	100	124	85	105	74	91
800	177	218	137	170	115	142	87	120	84	104
900	199	246	154	191	129	159	109	135	95	118
1000	220	272	171	211	143	177	121	149	105	130
1100	242	299	188	232	157	194	133	164	116	143
1200	264	326	205	253	171	211	144	179	126	156
1300	285	352	221	274	185	228	156	193	136	168
1400	307	379	238	294	199	246	168	208	147	181
1500	327	404	254	313	212	262	179	221	156	193
1600	347	428	269	333	225	278	190	235	166	205
1700	367	453	285	352	238	294	201	248	175	217
1800	387	478	300	371	251	310	212	262	195	228
1900	407	503	316	390	264	326	223	275	194	240
2000	427	527	331	409	277	342	234	289	204	252
2100	447	552	347	429	289	358	245	303	213	264
2200	467	577	362	448	302	374	256	316	223	276
2300	487	601	378	467	315	390	267	330	233	288
2400	506	626	393	486	328	406	278	343	242	299
2500	526	650	408	505	341	421	288	356	251	311
2600	545	674	424	523	353	437	299	369	261	322
2700	565	698	439	542	366	453	310	383	270	334
2800	584	722	454	561	379	468	320	396	279	345
2900	604	746	469	579	391	484	331	409	289	357
3000	623	770	484	598	404	499	342	422	298	368
3100	643	794	499	617	417	515	352	435	307	380
3200	662	819	514	635	429	531	363	449	317	391
3300	682	843	530	654	442	546	374	462	326	403
3400	701	866	544	672	454	561	384	475	335	414
3500	719	889	559	690	466	576	394	487	344	425
3600	738	912	573	708	478	591	404	500	353	436
3700	757	935	588	726	490	606	415	412	362	447
3800	775	958	602	744	502	621	425	525	371	458
3900	794	981	617	762	515	536	435	538	379	469
4000	812	1004	631	779	527	651	445	550	388	480
4100	831	1027	645	797	539	666	455	563	397	491
4200	850	1050	660	815	551	681	466	575	406	502
4300	868	1073	674	833	563	696	476	588	415	513
4400	885	1094	688	849	574	709	485	599	423	523
4500	902	1114	700	865	584	722	494	611	431	533
4600	918	1135	713	881	595	736	503	622	439	543
4700	935	1155	726	897	606	749	512	633	447	552
4800	951	1176	739	913	617	762	521	644	455	562
4900	968	1196	752	929	627	775	530	655	463	572
5000	984	1216	765	944	638	799	539	667	471	582
5100	1001	1237	778	960	649	802	548	678	478	591
5200	1017	1257	790	976	659	815	557	689	486	601
5300	1034	1278	803	992	670	828	567	700	494	611
5400	1050	1298	816	1008	681	842	576	711	502	621
5500	1067	1318	829	1024	691	855	585	723	510	630
5600	1083	1339	842	1039	702	868	594	734	518	640
5700	1100	1359	855	1055	713	881	603	745	526	650
5800	1116	1380	867	1071	724	894	612	756	534	660
5900	1133	1400	880	1087	734	908	621	767	542	669
6000	1149	1420	893	1103	745	921	630	779	550	679
6100	1166	1441	906	1119	756	934	639	790	557	689
6200	1182	1461	919	1135	766	947	648	801	565	699
6300	1199	1482	932	1150	777	961	659	812	573	709
6400	1215	1502	945	1166	788	974	666	823	581	718
6500	1232	1522	957	1182	798	987	675	835	589	725
6600	1248	1543	970	1198	809	1000	684	846	597	738
6700	1265	1563	983	1214	820	1014	693	857	605	748
6800	1281	1584	996	1230	831	1027	702	868	613	757
6900	1298	1604	1009	1246	841	1040	711	879	621	767
7000	1314	1624	1022	1261	852	1053	720	891	629	777
7000 +			For income greater than $7000, see Standard No. 8.							

Worksheet A
Computation of the Child Support Obligation

Mother _____   Father _____

County _____   Superior Court Case Number _____

Children and Ages:				
Part I: Basic Support Obligation (See Instructions)				
1. Monthly Gross Income		Father		Mother
a. Wages, Salaries, and Tips	$		$	
b. Interest and Dividend Income	$		$	
c. Business Income	$		$	
d. Other Income	$		$	
e. Total Gross Income (add lines 1a through 1d)	$		$	
2. Monthly Deductions from Gross Income				
a. Income Taxes	$		$	
b. FICA/Self-employment Taxes	$		$	
c. *Mandatory* Union/Professonal Dues	$		$	
d. *Mandatory* Pension Plan Payments	$		$	
e. Non-recurring Income	$		$	
f. Total Deductions from Gross Income (add lines 2a through 2e)	$		$	
3. Monthly Net Income (line 1e minus line 2f)	$		$	
4. Combined Monthly Net Income (add father's and mother's monthly net incomes from line 3)		$		

5. Basic Child Support Obligation
   (enter total amount in box>)
   Child #1 _____ Child #3 _____
   Child #2 _____ Child #4 _____
		$		

6. Proportional Share of Income (each parent's net income from line 3 divided by line 4)				
7. Each Parent's Basic Child Support Obligation (multiply each number on line 6 by line 5)	$		$	
Part II: Health Care, Day Care, and Special Child Rearing Expenses (See Instructions)				
8. Health Care Expenses				
a. Monthly Health Insurance Premiums	$		$	
b. Uninsured Monthly Health Care Expenses	$		$	
c. Total Monthly Health Care Expenses (line 8a plus line 8b)	$		$	

d. Combined Monthly Health Care Expenses
     (Add father's and mother's monthly health care
     expenses from line 8c)
		$		

e. Maximum Ordinary Monthly Health Care		$		
f. Extraordinary Monthly Health Care Costs (line 8d minus line 8e, if "0" or negative, enter "0")		$		
CONTINUED ON BACK OF FORM				

Part II: Health Care, Day Care, and Special Child Rearing Expenses (cont.)		
9. Day Care and Special Expenses	Father	Mother
a. Day Care Expenses	$	$
b. Education Expenses	$	$
c. Long Distance Transportation Expenses	$	$
d. Other Special Expenses (list below)	$	$
	$	$
	$	$
	$	$
	$	$
e. Total Day Care and Special Expenses (add lines 9a through 9d)	$	$
10. Combined Monthly Total of Day Care and Special Expenses (add father's and mother's total day care and special expenses from line 9e)	$	
11. Total Extraordinary Health Care, Day Care, and Special Expenses (line 8f plus line 10)	$	
12. Each Parent's Obligation for Extraordinary Health Care, Day Care, and Special Expenses (multiply each number on line 6 by line 11)	$	$
Part III: Total Child Support Obligation		
13. Total Support Obligation (line 7 plus line 12)	$	$
Part IV: Child Support Credits (See Instructions)		
14. Child Support Credits		
a. Monthly Health Care Expenses Credit	$	$
b. Day Care and Special Expenses Credit	$	$
c. Other Ordinary Expense Credit (list below, expenses must have court approval)		
	$	$
d. Residential Schedule Credit (from worksheet B, lines 27 and 28)	$	$
e. Total Support Credits (add lines 14a through 14d)	$	$
Part V: Net Support Obligation and Transfer Payment (See Instructions)		
15. Net Support Obligation (line 13 minus line 14e)	$	$
CONTINUE TO WORKSHEET C		

Worksheet B
Residential Schedule Adjustment

Mother _____   Father _____

County _____   Superior Court Case Number _____

Complete Worksheet B if a residential schedule credit is allowable and desired pursuant to Standard #10 and the instructions.				
16. List Children (first name only)				
17. Basic Support Obligation Per Child (from worksheet A, line 5 - individual amounts)	$	$	$	$
18. Ordinary Expenses *Per Child*				
a. Total Monthly Health Care Expenses	$	$	$	$
b. Maximum Ordinary Monthly Health Care	$	$	$	$
c. Ordinary Health Care Amount (lesser amount of 18a or 18b)	$	$	$	$
d. Other Ordinary Expenses	$	$	$	$
e. Total Ordinary Expenses Per Child				
e. (line 18c plus line 18d)	$	$	$	$
19. Adjusted Basic Support (line 17 minus line 18e)	$	$	$	$
20. Overnights with Father				
21. Proportional Overnights with Father (divide each entry on line 20 by 365)				
22. Overnights with Mother				
23. Proportional Overnights with Mother (divide each entry on line 22 by 365)				
24. Father's Credit Proportion (for each child subtract .25 from the entry on line 21 and multiply the resulting amount times 2) *Note:* For answers less than 0 enter "0" For answers greater than 1.0 enter "1.0" For answers between 0 and 1 enter exact amount				
26. Father's Residential Schedule Credits (for each child multiply the entry on line 24 times the entry on line 19)	$	$	$	$
27. Mother's Residential Schedule Credits (for each child multiply the entry on line 25 times the entry on line 19)	$	$	$	$
RETURN TO WORKSHEET A, LINE 14d				

This worksheet has been certified by the State of Washington
Office of the Administrator for the Courts.
Photocopying of the worksheet is permitted.

Worksheet C
Additional Factors for Consideration

Mother _____ Father _____

County _____ Superior Court Case Number _____

This worksheet must be completed regardless of whether or not a deviation is being requested. Pursuant to RCW 26.19.020 the resources and income of each parent's household must be considered.		
28. List the estimated present value of all major household assets (if there is a new marriage, include assets held in the new household)	Father's Household	Mother's Household
a. Real Estate	$	$
b. Stocks and Bonds	$	$
c. Vehicles	$	$
d. Boats	$	$
e. Pensions/IRAs/Bank Accounts	$	$
f. Cash	$	$
g. Insurance Plans	$	$
h. Other	$	$
29. List liens against assets owned by the household and/or any extraordinary debt.		
a. $	$	
b. $	$	
c. $	$	
d. $	$	
e. $	$	
30. List the monthly household income not attributable to these proceedings.		
a. Income of new spouse	$	$
b. Income of other adults in household	$	$
c. Child support rcvd. from another relationship	$	$
d. Extraordinary income of children	$	$
e. Income from any assistance programs (i.e., AFDC, SSI, Food Stamps, etc.)	$	$
f. Maintenance received from another relationship	$	$
g. Other (describe)	$	$
31. Monthly child support paid for other children	$	$
32. Maintenance Paid for Prior Relationships	$	$
33. Children not of this relationship living in the household (first names and ages) _____ _____ _____ _____ _____	a. b. c. d.	a. b. c. d.
34. New spouse's name	$	$
35. Names of other adults living in the household	$	$
Continued on Back of Form		

36. Use this section to list any other factors that should be considered in determining the child support obligation (for nonparental custody proceedings, see instructions).

_____
_____
_____
_____
_____
_____
_____
_____
_____
_____
_____
_____
_____
_____
_____
_____
_____
_____
_____
_____
_____
_____
_____

Signature and Dates

I declare, under penalty of perjury under the laws of the State of Washington, the information contained in Worksheet A, Worksheet B, and Worksheet C is complete, true, and correct.

Mother's Signature   Father's Signature

Date   City   Date   City

This worksheet has been certified by the State of Washington
Office of the Administrator for the Courts.
Photocopying of the worksheet is permitted.

SAMPLE CASE APPLICATION
WASHINGTON STATE CHILD SUPPORT SCHEDULE

EXAMPLE 1

After fifteen years the marriage of Robert and Edith Weaver has deteriorated from wedded bliss to mutual hate and resentment. After numerous unsuccessful attempts at reconciliation they have filed for a dissolution. Robert and Edith have two children, Gilbert and Yvonne.

Robert Weaver:

Robert is a construction worker whose gross income last year was $36,000. $5,000 of Robert's gross income for last year was unanticipated overtime pay. Robert's only additional income is from a joint savings account with Edith from which they earned $1,800 in interest income last year.

Robert's monthly deductions from gross income include federal income taxes of $436 (claiming one dependent and based upon gross income of $31,000), FICA withholding of $193, and union dues of $40.

Robert also has a child from a prior relationship for whom he pays a monthly child support obligation of $200.

Robert anticipates average monthly travel expenditures of $350 to maintain the agreed-upon residential schedule.

Robert's post-dissolution assets will include a 1985 Ford Ranger valued at $12,000, one-half of the joint savings account of $25,000, one-third of the net from the sale of the family home (estimated net is $25,000), an IRA with a $15,000 balance, and a whole life insurance policy with a trade in value of $10,000.

Edith Weaver:

Edith is employed as an accountant and has an annual gross income of $32,000. Shortly after her separation from Robert, she relocated from Spokane to Klamath Falls, Oregon. Monthly deductions from Edith's gross income include federal income taxes of $458 (claiming one dependent), state income taxes of $137 (claiming two dependents), and FICA withholding of $199. Edith's employee benefits provide full health care coverage for her family; however, she is currently paying $75 a month out of pocket for Gilbert's orthodontic work.

Edith's post-dissolution assets will include two-thirds of the net from the sale of the family home (estimated net is $25,000), a 1987 Honda Civic valued at $14,000, one-half of the joint savings account of $25,000, an IRA with a $15,000 balance, and a whole life insurance policy with a face value of $8,000.

There is an outstanding loan of $10,000 on the Honda for which monthly payments of $200 are being made.

Gilbert and Yvonne Weaver:

Gilbert Weaver is twelve years old. Gilbert is enrolled in an after-school computer science enrichment program. Tuition for the program is $75 per month. Each summer Gilbert goes to church camp at a cost to his parents of $250.

Gilbert's residential schedule (included with the parenting plan filed with the petition for dissolution) provides for him to reside with his mother in Klamath Falls for a majority of the year. He resides with his father one weekend per month, during winter and spring vacations for one week each, and for two months of his summer vacation. The annual number of over-nights Gilbert will spend with his father totals ninety-eight.

Yvonne Weaver is eight years old. Yvonne intends to be a ballerina veterinarian when she grows up and therefore, in pursuit of her ambitions, is enrolled in a dance academy and takes horseback riding lessons. Monthly cost of the program is $65.

Yvonne's residential schedule provides for a majority of residential time to be spent with her mother. She resides with her father for one weekend per month, during winter and spring vacations for one week each, and for one month during her summer vacation. The annual number of overnights Yvonne will spend with her father totals sixty-seven.

Worksheet A
Computation of the Child Support Obligation

Mother _Edith Weaver_   Father _Robert Weaver_

County _Spokane_   Superior Court Case Number _90-3-00000-0_

Children and Ages: _Gilbert, 12; Yvonne, 8._

Part I: Basic Support Obligation (See Instructions)

	Father	Mother
1. Monthly Gross Income		
a. Wages, Salaries, and Tips	$ 3000.00	$ 2667.00
b. Interest and Dividend Income	$ 75.00	$ 75.00
c. Business Income	$ —	$ —
d. Other Income	$ —	$ —
e. Total Gross Income (add lines 1a through 1d).	$ 3075.00	$ 2742.00
2. Monthly Deductions from Gross Income		
a. Income Taxes	$ 634.26	$ 494.00
b. FICA/Self-Employment Taxes	$ 225.30	$ 200.29
c. *Mandatory* Union/Professional Dues	$ 40.00	$ —
d. *Mandatory* Pension Plan Payments	$ —	$ —
e. Non-recurring Income	$ 417.00	$ —
f. Total Deductions from Gross Income (add lines 2a through 2e)	$ 1316.56	$ 694.29
3. Monthly Net Income (line 1e minus line 2f)	$ 1758.44	$ 2047.71
4. Combined Monthly Net Income (add father's and mother's monthly net incomes from line 3)	$ 3806.15	
5. Basic Child Support Obligation (enter total amount in box ——→) Child #1 _Gilbert_ 558.00 Child #3 _____ Child #2 _Yvonne_ 452.00 Child #4 _____	$ 1010.00	
6. Proportional Share of Income (each parent's net income from line 3 divided by line 4)	0.462	0.538
7. Each Parent's Basic Child Support Obligation (multiply each number on line 6 by line 5)	$ 466.62	$ 543.38
Part II: Health Care, Day Care, and Special Child Rearing Expenses (See Instructions)		
8. Health Care Expenses		
a. Monthly Health Insurance Premiums	$ —	$ —
b. Uninsured Monthly Health Care Expenses	$ —	$ 75.00
c. Total Monthly Health Care Expenses (line 8a plus line 8b)	$ —	$ 75.00
d. Combined Monthly Health Care Expenses (Add father's and mother's monthly health care expenses from line 8c)	$ 75.00	
e. Maximum Ordinary Monthly Health Care	$ 50.50	
f. Extraordinary Monthly Health Care Costs (line 8d minus line 8e. If "0" or negative, enter "0")	$ 24.50	

Continued on Back of Form

Part II: Health Care, Day Care, and Special Child Rearing Expenses (cont.)		
9. Day Care and Special Expenses	Father	Mother
a. Day Care Expenses	$ —	$ —
b. Education Expenses	$ —	$ —
c. Long Distance Transportation Expenses	$ 350.00	$ —
d. Other Special Expenses (list below)	$	$
	$ —	$ —
	$	$
	$	$
	$	$
e. Total Day Care and Special Expenses (add lines 9a through 9d)	$ 350.00	$
10. Combined Monthly Total of Day Care and Special Expenses (add father's and mother's total day care and special expenses from line 9e)	$ 350.00	
11. Total Extraordinary Health Care, Day Care, and Special Expenses (line 8f plus line 10)	$ 374.00	
12. Each Parent's Obligation for Extraordinary Health Care, Day Care, and Special Expenses (multiply each number on line 6 by line 11)	$ 173.02	$ 201.48
Part III: Total Child Support Obligation		
13. Total Support Obligation (line 7 plus line 12)	$ 639.64	$ 744.86
Part IV: Child Support Credits (See Instructions)		
14. Child Support Credits		
a. Monthly Health Care Expenses Credit	$ —	$ 75.00
b. Day Care and Special Expenses Credit	$ 350.00	$ —
c. Other Ordinary Expense Credit (list below, expenses must have court approval) Gilbert (camp/computer) — (ballet, riding lessons) Yvonne	$ — $ —	$ 96.00 $ 65.00
d. Residential Schedule Credit (from worksheet B, lines 27 and 28)	$ 15.63	$ 805.47
e. Total Support Credits (add lines 14a through 14d)	$ 365.63	$ 1041.47
Part V: Net Support Obligation and Transfer Payment (See Instructions)		
15. Net Support Obligation (line 13 minus line 14e)	$ 274.01	$ −296.61
Continue to Worksheet C		

Worksheet B
Residential Schedule Adjustment

Mother _Edith_   Father _Robert_

County _SPOKANE_   Superior Court Case Number _90-3-00000-0_

Complete Worksheet B if a residential schedule credit is allowable and desired pursuant to Standard #10 and the instructions.				
16. List Children (first name only)	Gilbert	Yvonne		
17. Basic Support Obligation Per Child (from worksheet A, line 5 - individual amounts)	$ 558.00	$ 452.00	$	$
18. Ordinary Expenses Per Child				
a. Total Monthly Health Care Expenses	$ 75.00	$ —	$	$
b. Maximum Ordinary Monthly Health Care	$ 27.90	$ 22.60	$	$
c. Ordinary Health Care Amount (lesser amount of 18a or 18b)	$ 27.90	$ —	$	$
d. Other Ordinary Expenses	$ 96.00	$ 65.00	$	$
e. Total Ordinary Expenses Per Child (line 18c plus line 18d)	$ 123.90	$ 65.00	$	$
19. Adjusted Basic Support (line 17 minus line 18e)	$ 434.10	$ 387.00	$	$
20. Overnights with Father	98	67		
21. Proportional Overnights with Father (divide each entry on line 20 by 365)	0.268	0.184	.	.
22. Overnights with Mother	267	298		
23. Proportional Overnights with Mother (divide each entry on line 22 by 365)	0.732	0.816	.	.
24. Father's Credit Proportion (for each child subtract .25 from the entry on line 21 and multiply the resulting amount times 2) Note: For answers less than 0 enter "0" For answers greater than 1.0 enter "1.0" For answers between 0 and 1 enter exact amount	0.036	0.000	.	.
25. Mother's Credit Proportion (for each child subtract .25 from the entry on line 23 and multiply the resulting amount times 2) Note: For answers less than 0 enter "0" For answers greater than 1.0 enter "1.0" For answers between 0 and 1 enter exact amount	0.964	1.000	.	.
26. Father's Residential Schedule Credits (for each child multiply the entry on line 24 times the entry on line 19)	$ 15.63	$ —	$	$
27. Mother's Residential Schedule Credits (for each child multiply the entry on line 25 times the entry on line 19)	$ 418.47	$ 387.00	$	$
Return to Worksheet A, line 14d				

This worksheet has been certified by the State of Washington Office of the Administrator for the Courts.
Photocopying of the worksheet is permitted.

WSCSS/07-01-89

Worksheet C
Additional Factors for Consideration

Mother __Edith__   Father __Robert__

County __SPOKANE__   Superior Court Case Number __89-3-00000-0__

This worksheet must be completed regardless of whether or not a deviation is being requested. Pursuant to RCW 26.19.020 the resources and income of each parent's household must be considered.		
28. List the estimated present value of all major household assets. (If there is a new marraige, include assets held in the new household)	Father's Household	Mother's Household
a. Real Estate	$ 8333.00	$ 16,667.00
b. Stocks and Bonds	$ —	$ —
c. Vehicles	$ 12000.00	$ 14000.00
d. Boats	$ —	$ —
e. Pensions/IRAs/Bank Accounts	$ 27500.00	$ 27500.00
f. Cash	$ —	$ —
g. Insurance Plans	$ 10000.00	$ 8000.00
h. Other	$ —	$ —
29. List liens against assets owned by the household and/or any extraordinary debt.		
a. Honda loan	$	$ 10000.00
b.	$	$
c.	$	$
d.	$	$
e.	$	$
30. List the monthly household income not attributable to these proceedings.		
a. Income of new spouse	$	$
b. Income of other adults in household	$	$
c. Child support received from another relationship	$	$
d. Extraordinary income of children	$	$
e. Income from any assistance programs (i.e., AFDC, SSI, Food Stamps, etc.)	$	$
f. Maintenance received from another relationship	$	$
g. Other (describe)	$	$
31. Monthly child support paid for other children	$ 200.00	$
32. Maintenance Paid for Prior Relationships	$	$
33. Children not of this relationship living in the household (first names and ages)	a.	a.
	b.	b.
	c.	c.
	d.	d.
34. New spouse's name.	$	$
35. Names of other adults living in the household.	$	$
Continued on Back of Form		

EXAMPLE 2

After a relatively short yet fertile marriage of two years, Steve and Judith Henderson have filed for a dissolution. Steve and Judith have two children, Ann and Deborah.

Steve Henderson:

Steve is a salesman with a monthly gross income of $2,074. Monthly income tax is $268 and FICA withholding is $156. Steve pays $75 per month for health insurance premiums for the children.

Steve's post-dissolution assets will include a 1980 Toyota Celica valued at $3,000 and an insurance plan with a face value of $5,000.

Judith Henderson:

Judith is a clerical staff worker for a private non-profit social service agency. Her monthly gross income is $984. Monthly income taxes amount to $110 and FICA withholding is $74.

Since her separation from Steve she has been responsible for payment of the children's monthly day-care costs of $250.

Judith's post-dissolution assets will include a 1983 Ford Fairmont station wagon valued at $5,000.

Ann and Deborah Henderson:

Ann Henderson is a precocious two-year-old. Deborah is twelve months younger than Ann. The girls' residential schedules with their parents calls for them to be with their father for 122 overnights per year and with their mother for 243 overnights per year.

Worksheet A
Computation of the Child Support Obligation

Mother ___Judith Henderson___   Father ___Steve Henderson___

County ___KING___   Superior Court Case Number ___90-3-00000-0___

		Father	Mother
Children and Ages: Ann, 2 ; Deborah, 1.			
Part I: Basic Support Obligation (See Instructions)			
1. Monthly Gross Income		Father	Mother
a. Wages, Salaries, and Tips		$ 2074.00	$ 984.00
b. Interest and Dividend Income		$ —	$ —
c. Business Income		$ —	$ —
d. Other Income		$ —	$ —
e. Total Gross Income (add lines 1a through 1d)		$ 2074.00	$ 984.00
2. Monthly Deductions from Gross Income			
a. Income Taxes		$ 304.00	$ 108.00
b. FICA/Self-Employment Taxes		$ 155.76	$ 73.90
c. *Mandatory* Union/Professional Dues		$ —	$ —
d. *Mandatory* Pension Plan Payments		$ —	$ —
e. Non-recurring Income		$ —	$ —
f. Total Deductions from Gross Income (add lines 2a through 2e)		$ 459.76	$ 181.90
3. Monthly Net Income (line 1e minus line 2f)		$ 1614.24	$ 802.10
4. Combined Monthly Net Income (add father's and mother's monthly net incomes from line 3)		$ 2416.34	
5. Basic Child Support Obligation (enter total amount in box ⟶) Child #1 Ann 393.00 Child #3 ____ Child #2 Deborah 393.00 Child #4 ____		$ 786.00	
6. Proportional Share of Income (each parent's net income from line 3 divided by line 4)		0.668	0.332
7. Each Parent's Basic Child Support Obligation (multiply each number on line 6 by line 5)		$ 525.05	$ 260.95
Part II: Health Care, Day Care, and Special Child Rearing Expenses (See Instructions)			
8. Health Care Expenses			
a. Monthly Health Insurance Premiums		$ 75.00	$ —
b. Uninsured Monthly Health Care Expenses		$ —	$ —
c. Total Monthly Health Care Expenses (line 8a plus line 8b)		$ 75.00	$ —
d. Combined Monthly Health Care Expenses (Add father's and mother's monthly health care expenses from line 8c)		$ 75.00	
e. Maximum Ordinary Monthly Health Care		$ 40.00	
f. Extraordinary Monthly Health Care Costs (line 8d minus line 8e, if "0" or negative, enter "0")		$ 35.00	

Continued on Back of Form

Part II: Health Care, Day Care, and Special Child Rearing Expenses (cont.)		
9. Day Care and Special Expenses	Father	Mother
a. Day Care Expenses	$	$ 250.00
b. Education Expenses	$	$
c. Long Distance Transportation Expenses	$	$
d. Other Special Expenses (list below)	$	$
	$	$
	$	$
	$	$
	$	$
e. Total Day Care and Special Expenses (add lines 9a through 9d)	$	$ 250.00
10. Combined Monthly Total of Day Care and Special Expenses (add father's and mother's total day care and special expenses from line 9e)	$ 250.00	
11. Total Extraordinary Health Care, Day Care, and Special Expenses (line 8f plus line 10)	$ 285.00	
12. Each Parent's Obligation for Extraordinary Health Care, Day Care, and Special Expenses (multiply each number on line 6 by line 11)	$ 190.38	$ 94.62
Part III: Total Child Support Obligation		
13. Total Support Obligation (line 7 plus line 12)	$ 715.43	$ 355.57
Part IV: Child Support Credits (See Instructions)		
14. Child Support Credits		
a. Monthly Health Care Expenses Credit	$ 75.00	$ —
b. Day Care and Special Expenses Credit	$ —	$ 250.00
c. Other Ordinary Expense Credit (list below, expenses must have court approval)		
	$ —	$ —
d. Residential Schedule Credit (from worksheet B, lines 27 and 28)	$ 125.32	$ 620.68
e. Total Support Credits (add lines 14a through 14d)	$ 200.32	$ 870.68
Part V: Net Support Obligation and Transfer Payment (See Instructions)		
15. Net Support Obligation (line 13 minus line 14e)	$ 515.11	$ -515.11

Continue to Worksheet C

WSCSS/07-01-89

Worksheet B
Residential Schedule Adjustment

Mother __Judith__ Father __Steven__
County __KING__ Superior Court Case Number __90-3-00000-0__

Complete Worksheet B if a residential schedule credit is allowable and desired pursuant to Standard #10 and the instructions.				
16. List Children (first name only)	Ann	Deborah		
17. Basic Support Obligation Per Child (from worksheet A, line 5 - individual amounts)	$ 393.00	$ 393.00	$	$
18. Ordinary Expenses Per Child				
a. Total Monthly Health Care Expenses	$ 37.50	$ 37.50	$	$
b. Maximum Ordinary Monthly Health Care	$ 20.00	$ 20.00	$	$
c. Ordinary Health Care Amount (lesser amount of 18a or 18b)	$ 20.00	$ 20.00	$	$
d. Other Ordinary Expenses	$ —	$ —	$	$
e. Total Ordinary Expenses Per Child (line 18c plus line 18d)	$ 20.00	$ 20.00	$	$
19. Adjusted Basic Support (line 17 minus line 18e)	$ 373.00	$ 373.00	$	$
20. Overnights with Father	122	122		
21. Proportional Overnights with Father (divide each entry on line 20 by 365)	0.334	0.334	.	.
22. Overnights with Mother	243	243		
23. Proportional Overnights with Mother (divide each entry on line 22 by 365)	0.666	0.666	.	.
24. Father's Credit Proportion (for each child subtract .25 from the entry on line 21 and multiply the resulting amount times 2) Note: For answers less than 0 enter "0" For answers greater than 1.0 enter "1.0" For answers between 0 and 1 enter exact amount	0.168	0.168	.	.
25. Mother's Credit Proportion (for each child subtract .25 from the entry on line 23 and multiply the resulting amount times 2) Note: For answers less than 0 enter "0" For answers greater than 1.0 enter "1.0" For answers between 0 and 1 enter exact amount	0.832	0.832	.	.
26. Father's Residential Schedule Credits (for each child multiply the entry on line 24 times the entry on line 19)	$ 62.66	$ 62.66	$	$
27. Mother's Residential Schedule Credits (for each child multiply the entry on line 25 times the entry on line 19)	$ 310.34	$ 310.34	$	$
Return to Worksheet A, line 14d				

WSCSS/07-01-89

Worksheet C
Additional Factors for Consideration

Mother ___Judith___   Father ___Steve___

County ___KING___   Superior Court Case Number ___90-3-00000-0___

This worksheet must be completed regardless of whether or not a deviation is being requested. Pursuant to RCW 26.19.020 the resources and income of each parent's household must be considered.		
28. List the estimated present value of all major household assets. (If there is a new marriage, include assets held in the new household)	Father's Household	Mother's Household
a. Real Estate	$ —	$ —
b. Stocks and Bonds	$ —	$ —
c. Vehicles	$ 3000.00	$ 5000.00
d. Boats	$ —	$ —
e. Pensions/IRAs/Bank Accounts	$ —	$ —
f. Cash	$ —	$ —
g. Insurance Plans	$ 5000.00	$ —
h. Other	$ —	$ —
29. List liens against assets owned by the household and/or any extraordinary debt.		
a.	$	$
b.	$	$
c.	$	$
d.	$	$
e.	$	$
30. List the monthly household income not attributable to these proceedings.		
a. Income of new spouse	$	$
b. Income of other adults in household	$	$
c. Child support received from another relationship	$	$
d. Extraordinary income of children	$	$
e. Income from any assistance programs (i.e., AFDC, SSI, Food Stamps, etc.)	$	$
f. Maintenance received from another relationship	$	$
g. Other (describe)	$	$
31. Monthly child support paid for other children	$	$
32. Maintenance Paid for Prior Relationships	$	$
33. Children not of this relationship living in the household (first names and ages)	a. / b. / c. / d.	a. / b. / c. / d.
34. New spouse's name.	$	$
35. Names of other adults living in the household.	$	$
Continued on Back of Form		

APPENDIX K
RESOURCES FOR DOMESTIC VIOLENCE

Domestic Violence Hotline: Crisis information or immediate referrals in Washington State, 1-800-562-6025.

ABERDEEN:

Domestic Violence Center Grays Harbor (Crisis Line evening and weekends, 1-800-562-6025; Monday-Friday, 9-5. (206) 538-0733; 2306 Sumner Avenue, Hoquiam, WA 98550). Services: Advocacy/counseling, shelter, support groups for domestic violence victims, domestic violence anger control for abusers.

BELLEVUE:

Eastside Domestic Violence Program (Crisis Line/24 hours, (206) 746-1940 (888-2763 toll-free from Snoqualmie Valley); business, Monday-Friday, 9-5; P.O. Box 6398, Bellevue, WA 98008-0398). Services: 24 hour crisis line, safe houses, counseling for victims, support groups for women, children's groups, legal advocacy, information, and referral.

Family Services (Business Monday-Friday, 8:30-5, or by appointment, (206) 451-2869; 2122 112th NE, Suite B101, Bellevue, WA 98004). Services: Counseling/groups for women, counseling/groups for men, counseling for sexual assault, Family Anger Management Institute, counseling for children through Seattle Child Guidance.

BELLINGHAM:

Whatcom County Crisis Services/Domestic Violence Program (Crisis line/24 hours, TTY/TDD (206) 734-7271; toll-free line for Whatcom County residents (206) 384-1485; business Monday-Friday, 8:30-4:30, (206) 671-5714 or 384-3748; 1407 Commercial Street, Bellingham, WA 98225). Services: Advocacy (legal, medical, financial, *etc.*), individual support sessions, support groups, anger control training, information and referral, programs at WCCS include 24 hour crisis line, information and referral outreach team and rape relief/domestic violence victim relief.

Womencare Shelter (Crisis Line/24 hours, (206) 734-3438, business, (206) 671-8539; 1026 N. Forest, #201, Bellingham, WA 98225). Services: Shelter (boys up to twelve), advocacy/counseling for women, support group for shelter, residents and ex-residents, referrals for men, interpreters for hearing impaired.

BREMERTON:

ALIVE/Kitsap County, YWCA (Crisis Line/24 hours (206) 479-1980; business, (206) 479-5118; c/o YWCA 611 Highland Avenue, Bremerton, WA 98310). Services: shelter and safe houses, advocacy/counseling for women, counseling for children, support group for women.

CENTRALIA/CHEHALIS:

C.A.R.E. Crisis Line/24 hours, (206) 748-6601, Lewis County 24-hour Hotline 1-800-458-3080; business (206) 748-0547; P.O. Box 337, Chehalis, WA 98532). Services: safe houses, advocacy/counseling for women, advocacy for children.

CLARKSTON, WASHINGTON; LEWISTON, IDAHO:

YWCA of Lewiston/Clarkston Crisis Services (Crisis Line/24 hours, (208) 746-9655; 300 Main Street, Lewiston, ID 83501). Services: shelter for victims of domestic violence and sexual assault, 24-hour advocacy, counseling, crisis intervention, information and referral.

COLVILLE:

Family Support Center (Crisis Line/24 hours, (509) 684-6139; business, Monday-Friday, 8-5, (509) 684-3796; N. 260 Oak, Colville, WA 99114). Services: safe houses, advocacy/counseling for women, support group for women, counseling for sexual assault.

ELLENSBURG:

Central Washington Comprehensive Mental Health (Crisis Line/24 hours, (509) 925-9861; 220 W. Fourth Street, Ellensburg, WA 98926). Services: Safe houses, counseling for women, counseling for children, counseling for men, advocacy/ counseling for sexual assault and domestic violence, support groups for women.

EVERETT:

STOP ABUSE (Crisis Line/24 hours, (206) 25-ABUSE; business (206) 252-2873; P.O. Box 2086, Everett, WA 98203). Services: advocacy/counseling for women, counseling for children, counseling for men, support groups for women and men, wheelchair accessible, interpreters of Spanish and Portuguese.

FORKS:

Forks Abuse Programs (Crisis Line/24 hours, (206) 374-2273; P.O. Box 1775, Forks, WA 98331). Services: safe houses (no housing for boys over twelve), advocacy/counseling for women, referrals for men.

FORT LEWIS:

Army Community Service Family Advocacy Program (Crisis/business, Monday-Friday 7:30-4:30; (206) 967-7166; Crisis/evenings and weekends, (206) 967-6972; Crisis/24 hours, 1-800-562-6025; Building 5218, Fort Lewis, WA 98433-5000). Services: Crisis counseling, shelter referrals, classes in domestic violence, classes in anger control, wheelchair accessible.

GOLDENDALE and WHITE SALMON:

Klickitat County Council on Domestic Violence (Crisis — Klickitat Valley Hospital (509) 773-4022. Services: safe houses, advocacy/counseling for women.

KENT/RENTON - SOUTH KING COUNTY:

DAWN (Crisis Line/24 hours, (206) 852-5529; P.O. Box 1521, Kent, WA 98035). Services: safe houses, advocacy/counseling for women.

Family Services (Business: Monday–Friday, 9:00-5 or by appointment, (206) 854-8705, 1851 S. Central Place, Kent, WA 98031; King County Crisis Lines, 461-3222, 1515 Dexter Avenue N., Seattle, WA). Services: Counseling/groups for women, counseling/groups for men, counseling for sexual assault, Family Anger Management Institute, counseling for children through Seattle Child Guidance.

LANGLEY:

Citizens Against Domestic Abuse (CADA) (Crisis Line/24 hours, (206) 675-2232; P.O. Box 796, Langley, WA 98260). Services: safe houses, advocacy for victims of domestic violence/sexual assault, support group for abused women, support group for children from violent families, referrals, interpreters for Japanese and Filipino.

LONGVIEW/KELSO:

Emergency Support Shelter (Crisis Line/evenings and weekends, (206) 636-8471; Crisis/business, Monday-Friday 8-5; (206) 425-1176; P.O. Box 877, Kelso, WA 98626). Services: shelter, advocacy/counseling for women, support group for women, counseling/group for children, interpreters for Spanish and hearing impaired, wheelchair accessible.

MOSES LAKE:

Nuestro Lugar ("Our Place") (Crisis Line/Monday-Friday, 8-5, (509) 765-1214; Crisis Line/after hours, (509) 765-1791, ask for 191; P.O. Box 1394, Moses Lake, WA 98837). Services: safe houses, advocacy/counseling for women, support group for women, support group for victims of incest, support group for victims of sexual assault, support group for parents of victims of sexual assault, Spanish-speaking advocates, and children's support group.

MOUNT VERNON:

Skagit Rape Relief/Battered Women's Program (Crisis Line/24 hours, (206) 336-2162; Crisis Line for Anacortes, (206) 293-3232; business, Monday-Friday, 8:30-4:30, (206) 336-9591; P.O. Box 301, Mount Vernon, WA 98273). Services: shelter, advocacy/counseling, support groups, group for children, interpreter for Spanish.

NASELLE:

Pacific County Crisis Support Network (Crisis Line/24 hours, Washington State Domestic Violence Hotline, 1-800-562-6025; business Monday-Friday, 9-4, (206) 484-7191; HCR 78 Box 336, Naselle, WA 98638). Services: safe houses, shelter, advocacy/counseling for women, advocacy for children, counseling for victims of sexual assault, AMP and parenting programs.

NEWPORT:

Family Crisis Network (Crisis Line/24 hours, (509) 447-5483; business, 447-2274, P.O. Box 944, Newport, WA 99156). Services: safe houses, advocacy/counseling for women, support group for women, counseling for children, counseling for men, groups for victims of sexual abuse and incest, interpreters for Spanish, French, and hearing impaired.

OAK HARBOR:

Citizens Against Domestic Abuse (CADA) (Crisis Line/24 hours, (206) 675-2232; P.O. Box 190, Oak Harbor, WA 98277). Services: safe houses, advocacy/counseling for victims of sexual assault/domestic violence, support group for abused women, support group for children from violent families, referrals, interpreters for Japanese and Filipino.

OLYMPIA:

Safeplace: Rape Relief/Battered Women's Shelter Services (Crisis Line/24 hours, (206) 754-6300; business, (206) 786-8754; P.O. Box 1605, Olympia, WA 98507). Services: wheelchair accessible, shelter, advocacy/counseling for women and children, support group for women and children, advocacy/counseling for victims of sexual assault, interpreters for Spanish-speaking people.

Domestic Violence Hotline (Statewide 24 hour, hotline 1-800-562-6025; business (206) 586-2380). Services: Crisis counseling on phone, referrals to services throughout Washington State and U.S.A., limited technical assistance.

Puget Sound Legal Assistance Program (Business, (206) 943-6260; 529 W. Fourth, Olympia, WA 98501). Services: Legal aid for people of low income, offers civil remedies for women who are victims of domestic violence and would like assistance in obtaining welfare or other public entitlements; dissolutions; assistance in custody battles.

OMAK:

The Support Center (Crisis Line/24 hours, (509) 826-3221; P.O. Box 2058, Omak, WA 98841). Services: Shelter, advocacy/counseling for women, support group for women, advocacy/counseling for sexual assault, interpreters for Spanish.

PORT ANGELES:

Safehomes Domestic Violence Program (Crisis Line/24 hours, (206) 452-4357 (or 452-HELP); business, Monday-Friday, 8-5, (206) 452-3811; c/o Umbrella Community Services, 708 E. Eighth Street, (Transition Housing), Port Angeles, WA 98362). Services: Safe houses, advocacy/counseling for women, support group for unchanged women, counseling for children.

PORT TOWNSEND:

Domestic Violence Program (Crisis Line/24 hours, (206) 385-5291; P.O. Box 743, Port Townsend, WA 98468). Services: Safe houses, advocacy/counseling for victims of domestic violence, support groups for women, advocacy/counseling for victims of sexual assault, medical and legal advocacy for victims, emergency housing assistance, individual and group counseling for children, interpreters for Spanish and hearing impaired.

REPUBLIC:

Ferry County Community Services (Crisis Line/24 hours, (509) 775-3341; Sheriff/24 hours, (509) 775-3132; P.O. Box 406, Republic, WA 99166). Services: Safe houses, advocacy/counseling for women, counseling for victims of sexual assault, counseling for children.

RICHLAND:

Columbia Basin Domestic Violence Service (Crisis Line/24 hours, (509) 582-9841; business, Monday-Friday, 8:30-5, (509) 943-2649; 640 Jadwin Suite C, Richland, WA 99352). Services: Safe houses, advocacy/support group for women, shelter for victims of domestic violence and their children, counseling for children, handicap accessible, resident and non-resident counseling, women, interpreters for Spanish.

SAN JUAN ISLANDS:

Volunteers Against Violence (Crisis Line/24 hours, call for referrals, 1-800-562-6025; San Juan Island, P.O. Box 325; Friday Harbor, WA 98250; Lopez Island, Route 1, Box 1180, Lopez Island, WA 98261). Services: Safe houses, advocacy/counseling for women.

SEATTLE:

YWCA Emergency Shelter (24 hour staffing, (206) 461-4882; 1118 Fifth Avenue, Seattle, WA 98101). Services: Three week shelter stay (no male children over six years old), crisis intervention, support group on-site, advocacy, referrals to other agencies, TTY available, wheelchair accessible.

Catherine Booth House (Crisis Line/24 hours, (206) 324-4943 with TTY; Box 20128, Seattle, WA 98102). Services: Shelter for battered/abused women and their children (no boys over twelve), advocacy/counseling for women and children, support group, parenting group, therapeutic childcare, legal and public assistance advocacy, some interpreters available.

Center for the Prevention of Sexual and Domestic Violence (business, Monday-Friday, 9:30-4:30, (206) 634-1903; 1914 N. 34th, Suite 105, Seattle, WA 98103). Services: Counseling on religious issues, community education with workshops for clergy and religious educators on family violence, including sexual assault, marital rape, and battering.

Family Violence Project 6 (Business, (206) 684-7770; Seattle City Attorney's Office, Room 1414 Dexter Horton Building, 710 Second Avenue, Seattle, WA 98104). Services: Legal advocacy in Seattle Municipal Court, referrals for civil concerns, including divorce and custody, crisis counseling, referrals to other agencies, interpreters for Spanish, wheelchair accessible, TTY.

Evergreen Legal Services (Business, Monday-Friday, 9-5, (206) 464-5911; 401 Second Avenue S., Suite 401, Seattle, WA 98104). Services: Legal advocacy: domestic violence — low income only; TTY available, wheelchair accessible.

Group Health Cooperative (Business, Monday-Friday, 8-5:30, (206) 287-2500; 1730 Minor Avenue, Seattle, WA 98101). Services for Group Health Cooperative members only: counseling/groups for women, counseling/groups for men, groups for adult women victims of incest, group for child sexual assault victims

Family Services (Business, Monday-Friday, 8:30-5 or by appointment, (206) 461-3883; 107 Cherry Street, Room 500, Seattle, WA 98104). Services: Counseling/groups for women, counseling/groups for men, counseling for sexual assault, Family Anger Management Institute, counseling for children through Seattle Child Guidance.

King County Crisis Lines (206-461-3222; 1515 Dexter Avenue N., Seattle, WA 98121).

New Beginnings (Crisis Line/24 hours, (206) 522-9472; P.O. Box 75125, Seattle, WA 98125). Services: Shelter (no boys over eleven), advocacy/counseling for women, community support groups for women and children, counseling for children, interpreters for Spanish and hearing impaired.

Stop Abuse: Counseling Center, (206) 254-BOSE.

Redmond: Greater Seattle Domestic Violence Program D.V.P. Education Counseling, (206) 869-8282.

SHELTON:

Recovery: Aid for Victims of Sexual and Domestic Abuse (Crisis Number, 1-800-562-6025 Hotline referral; business, (206) 426-5878, Monday-Friday, 10-4, P.O. Box 1132, Shelton, WA 98584). Services: Advocacy/counseling for women and children dealing with domestic and sexual abuse, safe houses, advocacy with legal and medical issues, accompaniment and transportation.

SPOKANE:

Alternatives to Domestic Violence/YWCA (Crisis Line, evenings/weekends, Hotline number (509) 838-4428; Crisis/business, Monday-Friday, 9-5, (509) 327-9534; W. 829 Broadway, Spokane, WA 99201). Services: Shelter, advocacy/counseling for women, anger management, counseling for children, support groups for women.

STEVENSON:

Skamania County Council on Domestic Violence (Crisis number, Hotline referral, 1-800-562-6025; P.O. Box 477, Stevenson, WA 98648). Services: Safe houses, advocacy/counseling, transportation, child care, information and referral

SUNNYSIDE:

Lore Valley Crisis and Support Services (Crisis line/24 hours, (509) 837-6689; 1001 E. Edison, Sunnyside, WA 98944; P.O. Box 93, Sunnyside, WA 98944). Services: Advocacy/counseling for women, parenting skills group, counseling for children, counseling for men, counseling/advocacy for sexual assault, transportation to Yakima and Richland shelters, interpreters for Spanish.

TACOMA:

YWCA Women's Support Shelter (Crisis line/24 hours, (206) 383-2593, (206) 383-2594, (206) 383-3263; 407 Broadway, Tacoma, WA 98402). Services: Shelter (no boys over twelve), advocacy/counseling for women, support group for women, counseling for children, interpreters for Korean.

Turtle Island Institute (Crisis/business (206) 474-2294; P.). Box 8004, Tacoma, WA 98408). Services: Safe houses (teenage boys OK), advocacy/counseling for battered women and their children, adult women incest survivors, abused elders, battered lesbians, women of color and those with low incomes, several support groups weekly, wheelchair accessible.

WALLA WALLA:

Community Abuse and Assault Center (Crisis line/Monday-Friday, 8:30-5, (509) 529-3300; Crisis Line, evenings and weekends, (509) 529-9090; 366 Chase, Walla Walla, WA 99324). Services: Safe houses, advocacy/counseling for women, support group for women, victims of incest group, advocacy/counseling for children, counseling for sexual assault, interpreters for Spanish.

WENATCHEE:

Wenatchee Rape Crisis and Domestic Violence Center (Crisis Line/24 hours, (509) 663-7446; P.O. Box 2704, Wenatchee, WA 98801). Services: Safe houses, advocacy/counseling for victims, support group for women, advocacy/counseling for sexual assault, interpreters for Spanish, wheelchair accessible.

VANCOUVER:

YWCA Women's Emergency House (Crisis Line/24 hours, (206) 695-0501; Business/Monday-Friday, M-F, (206) 696-0167; 1115 Esther, Vancouver, WA 98660). Services: Shelter, advocacy/counseling for women, support group for women, parenting group for women.

YAKIMA:

Family Crisis Program/YWCA (Crisis Line/24 hours, (509) 248-7796; 15 N. Naches, Yakima, WA 98901). Services: Shelter, advocacy/counseling for women, counseling for men, advocacy/counseling for children, interpreters for Spanish.

APPENDIX L
RESOURCES FOR ALCOHOL AND DRUG ABUSE

Bureau of Alcohol and Substance Abuse (BASA), Department of Social and Health Services (DSHS), Mail Stop OB-44W, Olympia, WA 98504 has compiled a directory of state-wide, DSHS approved treatment facilities. The directory lists available services for the treatment of drug and/or alcohol abuse, target populations, treatment type, and city/county location.

For further information or immediate referrals, call the Alcohol and Drug 24-hour HELP LINE, (206) 722-3700; toll free at 1-800-562-1240; Ann Forbes, Director. Al-Anon information center, (206) 625-0000.

DEFINITION OF SERVICES

DETOXIFICATION: Care and treatment, in a residential or hospital setting, of persons intoxicated or incapacitated by alcohol or other drugs during the period in which the person recovers from the transitory effects of acute intoxication.

EXTENDED CARE RECOVERY HOUSE: Care and treatment in a residential setting in excess of 60 days for clients needing prolonged treatment services.

INTENSIVE INPATIENT TREATMENT: A concentrated residential program consisting of a combination of educational sessions, individual and group therapy, and related activities for detoxified Alcoholic/addicts and their families.

INTENSIVE OUTPATIENT TREATMENT: A concentrated non-residential program consisting of a combination of educational sessions, individual and group therapy, and related activities for detoxified Alcoholic/addicts and their families.

LONG-TERM RESIDENTIAL TREATMENT: Care and treatment on a

long-term basis (90 days or more) in a residential setting with personal care services for Alcoholic/addicts with impaired self-maintenance capabilities needing personal guidance and assistance to maintain abstinence and good health.

METHADONE TREATMENT: A non-residential treatment program which includes the use of methadone (or other drugs approved by the DSHS) as a substitute for opiates, in addition to counseling and other types of therapy.

OUTPATIENT TREATMENT: Drug addiction and drug abuse treatment services according to a prescribed plan in a non-residential setting.

RECOVERY HOUSE: Care and treatment in a residential setting with social andrecreational activities for detoxified Alcoholics/addicts to aid their adjustment to abstinence and aid their engagement in occupational training, gainful employment, or other types of community service.

ALCOHOL/DRUG INFORMATION SCHOOL (ALCOHOL/DRUG INFO SCHOOL): An educational program providing students with information regarding the use and abuse of Alcohol and drugs. The goal of the school is to help students not currently presenting a significant Alcohol or drug problem to make informed decisions about the use of Alcohol and drugs.

CRISIS INTERVENTION: Services aimed at alleviating acute emotional, behavioral, and/or physical distress resulting from the individual's use of Alcohol and/or drugs.

DWI ASSESSMENT: A diagnostic service designed to evaluate and assess clients' involvement with Alcohol and/or other drugs, and to recommend an appropriate course of action. Agencies performing these assessments also perform assessments appropriate for other inquiries, legal or private.

TARGET POPULATIONS

YOUTH: Services are restricted to clients who are 19 years of age or less.

INVOLUNTARY ONLY: Services are restricted to involuntarily committed clients only.

WOMEN ONLY: Services are restricted to women clients only.

MEN ONLY: Services are restricted to men clients only.

PRIMARILY YOUTH: Services are designed primarily for clients who are 19 years of age or less, but not restricted to such an age group.

ADAMS COUNTY:

Adams County Community Counseling Service (509) 488-5162, Crisis Line (24 hours/day) 488-5611; 165 N. First, Othello, WA 98344. Alcohol/ Drug Services: outpatient treatment, alcohol/drug info school, DWI assessment.

BENTON COUNTY:

Comprehensive Alcohol Program (509) 735-1191; 5219 W. Clearwater, Suite 9, Kennewick, WA 98336. Alcohol/ Drug Services: outpatient treatment, intensive outpatient, DWI assessment, alcohol/drug info school.

CHELAN COUNTY:

Cascade Community Counseling(509) 662-4448; 1201 S. Mission, Wenatchee, WA 98801. Alcohol/Drug Services: outpatient treatment, intensive outpatient, alcohol/drug info school, DWI assessment.

The Center for Alcohol and Drug treatment (CASA, Inc.) Crisis Line, (509) 662-0460; Business, (509) 662-9673; 327 Okanogan, Wenatchee, WA 98801. Alcohol/Drug Services: outpatient treatment, intensive inpatient, DWI assessment, alcohol/drug info school; alcohol only detoxification, recovery house.

CLALLAM COUNTY:

Clark's Counseling (206) 452-4791; 934-1/2 Caroline, Port Angeles, WA 98362. Alcohol/Drug Services: outpatient treatment, intensive outpatient, DWI assessment.

North Olympic Alcohol and Drug Center (206) 452-2381; 315 E. Eighth St., Port Angeles, WA 98362. *Outreach Offices*: Sequim, Joyce. Alcohol/ Drug Services: outpatient treatment, intensive outpatient, alcohol/drug info school, DWI assessment.

West-End Outreach Services (206) 374-6177; Forks Community Hospital, RR 3, Box 3575, Forks, WA 98331. Alcohol/Drug Services: outpatient treatment, DWI assessment, alcohol/drug info school.

CLARK COUNTY:

Clark County Council on Alcoholism (206) 696-1631; John Owen Recovery House, 1950 Fort Vancouver Way, Vancouver, WA 98668. Services: Alcohol/drug detoxification, intensive outpatient, outpatient treatment, DWI assessment, alcohol/drug info school. alcohol only recovery house.

Veterans Administration Medical Center (206) 696-4061, ext. 3588; O Street and Fourth Plain Ward 3D, Vancouver, WA 98661. Services: outpatient treatment, intensive inpatient.

COWLITZ COUNTY:

Drug Abuse Prevention Center (206) 636-1050; 2112 S. Kelso Drive, Kelso, WA 98626. Alcohol/Drug Services: outpatient treatment, long term residential.

Recovery Northwest *Intensive Inpatient/Detoxification:* (206) 636-4859; 600 Broadway, Longview, WA 98632. *Outpatient Treatment:* (206) 425-1914; 828 12th Avenue, Suite A, Longview, WA 98632. Alcohol/Drug Services: DWI assessment, alcohol/drug info school. Alcohol Only: outpatient treatment, intensive outpatient.

FRANKLIN COUNTY:

Our Lady of Lourdes Health Center (509) 547-7704 ext. 377; Alcohol and Drug Treatment Unit, 520 Fourth Avenue, Pasco, WA 99302. Alcohol/Drug Services: intensive inpatient, detoxification, intensive outpatient, outpatient, DWI assessment, alcohol/drug info school.

GRANT COUNTY:

Grant County Alcohol and Drug Center (509) 765-5402; 1038 W. Ivy Avenue, Moses Lake, WA 98837. *Outreach Offices*: Quincy, Grand Coulee, Ephrata. Alcohol/Drug Services: outpatient treatment, intensive outpatient, DWI assessment, alcohol/drug info school.

GRAYS HARBOR COUNTY:

Chehalis Reservation Confederated Tribes Alcoholism Treatment Center (206) 273-5911; P.O. Box 536, Oakville, WA 98568. Alcohol/Drug Services: intensive outpatient, DWI assessment, alcohol/drug info school. Alcohol Only: outpatient treatment.

Kairos Detoxification and Recovery House (206) 533-2529; 611 Eighth Street, Hoquiam, WA 98550. Alcohol Only: Detoxification, intensive inpatient.

Saint Joseph's Hospital Care Unit (206) 533-8500; 1006 N. "H" Street, Aberdeen, WA 98520. Alcohol Only Services: Detoxification, intensive inpatient.

ISLAND COUNTY:

Recovery Northwest: (206) 679-4525; 2134 - 200 Avenue W., Suite 1, Oak Harbor, WA 98277. *Outreach Offices:* Langley and Stanwood.

KING COUNTY:

Alcohol and Drug 24-Hour Helpline Crisis line (206) 722-3700, Toll Free 1-800-562-1240. Alcohol/Drug Services: Crisis intervention.

Community Alcohol/Drug Centers *Central Area:* (206) 322-2970; 1401 E. Jefferson, Seattle, WA 98122. *Southeast:* (206) 854-6513; Titus Building, 232 S. Second, Kent, WA 98032. *Southwest:* (206) 242-3506; 15025 Fourth Avenue SW, Seattle, WA 98166. *Vashon:* (206) 463-9492; Sunrise Ridge Vashon-Maury, Vashon, WA 98070. Alcohol/Drug ServicesP: outpatient treatment, intensive outpatient, DWI assessment, alcohol/drug info school.

Eastside Alcohol Center (206) 454-1505 Park 120, Suite D204, 606 120th Avenue NE, Bellevue, WA 98005. Alcohol/Drug Services: intensive outpatient, outpatient treatment, DWI assessment, alcohol/drug info school.

Evergreen Treatment Services (206) 282-2959; 557 Roy St., Seattle, WA 98109. Drug Only Services: outpatient treatment, methadone treatment.

Federal Way Counseling Services (206) 874-4443; 32700 Pacific Hwy. S., Suite 11, Federal Way, WA 98002. Services: Alcohol outpatient treatment, intensive outpatient. drug only, DWI assessment.

First Step *Kent:* (206) 859-0951; 25608 74th Avenue S., Kent, WA 98032. *Bellevue:* (206) 746-3888; 14400 NE Bel-Red Road, #204, Bellevue, WA 98007. *Seattle:* (206) 363-0031; 12063 15th Avenue NE, Seattle, WA 98125. *Tacoma:* (206) 474-8777; 3640 S. Cedar Street, Suite Y, Tacoma, WA 98409. Alcohol/Drug Services: outpatient treatment, intensive outpatient, DWI assessment, alcohol/drug info school.

Group Health Cooperative *Alcohol and Drug Abuse Unit:* (206) 287-2700; 1600 E. John, Annex #15, Seattle, WA 98112. Alcohol/Drug Services: outpatient, intensive outpatient, DWI assessment, alcohol/drug info school. *Adapt:* (206) 885-9492; 2661 Bellevue-Redmind Road, Bellevue, WA 98005 Alcohol/Drug Services: intensive outpatient, outpatient treatment, DWI assessment, alcohol/drug info school. *Alcohol And Drug Abuse Unit:* (206) 883-5151 ext. 4366; 2700 152nd Avenue NE, Redmond, WA 9052. Alcohol/Drug Services: Detoxification, intensive inpatient.

Lakeside Recovery Counseling Center *Angle Lake:* (206) 824-9780; 19530 Pacific Hwy. S., The Shores, Building #1, Suite 102, Seattle, WA 98188. Alcohol/Drug Services: intensive outpatient, outpatient, DWI assessment, alcohol/drug info school. Lakeside *Recovery Center East:* (206) 822-5095; 10422 NE 37th Circle, Suite B, Kirkland, WA 98033. *Bothell-inpatient:* (206) 823-3116, 1-800-231-4303. Alcohol/Drug Services: intensive outpatient, outpatient treatment, DWI assessment, alcohol/drug info school. *Lakeside Recovery Center North:* (206) 542-6106; 17962 Midvale Avenue N., Seattle, WA 98133. Alcohol/Drug Services: intensive outpatient, outpatient treatment, DWI assessment, alcohol/drug info school. Alcohol/Drug

Mercer Island Youth and Family Services (206) 236-3523; 8236 SE 24th St.rtte Mercer Island, WA 98040. Alcohol/Drug Services: outpatient treatment.

Mt. Baker Youth Service Bureau Community Association (206) 322-7676; 1730 Bradner Place S., Seattle, WA 98144. Drug Only :outpatient treatment, (primarily youth).

Northwest Treatment Center (206) 789-5911; 9010 13th NW, Seattle, WA 98117. Alcohol/Drug Services: intensive inpatient, DWI assessment. *Kirkland:* (206) 789-5911; 1029 Market Street, Suite C, Kirkland, WA 98033. Alcohol/Drug Services: DWI assessment. *Seattle:* (206) 283-9101 or 283-9205 130 Nickerson Street, Seattle, WA 98109. Alcohol/Drug Services: intensive outpatient, outpatient, DWI assessment.

Renton Vocational Technical Institute (206) 235-2352; 3000 NE Fourth Street, Renton, WA 98056. Alcohol/Drug Services: DWI assessment, alcohol/drug info school.

Residence XII *South:* (206) 431-5327; 16255 Sylvester Road SW, Seattle, WA 98166. Alcohol/Drug Services: intensive inpatient (Women Only). *North:* (206) 823-8844; 14506 Juanita Dr. NE, Bothell, WA 98011. Alcohol/Drug Services: intensive inpatient (Women Only).

Ryther Child Center (206) 525-5050; 2400 NE 95th, Seattle, WA 98115. Alcohol/Drug Services: intensive inpatient, (youth only).

Saint Cabrini Recovery Program (206) 583-4344; St. Cabrini Hospital, Terry and Madison, Seattle, WA 98104. Alcohol/Drug Services: intensive inpatient, detoxification, intensive outpatient, outpatient treatment, DWI assessment. *Bellevue Branch:* (206) 455-4154; 1810 116th NE, Bellevue, WA 98004. Alcohol/Drug Services: intensive outpatient youth only, outpatient treatment, (youth only).

Schick Shadel Hospital (206) 244-8100; 12101 Ambaum Blvd. SW, Seattle, WA 98146. Alcohol/Drug Services: intensive inpatient, DWI assessment, alcohol only detoxification.

Seadrunar *Capitol Hill:* (206) 324-8500; 809 15th E, Seattle, WA 98112. *Queen Anne:* (206) 284-2431; 200 W. Comstock, Seattle, WA 98119. Drug Only: long term residential.

Square One *Issaquah:* (206) 392-7815; 1275 12th Avenue NW, Issaquah, WA 98027. *Redmond:* (206) 881-7084; 7811 159th Place NE, Redmond, WA 98052. Alcohol/Drug Services: outpatient treatment, intensive outpatient, DWI assessment, alcohol/drug info school.

KITSAP COUNTY:

Awareness Express (206) 876-9430; 614 Division, Port Orchard, WA 98366. Alcohol/Drug Services: outpatient treatment, intensive inpatient, DWI assessment, alcohol/drug info school.

Bennett Counseling Services (206) 842-1028; Plaza 305, Suites 305 and 207, 19045 Highway 305, Poulsbo, WA 98370. Alcohol/Drug Services: Outpatient treatment, intensive outpatient, DWI assessment, alcohol/drug info school.

Kitsap County Council on Alcoholism (206) 377- 0051or 377-0052; 532 Fifth Street, Bremerton, WA 98310. Alcohol/Drug Services: Outpatient treatment, intensive outpatient, DWI assessment, alcohol/drug info school. Alcohol Only: Detoxification, intensive inpatient.

Olalla Guest Lodge (206) 857-6201 or 857-6501; 12851 LaLa Cove Lane SE, Olalla, WA 98359. Alcohol/Drug Services: Intensive inpatient.

KITTITAS COUNTY:

Alcohol and Drug Dependency Services (509) 925-9821; 507 Nanum, Room 111, Ellensburg, WA 98926. Alcohol/Drug Services: Outpatient treatment, DWI assessment, alcohol/drug info school. Alcohol Only: Intensive outpatient.

KLICKITAT COUNTY:

Counseling and Resource Center (509) 773-5801; 112 W. Main Street, Goldendale, WA 98620. *White Salmon:* (509) 493-3400; 40 Skyline Hospital, White Salmon, WA 98672. Alcohol/Drug Services: Outpatient treatment, DWI assessment, alcohol/drug info school.

LEWIS COUNTY:

Addictions Recovery Center (206) 736-4357 or 736-2803; Centralia General Hospital, 500 SE Washington, Chehalis, WA 98531. Alcohol/Drug Services: Detoxification, intensive inpatient.

Recovery Northwest (206) 748-9204; 129 NW Chehalis, Chehalis, WA 98532. Alcohol/Drug Services: Outpatient treatment, intensive outpatient, DWI assessment, alcohol/drug info school.

LINCOLN COUNTY:

Lincoln County Counseling Center (509) 725-3001; P.O. Box 278, Davenport, WA 99122. Services: Crisis intervention, individual and group counseling; also Alzheimer's support and much, much more.

Lincoln County Alcohol and Certification Center (509) 725-2111, P.O. Box 152, Davenport, WA 99122.

MASON COUNTY:

Listening Post/Access (206) 426-9717; 107 N. Eighth, Shelton, WA 98584. Alcohol/Drug Services: Outpatient treatment, intensive outpatient, DWI assessment, alcohol/drug info school.

PACIFIC COUNTY:

Recovery Northwest 607 Oregon St., Long Beach, WA 98631. Alcohol/Drug Services: outpatient treatment, intensive outpatient, DWI assessment, alcohol/drug info school.

PEND OREILLE COUNTY:

Pend Oreille Community Alcoholism Center (509) 447-5651; 230 S. Garden Avenue, P.O. Box 5000, Newport, WA 99156. Alcohol/Drug Services: Outpatient, DWI assessment, alcohol/drug info school.

PIERCE COUNTY:

Allied Counseling Services (206) 922-6738; 4410 20th Street E., Fife, WA 98424. Alcohol/Drug Services: DWI assessment, alcohol/drug info school. Alcohol Only: Outpatient treatment, intensive outpatient.

Chemical Abuse Resource and Education-C.A.R.E. (206) 572-2273; 1502 Tacoma Avenue S., Tacoma, WA 98402. Alcohol/Drug Services: Crisis intervention.

First Step (206) 474-8777; 3640 S. Cedar Street, Suite Y, Tacoma, WA 98409. Alcohol/Drug Services: Outpatient treatment, intensive Inpatient, DWI assessment, alcohol/drug info school.

Counselor (206) 848-2242; 315 39th Avenue SW, Suite 11, Puyallup, WA 98373. Alcohol/Drug Services: DWI assessment, alcohol/drug info school. Alcohol Only: Outpatient treatment, intensive outpatient.

Gig Harbor Alcohol Counseling Service (206) 851-2552; 8803 State Highway 16, Suite F, Gig Harbor, WA 98335. Alcohol/Drug Services: DWI assessment, alcohol/drug info school. Alcohol Only: outpatient treatment, intensive outpatient.

New Beginning Adolescent Alcohol Unit (206) 582-4357; Lakewood General Hospital, 11315 Bridgeport Way SW, Tacoma, WA 98499. Alcohol/Drug Services: Detoxification, intensive inpatient, youth only.

Plaza HAll (206) 272-0906; 1415 Center Street, Tacoma, WA 98409. Alcohol/Drug Services: Outpatient treatment, intensive outpatient, DWI assessment, alcohol/drug info school, recovery house.

Puget Sound Alcoholism Center (206) 474-0533; P.O. Box 11412, 215 S. 36th and Pacific Avenue, Tacoma, WA 98411-0412. Alcohol/Drug Services: Detoxification, intensive inpatient.

SAN JUAN COUNTY:

San Juan Community Alcohol Center (206) 378-4994; P.O. Box 755, 955 Guard Street, Friday Harbor, WA 98250. *Outreach Offices:* Lopez, Eastsound. Alcohol/Drug Services: Outpatient treatment, DWI assessment, alcohol/ drug info school.

SKAGIT COUNTY:

Skagit County Council on Alcoholism (206) 428-7835; John King Recovery House, 1Continental Place, Mount Vernon, WA 98273. Alcohol/Drug Services: Outpatient treatment, intensive outpatient, DWI assessment, alcohol/drug info school. Alcohol Only: detoxification, recovery house.

SNOHOMISH COUNTY:

Community Alcohol and Drug Services *Everett:* (206) 258-2662; 2812 Hoyt Avenue, Everett, WA 98201. *Lynnwood:* (206) 775-4686; P.O. Box 729, Lynnwood, WA 98046-0729. *Arlington:* (206) 435-4463; Second Floor City Hall, Third and Olympic, Arlington, WA 98223. Alcohol/Drug Services: Outpatient treatment, intensive outpatient, DWI assessment, alcohol/drug info school

Norcross Clinic, Inc. (206) 771-1194; 209 Dayton, Suite 201, Edmonds, WA 98020. *Mill Creek:* (206) 742-5233; 16000 Bothell/Everett Hwy., Bothell, WA 98012. Alcohol/Drug Services: Outpatient treatment, intensive outpatient, DWI assessment, alcohol/drug info school.

Providence Recovery Program (206) 258-7300; P.O. Box 1067, Pacific and Nassau, Everett, WA 98206. Alcohol/Drug Services: Detoxification, intensive inpatient.

SPOKANE COUNTY:

Alcoholism Outptient Services (509) 534-3132; East 901 Second Avenue, Suite 100, Spokane, WA 99202. Alcohol/Drug Services: DWI assessment, alcohol/drug info school. Alcohol Only: Outpatient treatment, intensive outpatient.

The Colonial Clinic (509) 838-6004; W. 315 Ninth Avenue, Suite 201, Spokane, WA 99204. Alcohol/Drug Services: Outpatient treatment, intensive outpatient, DWI assessment, alcohol/drug info school.

THURSTON COUNTY:

Alpine Shared Health Services (206) 459-7122; 931 Poplar Street, Olympia, WA 98501. Alcohol/Drug Services: outpatient treatment, intensive outpatient, DWI assessment, alcohol/drug info school.

Crisis Clinic of Thurston and Mason Counties (206) 352-2211, P.O. Box 2463, Olympia, WA 98507. Alcohol/Drug Services: Crisis intervention.

St. Peter Hospital Chemical Dependency Program (206) 456-7575; 413 N. Lilly Road, Olympia, WA 98506. Alcohol/Drug Services: Detoxification, intensive inpatient, intensive outpatient.

Thurston and Mason Addiction Recovery Council (TAMARC) (206) 943-8510; 1625 Mottman Road SW, Tumwater, WA 98502. Alcohol/Drug Services: Outpatient treatment, intensive outpatient, DWI assessment, alcohol/drug info school, recovery house. Alcohol Only: Detoxification.

WALLA WALLA COUNTY:

Alcohol and Drug Recovery Program (509) 522-4357; Walla Walla General Hospital, 1025 S. Second Avenue, Walla Walla, WA 99362. Alcohol/Drug Services: Detoxification, intensive inpatient.

Walla Walla Community Alcohol and Drug Abuse Center (509) 525-7800; 180 S. Fifth, Walla Walla, WA 99362. Alcohol/Drug Services: Outpatient treatment, DWI assessment, alcohol/drug info school. Alcohol Only: Intensive outpatient.

WHATCOM COUNTY:

Community Alcohol and Drug Center (206) 733-1400; 1728 Iowa, Bellingham, WA 98226. Alcohol/Drug Services: Outpatient treatment, intensive outpatient, DWI assessment, alcohol/drug info school.

Recovery Center for Alcoholism and Addictions (206) 734-5400; St. Joseph Hospital, 2901 Squalicum Parkway, Bellingham, WA 98225. Alcohol/Drug Services: Detoxification, intensive inpatient.

WHITMAN COUNTY:

Whitman County Alcoholism Center (509) 332-6585; NE 340 Maple Street, #2, Pullman, WA 99163. *Outreach Office:* Colfax. Alcohol/Drug Services: Outpatient treatment, DWI assessment, alcohol/drug info school. Alcohol Only: Intensive outpatient.

YAKIMA COUNTY:

James M. Oldham Treatment Center (509) 457-1623; 308 N. Fourth Street, Yakima, WA 98907. Alcohol/Drug Services: Intensive inpatient. Alcohol Only: Recovery house.

Northwest Counseling Services (509) 453-2900; 401 S. Fifth Avenue, Yakima, WA 98901. Alcohol/Drug Services: Outpatient treatment, intensive outpatient, DWI assessment, alcohol/drug info school.

Valley Alcohol Council (509) 837-7700; 702 Franklin, Sunnyside, WA 98944. Alcohol/Drug Services: DWI assessment, alcohol/drug info school. Alcohol Only: Outpatient treatment, intensive outpatient.

SAMPLE PARENTING PLAN

IN THE SUPERIOR COURT OF THE STATE OF WASHINGTON
FOR KING COUNTY

In re the Marriage of	)	
	)	
MARY ELLEN JEFFREY,	)	
	)	NO. 90-3-00000-0
Petitioner,	)	
	)	PARENTING PLAN
and	)	
	)	
JAMES L. JEFFREY,	)	
	)	
Respondent.	)	
	)	

D. PARENTING PLAN

PREAMBLE: We, the parents of Justin and Kristin, enter into this Agreement in order to better meet our parental responsibilities and to safeguard our children's future development. We both recognize that Justin and Kristin wish to love and respect both of us, regardless of our marital status or our place of residence, and that Justin's and Kristin's welfare can best be served by our mutual cooperation as partners in parenting and by each of us providing a home in which the children are loved and to which each child belongs: their mother's house and their father's house.

I.   **DECISION MAKING**
      A. **General**
         1.   Each parent desires to remain responsible and active in
               Justin's and Kristin's growth and development consistent
               with the best interest of the children. The parents will make
               a mutual effort to maintain an open, ongoing communi-
               cation concerning the development, needs, and
               interests of the children and will discuss together any major
               decisions which have to be made about or for the children.
               1.1 Each parent shall have an equal say in all major
                   decisions. In the event of an irreconcilable conflict, the
                   matter shall be submitted to mediation and, if
                   necessary, arbitration or final disposition on the Family
                   Law Motion Calendar, in accordance with paragraph
                   XI below.
               1.2 The residential parent shall have authority to make
                   day-to-day decisions affecting the children's welfare;
                   HOWEVER, major decisions concerning the
                   children's welfare shall not be made without
                   agreement by both parents.
         2.   Major decisions are the following:
               2.1 Non-emergency medical and/or dental care and
                   providers thereof.
               2.2 Change of school not mandated by authorities.
               2.3 Moving the children more than ten (10) miles from
                   their present residence.
               2.4 Choice of care providers.
         3.   Before any of the three following events may occur prior to
               the children's eighteenth (18th) birthdays, parents must
               consent, in writing, to their: (a) acquisition of a driver's
               license; (b) marrying; or (c) entry into any type of military
               service. In the event of disagreement each parent has
               temporary veto power with reference to these three (3)
               decisions until referral to mediation or Court.
         4.   Each parent shall have equal and independent authority to
               confer with school, day-care, and other programs with
               regard to the children's progress and each shall have free
               access to school, day-care, and other records. Each parent
               shall have authority to give parental consent or permission
               as may be required concerning school, day-care, or other
               programs for the children while the children are in his or
               her custody.

5.   Each parent agrees to honor one another's parenting style, privacy, and authority. Neither will interfere in the parenting style of the other, nor will either parent make plans and arrangements that would impinge upon the other parent's authority or time with the children without the express agreement of the other parent. Each parent agrees to encourage the children to discuss his or her grievance with a parent directly with the parent in question. It is the intent of both parents to encourage a direct child-parent bond.

B. Education

1.   The children shall attend the school mutually agreed upon by the parents, recognizing that the decisions should be made in the best interest of the children's education needs, rather than the needs of the parents.

    1.1 All schools, health care providers, and counselors shall be selected by the parents jointly. In the event the parents cannot agree to the selection of a school, the children shall be maintained in the present school, pending mediation and/or further order of the court.

    1.2 Each parent is to provide the other parent promptly upon receipt with information concerning the well-being of the children, including, but not limited to, copies of report cards, school meeting notices, vacation schedules, class programs, requests for conferences, results of standardized or diagnostic tests, notices of activities involving the diagnostic tests, notices of activities involving the children, samples of schoolwork, order forms for school pictures, all communications from health care providers, the names, addresses, and telephone numbers of all schools, health care providers, regular day care providers, and counselors.

C. Health Care

1.   Each parent shall be empowered to obtain emergency health care for the children without the consent of the other parent. Each parent is to notify the other parent as soon as reasonably possible of any illness requiring medical attention, or any emergency involving the children.

    1.1 Each parent shall have equal and independent authority to provide routine and emergency medical and dental services for the children while the children are in his or her care and residence.

    1.2 Major decisions regarding non-routine, non-emergency medical care must be made jointly by the parents.

D.

    Religious Upbringing

    1.   Each parent shall have an equal right to include the children in his or her religious activities and expressions. The children shall have the right to make their own religious choice as they mature.

II.   **RESIDENTIAL ARRANGEMENTS**

A. **School Year Schedules**

From one week prior to the commencement of the child's school year through the Saturday following its conclusion, the following shall be the children's residential arrangements.

    1.   The children shall reside with their father on the first, third, and fifth weekends of each month from 5:30 p.m. Friday evening through 8:00 p.m. Sunday evening, and with their mother the remainder of the time. The weekends shall be extended if they include a holiday.

    2.   **Summer Schedule**

The residential arrangements of the children during the summer of the year shall be as follows:

    2.1 The children shall reside with the father for six uninterrupted weeks during the summer school vacation. Proposed dates should be submitted by the father prior to April 15 each year.

    3.   **Holidays**

The children's holiday time shall be allocated as follows:

    3.1 During odd-numbered years, the children shall reside with the father on Presidents Day, Fourth of July, and Thanksgiving. During even-numbered years, the children shall reside with the mother on Presidents Day, Fourth of July, and Thanksgiving.

    3.2 During even-numbered years, the children shall reside with the father on Memorial Day, Labor Day, Veterans Day, and Easter. During odd-numbered years, the children shall reside with the mother on Memorial Day, Labor Day, Veterans Day, and Easter.

3.3 The parent having the children for the weekend immediately before or after a national holiday shall have the weekend time expanded to include such holiday.

3.4 Thanksgiving shall be defined as beginning at 5:00 p.m., Wednesday preceding Thanksgiving, until 7:00 p.m., Sunday following Thanksgiving.

III. **BIRTHDAYS AND SPECIAL FAMILY DAYS**

A. The children shall celebrate their birthdays with their mother in even-numbered years, and with their father in odd-numbered years.

B. The non-residential parent shall be allowed to spend some time with the child to celebrate the children's birthdays, within a week of that birthday.

C. The mother shall have the children every year for Mother's Day and the father shall have the children every year for Father's Day from 9:00 a.m. to 6:00 p.m.

IV. **VACATIONS, WINTER AND SPRING BREAK**

A. The children shall spend a portion of the winter school holiday from the first day of school vacation until 10 a.m. Christmas Day with the father in even-numbered years, and with the mother in odd-numbered years.

B. The children shall spend every other spring vacation, as defined by the school schedule, with the father.

V. **PARENTS' VACATIONS**

A. In addition to the other arrangements, each parent shall have the children for vacation purposes during that parent's scheduled vacation from work for up to two weeks each year provided that 30 days' notice is given to the other parent and provided that such vacation time does not conflict with the children's school schedule. Each parent shall endeavor to arrange their vacation during the summer months, if possible.

VI. **TELEPHONE ACCESS**

The children shall have liberal telephone privileges with the parent with whom they are not then residing without interference of the residential parent.

VII. **PARTICIPATION IN CHILDREN'S EVENTS**

A. Children shall be accompanied by the parent with whom they are residing at the time of a given social event. The other parent shall not be limited from attendance at that event, providing said attendance by the non-residential parent is not disruptive to the other participants

B. Each parent shall be responsible for keeping themselves advised of school, athletic, and social events in which the children participate. Both parents may participate in school activities for the children such as open house, attendance at an athletic event, *etc.*

VIII. **REMOVAL OF CHILDREN FROM STATE**

A parent shall not remove the residence of the children from the State of Washington except by the advance written approval of the other parent or by court order entered after notice of hearing having been given to the other parent.

IX. **TRANSPORTATION**

A. Responsibility for providing transportation shall be divided between the parents. Each parent shall be responsible for providing transportation to his or her home.

B. The children shall be picked up and returned at the designated times. Should a delay become necessary, the receiving parent shall be notified immediately.

C. The father shall be responsible for all transportation to and from Justin's and Kristin's soccer and baseball practices and games. The mother shall be responsible for all transportation to and from cultural enrichment activities.

X. **OTHER**

A. It is the responsibility of the parent scheduled to have the children to arrange suitable alternative care if necessary and pay for needed care.

B. Each parent shall notify the other parent at least 48 hours in advance if he/she is unable to exercise the regular schedule.

XI. **DISPUTE RESOLUTION**

A. Any decision concerning the children shall be made only after consideration is given to the needs, feelings, and desires of the children.

B. In the event that there are difficulties or differences of opinion between the parents regarding provisions for the children, the matter shall be referred to a private mediator chosen by the parties.

C. In the event the parties are unable to agree on a private mediator, the matter shall be referred to the King County Family Law Motion Calendar for designation of a mediator. Should mediation not be successful in resolving the dispute, the same may be referred to the King County Superior Court Family Law Motion Calendar for final resolution.

   D. In undertaking this dispute resolution process, the parents agree:
1. That preference shall be given to carrying out the parenting plan;
2. That the parents shall use the designated process to resolve the disputes relating to implementation of the plan, except those related to financial support, unless an emergency exists;
3. If the court finds that a parent has used or frustrated the dispute resolution process without good reason, the court shall award attorneys' fees and financial sanctions to the prevailing party; and
4. The parents have the right of review from the dispute resolution process to the Superior Court.

XII. **RESIDENTIAL DESIGNATION (JURISDICTIONAL ONLY)**

The following designations shall not affect either parent's rights or responsibilities under this Plan:
1. The children's residence for the purposes of jurisdiction, venue and child support only is that of the mother.
2. The children's custodian for the sole purpose of compliance with all other state and federal laws is the mother.

XIII. **FINANCIAL SUPPORT**

   A. **Major Expenses**

Prior to either parent obligating any parent for major expenses on behalf of the children, such as orthodontia expenses, private educational expenses, tutoring, or other expenses in excess of the day-to-day standard expenses for public-school children, the parents shall in good faith attempt to amicably reach an agreement on the subject.

   B. **Health Care Insurance; Uninsured Expense**

Both parents shall continue to carry all health care insurance as may be available through their respective employment, provided that the employer or other organization pays part or all of the premium. Mother shall pay 30% and father shall pay 70% of all uninsured medical, dental, optical, and orthodontic expenses for the children. The parents shall cooperate in the prompt processing of all insurance claims and reimburse the other for all out-of-pocket expenditures.

C. Duration of Support

Child support for each child shall continue until such child is 18 years old or graduates from high school, whichever occurs later, provided that support continues through September of the year of graduation if the child is enrolled for college. In no event shall support continue past the child's 19th birthday.

D. Support Amount

Based upon the present financial circumstances and joint parenting arrangements of the parents, the father agrees to contribute to the mother the sum of $700 per month as child support for the two children, payable on or before the fifth (5th) day of each month. The monthly support provided herein shall be adjusted beginning March 1, 1989, and each successive year on March 1 based upon both parents' earned income from all sources and utilizing the Washington State Superior Court Judges Association Child Support Guidelines, as now or hereafter amended.

E. Dispute Resolution

Disputes in applying the Guidelines or any other financial matters affecting the children shall be mediated or referred to court for final resolution, in accordance with paragraph XI above.

F. Life Insurance as Security

The father shall maintain a policy of decreasing term life insurance on his life payable for the benefit of the children in the initial face amount of $100,000 during the time that he is still obligated to pay support. In the event there is insufficient life insurance (less social benefits or other entitlements payable for the children due to the father's death) to support his obligations, the mother shall have a continuing claim against the father's estate, which shall survive his death and which shall be treated with the same statutory priority as an Award of Homestead.

G. Exemptions

So long as he is current in his support obligation the father shall be entitled to claim the younger child as an exemption for IRS reporting purposes and the mother shall execute appropriate forms for this purpose. So long as there is a continuing support obligation, the parents shall exchange authenticated copies of tax returns upon request.

H. **College Expense**

Each parent shall contribute to the children's post-secondary educational expenses taking into consideration the income and expenses and other resources of each parent at the time and the ability of the children to obtain loans and scholarships and to work part-time. In no event shall a parent's obligation exceed that for a student attending the University of Washington full-time; nor shall the obligation extend beyond the child's 23rd birthday. Both parents agree that the Court shall retain jurisdiction for the purpose of adjudicating the parents' college expense obligation if they are unable to agree.

I. **Miscellaneous Financial Data**

1. Payor Parent: James L. Jeffrey, 4466 West Mercer Way, Mercer Island, WA 98040. Employer: Jeffrey Limited, 4466 West Mercer Way, Mercer Island, WA.

2. Payee Parent: Mary Ellen Jeffrey, 9102 90th Place Southeast, Mercer Island, WA 98040. Employer: Bank of California, Bank of California Center, Seattle, WA 98164.

3. Payments of support shall be made directly to the payee spouse.

4. Uninsured health care expense and day care expense shall be paid 30% by mother and 70% by father.

5. Monthly net income of parents: Mother - $2,675; Father - $2,900.

6. Social Security numbers:
   Mother: XXX-XX-XXXX
   Father: YYY-YY-YYYY
   Justin: SSS-SS-SSSS
   Kristin: DDD-DD-DDDD

XIV. **COMPLIANCE WITH THE PLAN**

1. If a parent fails to comply with a provision of this Plan the other parent's obligations under the Plan are not affected.

2. If a support payment as provided for is more than 15 days past due in an amount equal to or greater than the support payable for one month, the person entitled to receive support may seek a mandatory wage assignment without prior notice to the person who is obligated to pay support.

3. Violation of Restraining Orders set forth in this Plan or Order may constitute a civil contempt and/or a criminal misdemeanor

XV. ACKNOWLEDGMENTS

Both parents acknowledge, by their signatures below, that this plan has been proposed in good faith and that they are in agreement and have a copy of this plan.

DATED: this 1st day of June, 1990.

_____   _____
Mary Ellen Jeffrey,   James L. Jeffrey,
Petitioner   Respondent

APPENDIX N
ASSOCIATION OF FAMILY AND CONCILIATION COURTS POLICY RE: AIDS AND FAMILY LAW

NOTICE: Scientific knowledge changes rapidly. This policy may become rapidly outdated. Check with the Centers for Disease Control and your physician.

Presently almost 90,000 people in the U.S. have AIDS and 50,000 have died from it. One million to 1.5 million people are seropositive. By 1991, the AIDS population is expected to triple and the fatalities will reach 179,000.

The fiscal cost of AIDS in medical care and lost productivity is estimated to exceed $30 billion per year. An increasingly large percentage of people with AIDS have had AIDS for over a decade. Thus we must prepare for the people living with HIV as well as those dying of AIDS.

There is no evidence of AIDS being transmitted through normal parent/child contact. Such contact includes kissing both on the cheek and on the lips, hugging, holding, bathing, sharing utensils, *etc.* The AIDS virus is transmitted through blood-to-blood contact and sexual contact through semen and vaginal secretions. There is no evidence of transmission through tears, saliva, cuts, bites, or insects. Knowledge of HIV transmission and detection is constantly changing. The court should follow the current guidelines of the Centers for Disease Control.

1. **Courtroom Procedure.** Since there is no evidence of risk of transmission in normal courtroom settings, any measures taken by courtroom personnel, such as wearing gloves or gauze masks, are both unnecessary and potentially prejudicial to the person with AIDS (hereinafter "PWA").

2. Parenting Capacity. As there is no evidence that infection with the AIDS virus alone affects the capacity to parent, HIV status is not a basis for restricting parental rights. The unwarranted discrimination against a parent with AIDS is detrimental to the child. Contributing to the stigma of AIDS contributes to the spread of the disease.

3. Prevention. Preventing the further spread of AIDS is most effectively achieved (a) through enactment and enforcement of strong antidiscrimination laws, (b) through thorough drug education, prevention, and treatment programs, and (c) through comprehensive safe sex education and explicit instruction in condom usage. Education, not testing, is key to AIDS prevention.

4. HIV Allegations Against Parents. No allegations regarding AIDS infection should be made in any court proceeding prior to sealing the court file. Absent a demonstrated medical risk to the child, any public accusation of HIV infection should be considered detrimental to the child and the child's relationship to the accused parent.

5. Limiting Access. Parental access to a child should be rejected when:

A. Any parent willfully exposes their child to high-risk behaviors for HIV infection as defined by the Centers for Disease Control. Existence of such behaviors which place the child at risk shall be confirmed by a physician with demonstrated expertise in epidemiology and the treatment of AIDS; or,

B. The parent develops a degree of physical or mental incapacity which prevents him or her from meeting the parenting needs of the child. In this context, every effort should be made to assist the child to deal with the imminent death of the parent. Time spent between the child and the terminally ill parent should be structured to maximize the best interests of the child.

6. HIV Testing. Testing should be performed only according to current CDC (Centers for Disease Control) protocols. In the absence of clear and convincing evidence of medical necessity, HIV antibody testing of the parent or the newborn child is unwarranted and not in the best interests of the child. Where an HIV parent is accused of sexually abusing his or her child, testing the accused parent is unwarranted since the results do not prove transmission, and the disclosure of HIV status could significantly harm that parent's capacity to support the family. Testing the child immediately after the alleged abuse is ineffective since the virus antibody is not detectable until two to six months after exposure. However, if there is clear evidence of a possible transmission, a short course of AZT or other appropriate medication may be prescribed for the child to reduce the possibility of transmission.

7. The HIV Status of a Mother. The HIV status of a mother should not be considered grounds for limiting her right to conceive or her right to parent her child. There are many other diseases or genetic conditions which pose an equal or greater risk to newborns. We must examine our national reluctance to provide for children. In Sweden, wed or unwed mothers receive 18 months of materinity leave with pay. Mothers without jobs are provided 200% to 300% the support that they are in the U.S., plus comprehensive medical coverage. Fewer AIDS babies would be abandoned if we provided the same support as our European and Canadian neighbors.

8. Universal Health Care. Since most children and many people with AIDS live at or below the poverty line, adequate care is rarely available. Some form of universal health care should be available to all children in need. The U.S. and South Africa are the only Western industrialized nations without universal health care.

9. Universal Drug Treatment Programs. Since most HIV women of child-bearing age are intravenous ("IV") drug users or the sexual partners of an IV drug user, comprehensive drug treatment programs and post-treatment monitoring should be freely available to family courts. Bleach kits and sterilized needles should be provided to IV drug addicts and measure should reduce the number of children born with AIDS.

FACTUAL BACKGROUND

AIDS: What Is It?
There is substantial agreement in the scientific community that AIDS is caused by a virus called HIV. Testing positive to the presence of the virus antibody means only that the individual has been exposed. Many individuals have tested positive to the virus for over ten years without showing any signs of AIDS or AIDS Related Complex (ARC). AIDS may be likened to forms of cancer or syphilis, which may be *in remission* or *dormant* for many years.

AIDS: How Is It Transmitted?
AIDS is transmitted through blood to blood contact or sexual intercourse through semen and vaginal secretions. Unprotected sexual intercourse and sharing of IV drug needles is the most common way of transmitting the virus. IV drug abusers or street children who regularly engage in prostitution are increasingly at risk. AIDS is not as contagious as sexually transmitted diseases such as herpes or hepatitis-B.

Hospital Care of AIDS Patients. Over 1,750 health care workers with substantial exposure to patients with AIDS have been studied for evidence of infection. The research indicates that caring for AIDS patients, even when there is intensive exposure to contaminated secretions, is not a high-risk activity. **Each year approximately 300 health care workers die from exposure to the hepatitis-B virus. By contrast, fewer than .1% of health care workers have become exposed to AIDS as a result of working with AIDS patients.** The virus is easily prevented from transmission by taking precautions suggested for hepatitis-B such as wearing gloves. The virus is easily inactivated by a solution of bleach, alcohol, formaldehyde, and Lysol. Heating contaminated articles at 56 degrees centigrade for ten minutes will also inactivate the virus.

Saliva. Of 83 HIV individuals tested, only one exhibited the virus. The concentration of the virus in saliva was one one-thousandth the concentration found in blood. There is no evidence of transmission of AIDS through saliva.

Mosquitos. The national tension regarding possible mosquito transmission of AIDS focused upon Belle Glade, Florida. Transmission was demonstrated to be highly unlikely and detailed epidemiologic investigation concluded that the AIDS population in Belle Glade was infected through sexual transmission and intravenous drug use. There is no biological evidence from any source to credibly support the notion that the virus can be transmitted by mosquitos or any other insect.

AIDS: How Is It Passed to Children?

By and large, children with AIDS are children in poverty. AIDS can be passed to children while they are in the womb if the mother is HIV. However, there may be a 50% to 67% chance that the child will not contract AIDS from the HIV parent. Of the 1,300 documented cases of children with AIDS, there is not one transmission attributed to causes other than transfusion, hemophilia, and perinatal contact. The HIV virus is also present in breast milk but there is no case of children contracting AIDS solely from consuming such breast milk.

There is no evidence of HIV transmission to children through normal parent/child contact. Extensive studies continue to clearly document the lack of transmission of the AIDS virus from the HIV parent to the child or to other adults living closely together in the same household. Parents and children engaged in hugging, kissing, sharing of cups, sharing of utensils, sharing of food, toothbrushes, nail clippers, combs, towels, drinking glasses, *etc*. A table summary of household contacts and a table summary of other studies that corroborate the absence of risk are provided below.

In the 1990s the new AIDS cases will become predominantly heterosexual, not homosexual. Nevertheless we must face the fact that our failure to address our discrimination against gays, drug users, minorities, and the poor ensures the continuing spread of AIDS. **Curing AIDS is a medical issue. Preventing AIDS is a social issue, where each of us must address our moral qualms about the poor, gays, minorities, and IV drug users.**

Table 1.
Type of Contact* with Patients with AIDs
among 101 Household Members

Activity	Percentage of Members in Activity
Sharing of household items	
Razors	9%
Toothbrushes	7%
Nail clippers	42%
Combs	51%
Towels	37%
Clothes	15%
Eating utensils	25%
Eating plates	46%
Drinking glasses	48%
Sharing of household facilities	
Bed	37%
Toilet	90%
Bath or shower	2%
Kitchen	93%
Washing items used by patients	
Dishes	65%
Toilet	49%
Bath	55%
Clothes	38%
Interacting with patient	
Helping to bathe	10%
Helping to dress	16%
Helping to eat	13%
Shaking hands	21%
Hugging	79%
Kissing on cheek	83%
Kissing on lips	17%

* The findings of no household contact transmission of AIDS to children in the above study are given further weight by the summary of studies printed below in Table 2.

Table 2.
Studies of the Risk of HIV Infection among
Household Contacts of Patients with AIDS

Study	Index Patients*	No. of Index Patients	No. of Household Contacts	No. Positive	No. Positive w/o other Risk Factors
Salzmann et al. 110	Adults (IV drug users)	61	145	1	0
Rogers et al. 106	Children (transfusion recipients)	24	85	0	0
Fischi et al. 56	Adults (Haitians, IV drug users)	45	135	19	0
Redfield et al. 57	Adults (heterosexuals, IV drug users)	7	11		0
Thomas et al. 107	Women	28	25	3	0
Lawrence et al. 108	Adults and children (hemophiliacs)	29	42	0	0
Jason et al. 109	Adults and children (hemophiliacs)	34	45	0	0
Total		228	491	24	0

* IV denotes intravenous

Although AIDs has been isolated in saliva and tears, there is no evidence of transmission through either. This includes close interaction between kids including biting of other children by HIV-infected children. Likewise, there is no documented case of transmission of AIDS to health care workers who are bitten by adult HIV patients.

HIV ANTIBODY TESTING: WHETHER AND WHEN

It is possible, with a reasonably high degree of accuracy, to determine who is infected with HIV and therefore capable of transmitting the virus to others. As noted above, the transmission occurs only as a result of specific behaviors that are usually not part of a household situation involving children. When such behaviors occur, they are illegal in their own right. Therefore, testing would seem irrelevant to decisions about child custody.

Testing for HIV antibodies is a two-step process: first one performs an ELISA (Enzyme Linked Immunosorbant Assay) as a screening test. The ELISA is better than 99% sensitive in identifying HIV-infected persons; and it is also better than 99% specific — i.e., fewer than 1% of uninfected persons will register positive. In persons with a history of high-risk behaviors, the ELISA test alone may be predictive of infection; however, because of the extreme emotional, political, and economic impact of the HIV infection and the possibility of significant discrimination, the standard of medical care is to perform confirmatory testing whenever the ELISA test registers positive.

First, the ELISA should be repeated to ensure that the first test result was not in error. If the second ELISA is positive, a different confirmatory test (a Western Blot) is performed. Generally, laboratories do not report ELISA tests alone, but only the results from the full sequence (repeated ELISA, then confirmatory tests). In persons without known risk behaviors, only about 20% of the repeat ELISA tests are confirmed to represent HIV infection. Roughly another 20% of positive ELISA specimens are read as "indeterminant" on the confirmatory tests. These persons may be infected, but more likely are not — only future testing may reveal whether HIV infection actually exists. The remainder (60%) are ELISA positive but not confirmed — not infected.

In low-risk persons (without known risk of infection), perhaps one in one-hundred persons positive by ELISA and confirmatory tests are actually not infected (false positive). In persons with high-risk histories, this figure would be lower. False negatives also occur most commonly because the infected person was too recently infected to have developed detectable antibody levels.

The period between infection and development of a detectable antibody is usually two to four months, although much longer periods have been reported. There are also some persons (perhaps 4%) with later stage infection — even AIDS — who lack antibodies detectable by the ELISA test.

Present evidence suggests that most persons who become infected will eventually develop disease. However, many remain well for years. Of sexually active gay men in San Francisco known to be infected ten years ago, the majority have either developed AIDS or AIDS-related diseases; however, about one-third remain well.

Given the established prejudice against minorities, gay people, and those in poverty in America, an allegation of AIDS/HIV should not be used to further discriminate against an already persecuted group. Harm to children can only be prevented by protecting parents from persecution.

BIBLIOGRAPHY AND REFERENCE ARTICLES

1. Friedland, Gerald H. and Robert S. Kline, M.D. "Transmission of the Human Immunodeficiency Virus," *New England Journal of Medicine,* vol. 317, no. 18, p. 1125, October 28, 1987.

2. Friedland, Gerald H., *et al.* "Lack of Transmission of HTLV-III/LAV Infection to Household Contacts of Patients with AIDS or AIDS-Related Complex with Oral Candidiasis," *New England Journal of Medicine,* February 6, 1986, pp. 344-349.

3. Sande, Dr. Merle "Transmission Against AIDS: The case against casual contagion," *New England Journal of Medicine,* February 6, 1986, pp. 314, 380, 383.

4. "Summary: Recommendations for preventing transmission of HTLV-III/LAV in the workplace." 34 MMWR, no. 45, Nov. 15, 1985.

5. Tsoukas, Chadjis T., *et al.* "Risk of Transmission of HTLV-III/LAV from Human Bites," presented at Second International Conference on AIDS, Paris, June 23-25, 1986; Rogers, Sanders, White, *et al.* "Can Children Transmit Human T-Lymphotrophic Virus Infection?" presented at Second International Conference on AIDS, Paris, June 23-25, 1986, as cited in *New England Journal of Medicine,* vol. 317, no. 18, p. 1132.

ADDITIONAL COPIES

Additional copies of **Divorce in Washington: A Humane Approach** may be obtained from your local bookstore or clip and mail the order form below. If you just want a blank set of divorce forms, indicate in the appropriate box.

Humane Approach
Eagle House Press
P.O. Box 1357
Mercer Island, WA 98040

Please send me

Divorce in Washington: A Humane Approach

_____ copies @ $14.95 each $_____

Wash. State sales tax, postage and handling @ $2.00 each $_____

☐ I just want a blank set of divorce forms and enclose my check for $9.00,
    including Wash. State sales tax, postage and handling.

I enclose check or money order in the amount of $_____
(no cash or COD's, please — allow 4 weeks for delivery).
(25% discount off per-copy price on orders of 5 or more.)

Name_____

Address _____

City _____   State/Zip _____